*Saving American Birds*

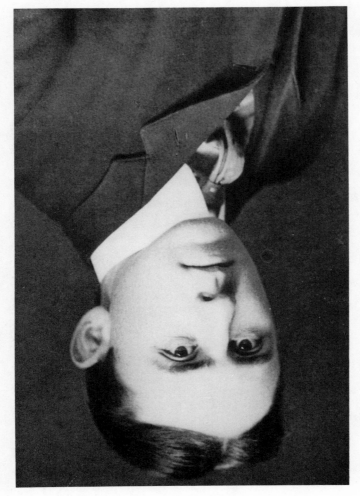

T. Gilbert Pearson, about 1902. Friends Historical Collection, courtesy of Guilford College.

# Saving
## American
## Birds

### T. Gilbert Pearson
### and the Founding of
### the Audubon Movement

OLIVER H. ORR, JR.

*University Press of Florida*
*Gainesville / Tallahassee / Tampa / Boca Raton*
*Pensacola / Orlando / Miami / Jacksonville*

Library of Congress Cataloging-in-Publication Data

Orr, Oliver H.
  Saving American birds: T. Gilbert Pearson and the founding of the
Audubon movement / Oliver H. Orr, Jr.
  p.  cm.
  Includes bibliographical references and index.
  ISBN 0-8130-1129-9 (alk. paper)
  1. Birds, Protection of—United States—History.   2. Pearson, T.
Gilbert (Thomas Gilbert), 1873-1943.   3. National Audubon Society—
History.   4. Audubon societies—United States—History.
5. Ornithologists—United States—Biography.   I. Title.
QL676.55.O77   1992
333.95'816'0973—dc20          91-34730

The University Press of Florida is the scholarly publishing agency of the
State University System of Florida, comprised of Florida A & M
University, Florida Atlantic University, Florida International University,
Florida State University, University of Central Florida, University of
Florida, University of North Florida, University of South Florida, and
University of West Florida.

Orders for books should be addressed to
University Press of Florida, 15 Northwest 15th Street,
Gainesville, FL 32611.

*to* ADRIANA, *who endured*

# Contents

# Illustrations

# Preface

I AM DEEPLY INDEBTED to Eloise F. Potter, North Carolina State Museum of Natural Sciences, who read the manuscript as a copyeditor might, pointing out innumerable places for making improvements, and to Henry Gemmill, Washington, D.C., who suggested ways of reducing the text's length without sacrificing the most important content. Dean Amadon, formerly chairman of the Department of Ornithology, American Museum of Natural History, allowed me to examine and copy correspondence in the department's files. Donald R. Lyman did research for me when he was a graduate student at the University of North Carolina at Chapel Hill. Emilie W. Mills, Walter Clinton Jackson Library, University of North Carolina at Greensboro, sent me photocopies and lent me duplicate copies of the university's catalogs and student literary publications. Likewise, Carole Treadway, Friends Historical Collection, Guilford College, provided photocopies and photographs and performed numerous other indispensable services. Additional help has come from many others, including Richard C. Banks, U.S. Fish and Wildlife Service; Charles H. Callison, then assistant to the president, National Audubon Society; staff members of the National Audubon Society library; Harry T. Davis, then director of the North Carolina State Museum of Natural Sciences; Helen Cubberly Ellerbe, Gainesville, Florida; Robert W. Hill, then keeper of manuscripts, New York Public Library; Michael Hyman, then J. Franklin Jameson Fellow, Library of Congress; and Carolyn A. Wallace, then manuscripts curator, Southern Historical Collection, University of North Caro-

xi

lina at Chapel Hill; as well as staff members of the Library of Congress and the North Carolina Division of Archives and History.

I have inserted the modern equivalents of the English names of birds and provided the scientific name of each species, usually wherever the English name first appears. My source for the scientific names is the U.S. Department of the Interior's Fish and Wildlife Service publication, *Checklist of Vertebrates of the United States, the U.S. Territories, and Canada* (Resource Publication 166. Washington, D.C.: 1987), edited by Richard C. Banks, Roy W. McDiarmid, and Alfred L. Gardner, who followed the *Check-list of North American Birds* (6th ed. Washington, D.C.: American Ornithologists' Union, 1983) and its supplements. The Fish and Wildlife Service has also published the extremely helpful *Obsolete English Names of North American Birds and Their Modern Equivalents* (Resource Publication 174. Washington, D.C.: 1988) by Richard C. Banks.

Some of the information in this book has appeared in "T. Gilbert Pearson: Young Ornithologist in Florida" in the *Florida Historical Quarterly* for October 1983, and "T. Gilbert Pearson: The Early Years" in the Spring 1986 issue of *Chat*.

# Introduction

IN THE LATE nineteenth century, a small group of self-taught, chiefly part-time ornithologists organized themselves into the American Ornithologists' Union (AOU) and as one of their accomplishments generated a movement, largely in the form of Audubon societies and the National Association of Audubon Societies (now the National Audubon Society), that changed the status of wild birds in America. Although numerous state laws protecting game birds had been passed at the request of sportsmen, nongame birds—that is, species generally unsuitable for food—had been killed with relatively little restraint for almost three hundred years. In response to the Audubon movement, state and national lawmakers were persuaded to adopt measures to stop the destruction of nongame birds and to begin protecting decimated populations.

This book is about the founding of the Audubon movement and the person who best represents the founders. Thomas Gilbert Pearson and other Audubon leaders not only asserted their own liking for birds but also insisted that everyone else ought to like birds—or at least recognize their value and help protect them. Alarmed by the extinction of the Great Auk *(Pinguinis impennis)* and the Labrador Duck *(Camptorhynchus labradorius)*, the rapid decline of the Passenger Pigeon *(Ectopistes migratorius)* and the Carolina Parakeet *(Conuropsis carolensis)*, and the spreading destruction of other birds, particularly to supply the feather market, Audubon leaders (with occasional misgivings about a few species that seemed at times to be pests) sought to save as many species in America as possible.

1

No method of historical analysis appears adequate to satisfactorily explain why some persons are entranced by wild birds and others are not, or why some persons believe they would experience a sense of great personal loss if all or most wild birds were to disappear whereas other persons are indifferent to the prospect. Likewise, historical research cannot reveal how many, or which, species of plant and animal life should be preserved for human society's future benefit, from either a narrow economic viewpoint or from various emotional, spiritual, intellectual, and scientific perspectives. The ornithologist bird protectors I have written about here were not sufficiently advanced to make a case for the importance of biological diversity. Nonetheless, they shared an appreciation of birds, a desire to save them, and a readiness to take action to protect them. Laboring before the widespread use of chemical pest controls, they found their most persuasive argument in the significance of birds in agriculture.

I have tried to identify the Audubon movement's foremost leaders, report what they said birds meant to them, and trace the ways in which they encouraged other Americans to value birds and to take steps protecting them. Because I found impracticable the idea of recreating in one book the lives of all major founders of the Audubon movement, I chose Pearson as their representative and detail only his activities.

Pearson's inclination from boyhood to write about his experiences makes him an especially appropriate choice for illustrating what it was like to become an ornithologist a hundred years ago. He recorded many of his field excursions and was eager to convey to others the excitement he often felt in studying birds. Ornithologists of his time learned by observing and collecting and by reading the writings of others who, in most instances, were their contemporaries or nearly so. No specific academic training in ornithology was available. Insofar as seemed potentially helpful, I have identified birds Pearson studied and collected, largely in

Florida and North Carolina, and described his role as a builder of museum collections, beginning with his own. The way he used his collecting skills to finance the earning of undergraduate degrees at two colleges exemplifies the ingenuity of many young persons of his time, especially in the impoverished South, as they sought advanced education. Pearson's surroundings encouraged religious faith, which in his case became the basis for justifying an interest in nature, and in the protection of bird species.

Although he was not among the earliest Audubon founders, Pearson is an appropriate representative because he became their leader. At eighteen, he was admitted to the AOU, which had already taken the first steps toward saving nongame birds. In 1902, while teaching at the State Normal and Industrial College for women in Greensboro, North Carolina, Pearson entered the Audubon movement by founding the Audubon Society of North Carolina. Through it, he persuaded the state legislature to enact the AOU model law (later more commonly known as the Audubon model law) protecting nongame birds. He also successfully added to the law provisions requiring out-of-state hunters to buy licenses and authorizing the society to use the revenue to enforce all the state's laws protecting wildlife. Thus North Carolina became the first southern state to undertake, at the state level, enforcement of wildlife laws, and the Audubon Society of North Carolina became the first Audubon organization to function as a state wildlife or game warden force. Because of the pioneering roles played by the North Carolina society and by Pearson as its administrator, in this study considerable attention is given to the details of the organization's structure and operation and of Pearson's adroit maneuvering to keep it going for the six years it retained full jurisdiction. During that time, it was held up as an example for other state Audubon societies to follow. The curtailment of its power, as this study indicates, is in retrospect less surprising than its having been given the power in the first place.

Pearson became even more fully caught up in the Audubon movement in 1905, when he began serving simultaneously as executive officer of the Audubon Society of North Carolina and as both special agent and secretary of the National Association of Audubon Societies. At thirty-one he was the only full-time Audubon executive in the nation, second in power and influence to the National Association's president, William Dutcher. As special agent, Pearson was the association's fundraiser. As secretary, he promoted the movement widely, primarily in the South, Midwest, and Northeast, particularly in New York, where traffic in bird feathers created special problems. Audubon leaders found considerable sympathy for their cause among school teachers and administrators. In North Carolina and other southern states, the movement coincided with a broad campaign for education. Pearson drew educators to the cause and promoted the teaching of bird study in schools and colleges. Farmers were approached through fairs and institutes. In this study I trace both Pearson's activities and the ups and downs of the Audubon movement, including its disappointing relations with the "conservation movement" led by Gifford Pinchot and Theodore Roosevelt.

When Dutcher was disabled by a stroke in 1910, Pearson was appointed full-time executive officer of the National Association, and he bought a house in New York to which he moved his family in January 1912. The move meant the sacrifice of opportunities for college teaching, museum building, and, to a large extent, field ornithology. Although his *Birds of North Carolina*, written in collaboration with H. H. and C. S. Brimley, would not be published until 1919, it would be based largely on field work and research performed before Pearson left North Carolina. He would guide the National Association until 1934, substituting for Dutcher from 1910 to 1920 and serving from 1920 to 1934 as the first full-time president, thus completing a tenure of a quarter-century. He would also found and preside over the International Committee for

Bird Protection (today the International Council for Bird Preservation), write books and articles, make many speeches, raise money, and carry his message widely in the United States and into foreign countries. In the 1920s and early 1930s he would be the world's best known and most influential protector of birds.

I conclude this study with the events of 1911, which marked the end of a distinct period in the Audubon movement and in Pearson's life. The movement's foundations were in place. An Audubon society existed in almost every state, and almost every state with an Audubon society had adopted the AOU model law protecting nongame birds. Congress had passed the Lacey Act to support state laws. In New York, where the nation's largest feather market operated, the legislature had adopted a law forbidding the sale of the feathers of most species. A basic legal structure was thus in place, and the idea that most nongame birds should be protected by law generally prevailed. The U.S. Biological Survey, employing ornithologists and befriending birds, had been established, and President Theoore Roosevelt had been persuaded to create national bird refuges. The National Association of Audubon Societies, having itself become a strong membership society as well as the representative of state societies, was sufficiently prosperous to employ Pearson full-time. Thereafter, the Audubon movement's objectives and strategies would evolve to include more emphasis on international cooperation, for example, and even greater interest in protecting game birds and other wildlife. With the Migratory Bird Treaty Act of 1918, the U.S. government would begin helping the states.

# 1

# "Oologically, T. G. Pearson, Archer, Fla."

*(1873–1891)*

IN 1886, WHEN Thomas Gilbert Pearson, age thirteen, with his first gun killed a "grackle" (probably a Common Grackle, *Quiscalus quiscula*) in Archer, Florida, he tacked its glossy black wings to a wall of his room. A few days later, the wings disappeared. They soon reappeared on his sister's hat, modeled after fashionable city hats.[1]

Hundreds of thousands of birds were killed annually in America for the millinery industry, which produced women's hats richly ornamented with bird feathers and bodies. In an article published early in 1886 and reissued as a pamphlet, the American Ornithologists' Union (AOU) bird protection committee had discussed the "whole-sale" destruction of birds and had recommended laws to protect them. Pearson did not yet know about the pamphlet. In Archer, as in most towns, few persons, if any, realized that bird populations were significantly diminishing, and few would have cared had they been told. Pearson could not perceive the irony in his killing the grackle and letting his sister decorate her hat with the

7

bird's wings. He did not know that in collecting his first bird he had promoted the fashion he would spend the early years of his adult life making illegal.

Gilbert Pearson was born on November 10, 1873, at Tuscola, Illinois, the fifth and last child of Thomas Barnard Pearson and Mary Eliott Pearson, a Quaker farm couple looking for a setting in which to prosper. They had already lived in Ohio and Indiana. After Gilbert's birth, they returned to Indiana, to the village of Dublin. In January 1882, they moved to Archer, a small town in Alachua County, about fifteen miles from Gainesville, the county seat.[2]

Thomas Pearson had been advised by a physician to leave the cold winters of the Midwest; William B. Lipsey, another Quaker farmer from Indiana, had encouraged him to come to Archer. Lipsey had moved to Archer about 1878 and had become partner in a nursery, Lipsey and Christie. In Archer, Lipsey had written to Pearson, the weather was pleasant, the land cheap, and the soil rich. Pearson purchased a log house as a temporary home, cleared several acres of woodland, and built a new house "odorous of yellow pine." He planted a garden and a grove of orange trees and in partnership with his son Charles, already twenty-five years old, opened a nursery near the Lipsey and Christie nursery. Gilbert was enrolled in a school conducted in a merchant's buggy shed.[3]

Almost immediately the boy showed more interest in exploring the countryside to stare at birds and other wildlife than in going to school or working on the farm and at the nursery. Perhaps his parents' indulgence was natural in his case. He was so much younger than the rest of the family—almost eighteen years younger than his brother and twelve years younger than the youngest of the three sisters—that he was possibly treated as the child of all of them.[4] They were probably puzzled and amused, as well as sometimes exasperated, by the behavior of this small boy, so unlike themselves in his interests and so stubborn in his determination to pursue them.

By age twelve, Pearson had met two other boys who liked wildlife. One was W. Morgan Martin, who came to Archer about 1885 when he was nineteen and moved away the following year. The other was Altus Lacy Quaintance, who at fifteen became Pearson's closest friend. Martin owned a gun and "often wandered about the country shooting at ducks, blue jays [*Cyanocitta cristata*], bullfrogs, or any other creature he happened to find." Pearson watched him shoot birds and other animals and examined whatever he killed. Martin also collected bird eggs. He showed Pearson how to make a hole in an egg with a small steel drill and force out the contents by blowing into the hole with a brass blowpipe. Emulating Martin, Pearson became a "zealous" egg collector.[5]

Pearson became acquainted with the *Oologist*, a monthly magazine published in Albion, New York, and edited by Frank H. Lattin, who directed it toward boys interested in birds, eggs, and taxidermy. Lattin published queries, letters, and articles contributed by readers, answered many questions himself, and sold pamphlets, books, eggs, and oologists' equipment. Pearson acquired a copy of Lattin's catalog of eggs and supplies, *The Oologists' Hand-Book, 1885*, from Quaintance for eleven alligator eggs.[6]

When Martin and Quaintance planned an egg-collecting hike to Bird Pond, about five miles from Archer, the younger and much smaller Pearson asked to go along. Martin said no. Pearson would be unable to keep up; he would have difficulty wading through the water to the bird nests; he would be vulnerable to snakes and alligators. Pearson won Martin's consent by promising to give him almost all the eggs he collected.[7]

The expedition occurred on April 27, 1886. With the help of the local druggist's wife, Pearson described it briefly in the *Oologist* for January 1888 in the first of nine reports he ultimately contributed to that periodical. He later recalled having "wanted to tell the world" about the hike and the birds. "Hundreds of herons" rested on buttonwood bushes growing in the pond. The "confused medley" of their calls was "pleasant music." The boys waded from bush to bush, collecting eggs in their hats, while the "terrified Herons quacked and flapped." On the basis of names used locally and in Lattin's catalog, the eggs of seven heron species were identified: "Snowy Heron [Snowy Egret, *Egretta thula*], Little Blue Heron [*Egretta caerulea*], Louisiana Heron [Tricolored Heron, *Egretta tricolor*], Green Heron [Green-backed Heron, *Butorides striatus*], Night Heron [either the Black-crowned Night-Heron, *Nycticorax nycticorax*, or the Yellow-crowned Night-Heron, *Nycticorax violaceus*], American Egret [Great Egret, *Casmerodius albus*], and Snake Bird [Anhinga, *Anhinga anhinga*]." The article was signed "Oologically, T. G. Pearson, Archer, Fla."[8]

To build an egg collection, Pearson needed calipers for measuring eggs, drills for making holes in them, and blowpipes for expelling the contents. Hooks and scissors were used for extracting embryos; the insides of the shells were washed with syringes. When the shells had dried, holes were patched with tissue paper, which could be bought already gummed. Cracks were mended with cement. There were pens and pencils for labeling and forms for keeping records. All these items could be bought through Lattin's catalog. Drills of varying quality cost from $0.10 to $1.50; blowpipes, $0.15 to $0.35; embryo hooks, $0.30 to $0.75; and embryo scissors, $0.25 to $1.50. Data sheets were $0.06 per dozen; climbing irons were $2.50 per pair. Pearson's parents could not afford to buy him such things for activities that would produce no income, but they often spared him from chores while he worked for others to earn money for his equipment. He picked blackberries and sold them at three cents a quart. From black farm boys he bought trapped "quail" (Northern Bobwhites, *Colinus virginianus*) for three cents apiece, dressed them, and sold them for five cents. He worked successively in a store and in a blacksmith's shop.[9]

Later he expressed pride in having "started right" as a scientist. He learned to prepare eggshells, remove and preserve skins, and keep records of observations and specimens. He noted characteristic shapes and structures, variations and aberrations, and, in the case of skins, differences between male and female, young and adult. He learned how to collect eggs while minimizing damage to the birds' welfare. Taking all the eggs from a nest was better than taking some of them, he observed. If he left any, the birds usually incubated them and thus raised only part of a brood. If he removed all the eggs, the female bird ordinarily laid another complete set. "One spring," Pearson wrote later, "I robbed a pair of red-headed woodpeckers [*Melanerpes erythrocephalus*] four times, whereupon the birds built a fifth nest in a tree so high I could not climb to it. In a few weeks a family of young woodpeckers with grayish-brown heads emerged from the cavity." [10]

On one day of collecting (Monday, May 6, 1889), he successively climbed, using irons, a dead tree containing the nest of a "sparrow hawk" (American Kestrel, *Falco sparverius*) in which he found four incubated eggs; another dead tree from which he took five kestrel eggs, forty feet up; an "old stub" of a tree containing the nest of a "flicker" (Northern Flicker, *Colaptes auratus*) from which he took five eggs; and a hundred-foot pine in which a pair of "crows" (either Fish Crows, *Corvus ossifragus*, or American Crows, *Corvus brachyrhynchos*) had built a nest. "I had to look at the [crow's] nest a long time before I could make up my mind to climb it," he reported in the *Oologist*. "But finally I could stand it no longer." Up he went. The nest of sticks, twigs, grass, and cow hair held five eggs. His next problem was to climb down without breaking the eggs. "Putting three of the eggs in my mouth and taking two in my hand I descended without mishap." On the same day, he took eggs from the nest of a Northern Mockingbird (*Mimus polyglottos*) in a small bush, "blowed" two slightly incubated eggs he found in the nest of a Common Nighthawk (*Chordeiles minor*) on the ground, bailed out a leaky boat in which he rowed to bushes where he gathered five sets of "grackle" eggs, and located two Common Ground-Dove (*Columbina passerina*) nests, one with eggs, the other with two young birds. [11]

He thought about birds much of the time and was occasionally

willful in his determination to study them. While plowing for his
father, he heard an American Kestrel call. Leaving the horse tied to
a fence, he went into the woods to look for the kestrel's nest. When
he returned, his father had taken up the plowing. "I hid in a pine
thicket and did not approach the house until darkness and hunger
drove me to face my father's displeasure." On a school day, he and
Quaintance left the grounds at noon recess to examine a Red-
headed Woodpecker's nest and returned late. The teacher whipped
them. Smarting, they left school, went to their respective homes
for food, took a quilt from Pearson's home, disregarded admoni-
tions from their mothers, and walked to Levy Lake, about eleven
miles away. They camped out for three days, watching birds and
hunting for eggs.[12]

The Archer public school, which had been moved from the
buggy shed to a moderately large, one-room building with a bell on
the roof, offered Pearson little inspiration. The school term was
short (four and one-half months was the average length of a school
term in Alachua County in 1883–84), and rarely did a teacher
remain for an entire term, possibly because the pay was low (the
county's average monthly salary in 1883–84 was $23.10). Few
teachers were trained. A list of teachers holding first-class certi-
ficates in Florida in 1888 shows only six in Alachua County and
none in Archer. "Every year," Pearson wrote later, "we started in
with our studies about where we had begun the year before and
went over the same subjects using the same textbooks." Reluctant
to perform his assignments, Pearson was called "stupid" by the
same teacher who had whipped him.[13]

One teacher, who stayed only two weeks, impressed Pearson
with his learning and grace of manner. When Pearson told his
father he wanted to be learned and gracious, his father suggested
he read good books. The books at home, where prayers and
evening readings aloud were routine, were largely on religion. John
T. Fleming, who ran a general store in Archer and was considered

civic-minded and generous, might have biographies of great men he would lend, Thomas Pearson suggested. Gilbert approached Fleming in his store, where several men were idling, put his question awkwardly, and was teased rather than helped. Without success, he wrote letters offering to trade bird eggs for used books. A wealthy man whose name he had seen in a newspaper did not reply. A publishing firm, Century Company, responded it had no used books to exchange for bird eggs.[14]

Thomas Pearson allowed Gilbert to take a horse or a horse and wagon on explorations several miles from home. Boys in the community told him where they had seen unusual looking birds or nests. Often he went to Ledworth Lake, about fifteen miles south of Gainesville, to watch White Ibises (*Eudocimus albus*) and "wood ibises" (Wood Storks, *Mycteria americana*). Whenever a large flock took off, the sound of their wings "was like the rumbling of thunder or the distant roar of cannon." Among these birds he saw and collected his first specimen of the "rare and beautiful" Roseate Spoonbill (*Ajaia ajaja*). Birds seemed to be unafraid of horses and cattle. Occasionally Pearson saw a "blackbird" (probably a Red-winged Blackbird, *Agelaius phoeniceus*), a Snowy Egret, or a Little Blue Heron standing on a cow's back. He learned to use his horse as a screen and walk to within a few yards of feeding herons.[15]

As his knowledge increased, he began to read and contribute to the *Ornithologist and Oologist*, a popular journal published by Frank B. Webster in Hyde Park, Massachusetts, for advanced bird students. Pearson's first report described studies he made of Pied-billed Grebe (*Podilymbus podiceps*) nests in the spring of 1890. Within the next two years, he published articles on the Anhinga, the Wood Duck (*Aix sponsa*), and the herons of Alachua County. His pursuit of knowledge advanced from random, exploratory trips and collecting to systematic studies. He examined sixteen Pied-billed Grebe nests; no bird was ever there. Eggs were covered, partially or wholly, with decaying vegetation. Whenever he uncovered them, they felt warm. "And although further observations may lead me to change my views," he reported, "for the present I must believe that the Grebe does not sit on her eggs in the daytime for the purpose of incubating; but that the incubation is carried on largely by heat generated from the decaying vegetation of which the nest is composed." His belief changed when he went to a Kanapaha Prairie pond to search for an alligator's nest and saw a grebe's nest floating, in typical fashion, on a small raft of dead vegetation anchored to a few strong reeds. A little more than one hundred feet from the grebe's nest he found the alligator's nest. After removing the alligator eggs, he sat on the nest, screened by reeds from the grebe's nest. At intervals of about five minutes, he rose slowly and looked over the reeds. About an hour passed. Suddenly the grebe was there, sitting on its nest, when Pearson rose to look. The bird saw him at once. Swiftly it covered its eggs with vegetation, slipped into the water, and swam out of sight through the reeds. Pearson did not linger. He had learned what he wanted to know. The grebe did, after all, sit on its eggs in the daytime.[16]

Apparently Pearson tried raising a wild bird in captivity only once. While camping at Levy Lake in March, he and Quaintance rowed to a small marshy island where Great Egrets nested in buttonwood bushes. After examining the colony, they picked up a young bird and put it in the boat. "He was an awkward creature with long weak legs and slender toes. Thin white down covered the dark green skin, and the wing quills had been growing but a short time." Restless and frightened, the bird repeatedly tried to climb out of the boat. When restrained, he "squawked piteously." On shore, Pearson, using worms taken from water lilies for bait, caught several perch for the young egret. Offered a perch, the bird refused to take it. "He had been accustomed to put his beak between the mandibles of his mother's bill and receive his food from her throat." Pearson and Quaintance, working together, cut the perch into pieces and forced them, one at a time, down the bird's throat. At first the bird resisted vigorously, crying, twisting his head, and scratching the hands that held him. Nonetheless, whenever a piece of fish was successfully thrust well down his throat, the bird swallowed it. After a few repetitions, he adjusted to this new manner of being fed and welcomed food merely placed in his beak.

On the second day, the bird picked up fish placed on the ground and began to search for other food. In the wagon during the trip back to Archer, he tried to swallow an Osprey (*Pandion haliaetus*) the boys had collected. Choking, the young egret fell on his back, a foot and leg of the Osprey caught in his throat, and made "loud, strangled squawking" noises. Pearson clambered over the camping gear to the bird and pulled the Osprey free.

At home, Pearson fed the egret on raw beef. The bird ate without hesitation and was never satisfied for long. Pearson's parents soon expressed concern. When the egret killed a young chicken with one peck of his heavy bill, Pearson was told he must get rid of the bird. He had no desire to keep him in a cage or spend time every day catching fish for him. Under pressure to act quickly, he took the egret to a lake on Horse Prairie, rather than going the eleven miles to Levy Lake. The bird now had to catch food for himself. Pearson never knew whether the bird survived. A year later, when he saw a "magnificent" Great Egret standing in the shallow waters of the lake, he welcomed the thought that the bird might be his former pet.[17]

Studying Bald Eagles (*Haliaeetus leucocephalus*) could be dangerous but Pearson was careful. He found a tall pine tree bearing a nest used for several years by a pair of eagles. "For ninety-one feet the great pine raises its slender trunk without a branch. Thirty feet higher is the nest in the main fork of the tree, which here sends out three limbs." With a rope looped around his waist and the tree, Pearson made his way up to the nest by using climbing irons and narrow boards nailed on the trunk with a hatchet. When he reached the bottom of the nest, after building his ladder for an hour and a half, he found no way to get to the top except by making a channel at the edge of the nest. "The dust from the decaying wood showered continually upon me as I worked, getting into my eyes, ears and hair. As I proceeded slowly upward, layer after layer of decaying twigs and green stained fish bones were uncovered, showing where the floor of each season's nursery had been." Two eaglets squatted in the nest. "They were near the size of half grown chickens, and had bodies covered with whitish down." Occasionally they made a "low whistling cry" but otherwise did not protest his presence, even when he put his hands on them. The parent birds soared at a distance, screaming now and then. Only one time did they threaten Pearson. The bird he believed to be the female, while flying at the height of the nest about one hundred yards away, suddenly turned toward it. Pearson raised his hatchet, aware she might attack, but thirty feet away she turned aside. After examining the nest and young carefully, Pearson backed out and down without mishap.[18]

One winter Pearson noted that a male American Kestrel perched regularly in a pine tree killed by lightning. In early spring, a female joined the male at the perch. Pearson watched as the male, apparently for the female's benefit, "began a series of elaborate circles and evolutions." "At times he flew slowly, and again with high speed, now skimming low, now soaring high above the earth." He brought food to her and seemed to Pearson to be "delighted" whenever she accepted it. The birds nested in a cavity made by flickers in another dead pine tree nearby. As Pearson studied their behavior, he heard the male making a "strange low sound" he decided was the kestrel's "love call." He took the birds' first set of eggs, their second set, and their third. They did not attempt to nest again that season. The following year they returned to the flicker hole. Pearson did not disturb them. With "much care and great labor," four young birds were reared.

After the offspring went away, the parents stayed together. At night they roosted under the eaves of a building "within the border of their domain." The female became too trustful of humans and allowed a boy to come close enough to hit her with a thrown stick; he killed her as she lay on the ground. The male, more wary, lived for at least three more years, guarding the same territory he had shared with her. He was still there when Pearson left Archer in 1891 and had not taken another mate in that time.[19]

# 2

# A Union of Ornithologists

## *(1891)*

ORNITHOLOGY IS A relatively accessible science to which anyone making systematic field studies can contribute. For Pearson,
almost every observation was an exciting discovery. He watched,
collected, talked, and wrote with an enthusiasm that lasted
throughout his life. As he gradually became a skilled field ornithologist, he acquired a strong private collection and a body of
first-hand observations on which to draw in persuading other
people to know, like, and, beginning in 1892, protect birds.

On January 16, 1891, a date he recorded, he acquired a copy of
Elliott Coues's *Key to North American Birds*. Later he recalled having
traded all his duplicate bird eggs for the book. Perhaps he traded
with Frank H. Lattin, who in the *Oologist* for December 1890
advertised the fourth edition of Coues's *Key* for $7.50, and who
accepted trades in lieu of purchases. First published in 1872,
Coues's *Key* was the basic American textbook in ornithology for
several decades. Years later, Pearson associated with ornithologists
like Witmer Stone, who praised the book as the "classic which
unlocked the secrets of ornithology for so many of us." An army
surgeon more interested in birds than medicine, Coues collected
specimens and took notes wherever he was stationed. In the *Key*, he
set forth the "Darwinian logic of observed facts, upon which the

modern Theory of Evolution is based" and defined a bird as a "greatly modified Reptile."[1]

Reading Coues's *Key,* Pearson perhaps first encountered an author who accepted the theory of evolution. Little else in the book conflicted with what he was taught at home. Coues was concerned with hard work and excellence in performance. Although he did not refer to God, he espoused a stern creed of behavior. "I wish the work were better than it is, for my reader's sake; I wish the author were better than he is, for my own sake; and above all I wish that every author may rise superior to his best work, to the end that the man himself be judged above his latest achievements." The *Key* had one illustration in color (the first colored picture of a bird Pearson had ever seen), many black-and-white drawings that helped him identify species, almost two hundred pages of text on structure and classification, and instructions for preserving bird eggs and skins and for mounting birds.[2] Studying birds at a heightened level of accuracy and understanding, Pearson began to mount skins as well as collect them.

In Gainesville, he met other naturalists with whom he shared experiences. James H. U. Bell, volunteer director of the small Florida Museum of Natural and Political History, had initially visited Florida to collect specimens for the Smithsonian Institution. Subsequently, he left a judgeship in Monticello, New York, to take a position with the General Land Office in Gainesville. His son J. P. Hovey Bell and Pearson became friends. Hovey Bell earned his living as an employee of the railway postal service and studied wildlife in his free time. He also collected specimens for Frank M. Chapman.[3]

Chapman had come to Gainesville in 1886, at twenty-two. The son of a Wall Street attorney who was also a gentleman farmer, he had been raised on a forty-acre farm near Englewood, New Jersey, where he became interested in birds. Like other young naturalists, he did in ignorance things he would not have done later: he made plans to trap birds for the market and killed and ate two Passenger Pigeons. As his interest in birds grew, his position as department head in a New York bank lost its appeal. After joining the American Ornithologists' Union (AOU), Chapman made notes on bird arrivals and departures in New York for Albert K. Fisher, of the committee on bird migration, and helped William Dutcher, of the committee on bird protection, mail circulars to New Jersey legislators.

During all the winter of 1886–87 and part of the following one, Chapman lived in Gainesville with his mother, who sought respite from New Jersey's cold weather. He recorded observations, collected specimens, made some of the earliest American photographs of birds, and published a list of birds observed in Gainesville. In 1888, he became assistant to Joel A. Allen, curator of birds and mammals at the American Museum of Natural History. From time to time, Chapman returned to Gainesville to visit his mother and to collect specimens.[4]

In March 1891, Pearson drove a wagon to Gainesville. He ran errands for his mother and at noon went into the Good Samaritan Restaurant for dinner. The only other customer was Chapman, whom Pearson had seen before but did not know. Taking a seat across the table, he noted Chapman to be "carefully attired," with "the confident bearing of an experienced man of the world" and a "nice way of eating." On the assumption Chapman was a visitor who should be made to "feel at home" in Gainesville, Pearson spoke to him: "Well, I got a pair of kitty hawk [American Kestrel] eggs today." Chapman smiled and said little as Pearson talked about birds and nests. After finishing his meal, Chapman left without having shown interest in what Pearson was saying. "This did not particularly disturb me," Pearson recalled, "as people seldom responded to my enthusiasm about birds." Later in the day, Pearson reported the incident to Hovey Bell, who told him he had had dinner with Frank Chapman, an ornithologist from New York.[5]

Meeting Chapman was fortunate for Pearson. Although the two men never became close personal friends (neither ever had many intimates), Chapman encouraged Pearson in his work and promoted his career. After the accidental meeting in Gainesville, Pearson introduced himself in a letter. "Although I had often seen you I never really knew you to be F. M. Chapman." Unaware Chapman had published a list of birds seen in the Gainesville area, Pearson announced his intention to publish a list of Alachua County birds. "I now have on my list nearly one hundred varieties that I have either seen or actually taken. And I thought that perhaps you would just as soon help me in my list as not, as you have traveled around over the County a good deal." He concluded by inviting Chapman to visit him in Archer. "I would be *very* glad to have the pleasure of entertaining you."[6]

Chapman answered Pearson's letter promptly, affirming his willingness to begin a relationship with this somewhat awkward young man who knew a great deal about birds. Apparently he never accepted Pearson's invitation to visit. In May 1891, he was possibly in Gainesville, but in that month Pearson went on a collecting trip to Cedar Key and up the Suwanee River. He wrote Chapman he had a "splendid view" of a Mississippi Kite (*Ictinia mississippiensis*), the first he had ever seen, and was "so fortunate as to find a nest containing a set of three eggs of the Fla. Sea-side Finch [Seaside Sparrow, *Ammodramus maritimus*]." Shortly after the trip, Pearson was bitten by an alligator. He wrote Chapman, "I had my left wrist badly torn not long ago by a four foot alligator I was capturing, having to lay down on him in the water to hold him. I now have him mounted and placed in my museum, and as I enter the room his glass eyes glare at me as though he would like to fasten on me again."[7]

Apparently he had decided to try to make a living as a naturalist-ornithologist, operating a museum and selling his services. He bought stationery headed "T. G. Pearson. Field Ornithologist and Oologist. Birds Mounted in first class order. Nests & Eggs

Collected and Exchanged." Although his letterhead limited his specialities to ornithology and oology, his museum held more than birds. He questioned Chapman about muskrats and manatees and said he had "gotten in several minerals, arrow-points, and chards." In a two-week period, he collected and mounted a Tricolored Heron, a Little Blue Heron, a Yellow-crowned Night-Heron, an American Coot (*Fulica americana*), an Anhinga, two American Kestrels, and three Green-backed Herons.[8]

On being elected an associate member of the AOU following Chapman's nomination, Pearson came into fellowship with the small group of men who were establishing ornithology as an orderly field of study and generating a movement to protect non-game birds. The AOU had grown out of the Nuttall Ornithological Club founded in Cambridge, Massachusetts, in 1873. Made up largely of Cambridge and Boston ornithologists, the club was named for Thomas Nuttall, author of *Manual of Ornithology of the United States and Canada* (1832–34), which could be considered the first handbook on American birds. Although the active membership was less than twenty, the club's corresponding membership included all American ornithologists of note and its quarterly *Bulletin* was the major medium of communication for advanced ornithologists. It was only a club, however, not large enough in active membership or earnest enough in spirit to deal with major problems confronting ornithologists, the most pressing of which was the lack of a uniform system of classification and nomenclature.[9]

Three club members, Joel A. Allen, Elliott Coues, and William Brewster, curator of birds and mammals for the Boston Society of Natural History, sent a form letter to forty-eight ornithologists in the United States and Canada, inviting them to a convention in New York on September 26, 1883, to found an American Ornithologists' Union similar to the existing British Ornithologists' Union. Twenty-one persons attended the three-day meeting, and six committees were appointed, the most important of which were the committees on classification and nomenclature, migration, and geographical distribution. Later, after the new organization's governing council voted to establish a journal, the Nuttall Ornithological Club transferred the *Bulletin* to the AOU, which continued it as the *Auk*.[10]

*Bulletin* editor Allen became editor of the *Auk* and was also elected AOU president. Thirty-five years older than Pearson, he too had been born on a farm (in Massachusetts) to deeply religious parents (Puritan stock). As a boy he too had collected natural history specimens, particularly birds. The sale of his collection enabled him to attend Wilbraham Academy. Later he enrolled at Harvard, where he studied under Louis Agassiz, whom he assisted on an expedition to Brazil. In 1876, Allen published two articles lamenting the destruction of birds. Beginning in 1885, he was curator of mammalogy and ornithology at the American Museum of Natural History. He presided over the AOU for seven years and edited the *Auk* for almost thirty years.[11]

At the AOU's second meeting, in 1884, William Brewster expressed distress about the slaughter of birds, particularly terns, for decorating women's hats. He offered statistics "startling" to some members and moved the appointment of a committee for the protection of North American birds. Sporadic state legislative action to protect some song and insectivorous birds, such as had been taken in Georgia, was not enforced by police action. Brewster's motion passed unanimously, and he was made committee chairman. Other members were William Dutcher, an insurance agent in New York who studied birds on Long Island; C. Hart Merriam, a physician who, like Coues, preferred being a naturalist; George Bird Grinnell, who held a doctoral degree in osteology from Yale and edited and published *Forest and Stream*, a weekly outdoor magazine; and Eugene P. Bicknell, who published studies in botany and ornithology while earning his living in a banking house.[12]

The AOU committees produced lasting results in a relatively

short time. Under Coues's leadership, the committee on classification and nomenclature published, after three years, *The Code of
Nomenclature and Check-List of North American Birds*. The committees on geographical distribution and on migration were merged
under Merriam, who wrote to eight hundred newspaper editors
asking for volunteers to collect data on the location and seasonal
movement of birds. About twelve hundred observers eventually
volunteered and sent in such voluminous reports that Merriam's
committee could not cope with them. The AOU council recommended creating a division of economic ornithology in the U.S.
Department of Agriculture to study the food habits of birds, their
relationship to agriculture, and their distribution and migration. In
the AOU's behalf, Merriam wrote a memorial to Congress and
testified before the House committee on agriculture. Congress
appropriated five thousand dollars for a bird study program in the
Division of Entomology. Asked by the commissioner of agriculture to nominate someone to conduct the work, the AOU
selected Merriam, who was appointed. His AOU committee
transferred to him in the Department of Agriculture the data it had
collected and notified observers to send future reports to that
agency. Within a year, Merriam's office became the Division of
Economic Ornithology and Mammalogy, and he employed two
other AOU members, Albert K. Fisher and Walter B. Barrows. By
1890, the annual appropriation was twenty-five thousand dollars
and Merriam had five assistants.[13]

The bird protection committee began work more slowly than
the other AOU committees. Weakened by illness, Brewster resigned as chairman after a year without having called the members
together, but at the AOU meeting in November 1885 he urged the
committee's continuation. In the ensuing discussion, statistics
were again offered on the "enormous destruction of bird life for hat
decoration." Dutcher and Allen spoke, as did Merriam, who said
bird protection was the most important work the AOU could

undertake. Less than a month later, on December 12, the committee met in Dutcher's office at 51 Liberty Street, New York. Three members—Dutcher, Grinnell, and Bicknell—attended. By their invitation, also present were Allen; George B. Sennett, a wealthy manufacturer who had placed his large collection of bird nests and eggs in the American Museum of Natural History; and Joseph B. Holder, a former army physician who had become a curator in the museum. All three guests were added to the committee, as were three other men, including Lyman S. Foster, a dealer in natural history books in the city. Sennett was elected chairman.[14]

For a time, committee meetings were held regularly on Saturday afternoons in the American Museum of Natural History. Then came a shift to evening meetings in residences of members, chiefly of Dutcher and Sennett. Committee minutes reveal agreement on the need for prompt action, for as quickly as possible "collecting the facts in the matter and giving them wide publicity," and for "creating public sentiment" favoring bird protection. Ideas were introduced and discussed; chores were performed, some on assignment, others voluntarily. Holder gathered information on the millinery trade in bird skins and feathers; Foster examined digests of state laws for evidence of legal protection already given to nongame birds. Dutcher composed a model state law the committee worked upon with care. Allen's draft statement on the committee and its objectives was adapted by Bicknell for release to the press and published in Grinnell's *Forest and Stream* for January 21, 1886. The printer donated to the committee one thousand reprints of the statement. These, as well as additional copies acquired later, were distributed with a covering letter throughout the United States.[15]

In the statement, the committee announced its formation, membership, and purposes. It would gather and distribute information, offer a model state bird protection law, and suggest law enforcement methods. It would also encourage the formation of bird

protection associations and women's "anti-bird-wearing leagues."
It would inform and guide; other organizations, new and old,
would get laws passed and enforced. Because game birds were,
"thanks to true sportsmen," given "a more or less effective protection by law through a great part of the year," Bicknell explained in a
letter published in the *New York Evening Post*, the committee was
concerned with the "great host of the feathered tribe native to this
country" living "among us solely at the mercy of chance." Bicknell
repeated the call for organization. "The committee will gladly lend
its assistance to the formation of bird protective societies or
women's leagues bent on discountenancing the use of birds for
purposes of adornment."

Grinnell volunteered to use *Forest and Stream* for forming a
national bird protection organization to support the AOU committee. "We propose the formation of an association for the protection
of wild birds and their eggs, which shall be called the Audubon
Society," he announced in *Forest and Stream* for February 11, 1886.
The society's name honored John James Audubon, who in Grinnell's opinion had done "more to teach Americans about birds of
their own land than any other who ever lived." The "work to be
done" would be "auxiliary to that undertaken by the Committee of
the American Ornithologists' Union" and would "further the
efforts" of the committee, "doing detail duties to which they
cannot attend." Recognizing the society as "an offshoot of the
Committee," Sennett appointed Grinnell a subcommittee of one to
"take charge" of organizing it. On Grinnell's motion, unanimously
adopted, Sennett wrote to *Forest and Stream* on the committee's
behalf, "I am authorized to communicate to the Audubon Society
our approval of its plan and the sanction of our authority in the
work it undertakes." [16]

On February 26, a group of articles by bird protection committee members was published, through Allen's arrangement, as a
supplement to the weekly magazine *Science*. Allen's "general state-

ment" was followed by an unsigned essay on the killing of birds for millinery purposes, Dutcher's report on bird destruction in the vicinity of New York City, Sennett's indictment of "eggers," and unsigned articles on birds and agriculture, the need for protective laws, and the role that women could play in saving birds. That birds would be destroyed as humans moved into their habitats was, in Allen's words, "unavoidable, sooner or later." Avoidable destruction included killing birds to market as food (unnecessary "pot-hunting"), taking eggs of large birds for shipping to market (an uneconomical business with "no excuse or necessity"), killing birds for sport (for "the mere desire to kill something" or to own something and display it), and, most important, killing birds so women could decorate with them ("many times exceeding all the others together" in its effect on all species of birds).

Almost no bird was safe. "Scarcely a species can be named . . . that is not to be met with as an appendage of the female headdress." Bird feathers, wings, and heads, even entire birds and sometimes as many as six small birds appeared on the hats of many of the ten million women of "bird-wearing age" in the United States. Gulls and terns were the most likely to be killed by feather hunters, partly because of their habit of nesting in large colonies. One dealer in New York obtained forty thousand "gull" and "tern" skins from Cobb Island, Virginia, in one summer; seventy thousand skins came from one village on Long Island during a four-month period; forty thousand "terns" were taken in a single season on Cape Cod. Allen estimated at least five million birds were killed annually for milliners.

Few birds were too small to be taken for food. On a day in March in a market in Norfolk, Allen reported, hundreds of birds, including "woodpeckers," "robins," "meadow-larks," "black-birds," "sparrows," "thrushes," "wax-wings," "vireos," and "warblers," were displayed on strings.

Something had to be done soon if the birds were to be saved

from the "fate of extermination, which, to the shame of our country, has already practically overtaken the bison." One approach was to remind people frequently that birds are pleasant to see and hear. "Birds considered aesthetically," said Allen, "are among the most graceful in movement and form, and the most beautiful and attractive in coloration, of nature's many gifts to man. Add to this their vivacity, their medodious voices and unceasing activity,— charms shared in only small degrees by other forms of life,—and can we well say that we are prepared to see them exterminated in behalf of fashion, or to gratify a depraved taste?" Beyond that line of argument, difficult for most ornithologists to develop, was the stronger, more practical defense of birds as beneficial to agriculture. "It has been found . . . that all birds are to a large degree insectivorous, including hawks and owls, and even plovers and sandpipers." Many species, especially hawks and owls, also eat mice and other rodents. Poultry killing by such birds had been shown to be minimal, "their infrequent raids—mostly by a few species—on the poultry being much more than offset by their destruction of mice, grasshoppers, and other injurious insects."

In the model bird protection law, game birds were defined and excluded from coverage, the committee having concluded such birds should be protected by organizations established for that purpose. Hunters had already formed organizations to lobby for legislation, many states had adopted laws regulating the killing of several game bird species, and Grinnell's *Forest and Stream* and other outdoor magazines circulated widely among sportsmen.

Many AOU bird protection committee members, including Allen, Dutcher, Brewster, and Grinnell, thought of themselves as being simultaneously sportsmen, scientists, and humanitarians. They also acknowledged their role as "bird-lovers." It seemed appropriate that game birds should be protected by hunters and sportsmen and that all other species should be left to the care of "bird-lovers and humanitarians," with ornithologists showing the way. The model law made killing, buying, or selling wild birds other than game birds a crime punishable by a fine of five dollars or imprisonment for ten days. Taking or needlessly destroying the nest or eggs of a wild bird was subject to the same penalty.[17]

Thousands of copies of the *Science* supplement, reprinted as the bird protection committee's Bulletin No. 1, were distributed throughout the United States. Help came from G. E. Gordon, American Humane Association president, who met with the committee and offered to buy and distribute one hundred thousand copies.[18]

Response to the bulletin and to the invitation to join the Audubon Society was immediate and enthusiastic. The society won the endorsement of such eminent persons as Henry Ward Beecher, John Greenleaf Whittier, and Oliver Wendell Holmes. In lieu of a membership fee, men and boys pledged not to kill wild birds except for food and not to rob or damage any bird nests; women and girls agreed not to use bird feathers as ornaments of dress or household decoration. More than five thousand pledges had been signed by May 1886. In August, the society was incorporated in New York, with Grinnell as "President pro tem." That same month, Allen reported in *Science* that the response to Bulletin No. 1 "far exceeded the most sanguine hopes of the committee: the press of the country took up the subject vigorously, there being scarcely a newspaper, magazine or journal of any sort . . . that did not publish copious extracts." A second committee publication, "Protection of Birds by Legislation," drafted by Allen, appeared in the November 11 issue of *Forest and Stream* and was reprinted as the committee's second bulletin. By the end of 1886, the Audubon Society had more than three hundred local secretaries and almost eighteen thousand recorded members, with another three thousand members "not yet registered." The future was "full of promise," Sennett reported at the AOU meeting in November. In January 1887, Grinnell began publishing the *Audubon Magazine*, a monthly journal designed to "spread the Audubon movement as widely as possible."[19]

Despite this promising beginning, the AOU effort to generate a movement to protect birds appeared to have failed. Although Audubon Society membership reached almost fifty thousand in two years, with no treasury and too few local groups, neither the society nor *Audubon Magazine* was self-supporting. In New York, a bird protection law adopted in May 1886 was not enforced. "The headgear of women is made up in as large a degree as ever before of the various parts of small birds," Grinnell wrote. "Thousands and millions of birds are displayed in every conceivable shape on the hats and bonnets." He stopped publishing the *Audubon Magazine*. To Dutcher, looking back more than fifteen years later, the "organized effort for bird protection" also seemed stalled. During 1889, he noted, "the subject received no attention from the press."[20]

Pearson was unaware of the AOU bird protection committee's early work and of the Audubon Society's birth and death. After buying his first gun, he briefly tried plume hunting, but in 1886 he was still so ignorant about birds he could not distinguish the plumeless Little Blue Heron in the white phase from the Snowy Egret bearing marketable feathers. After one heron skin was rejected by a New York firm, he abandoned the effort. Later, he saw the damage plume hunters were doing to heron colonies near Archer, where they shot adult birds during the breeding season for their valuable nuptial plumes and left the young to starve. At Horse Hammock in 1888, Pearson visited a colony of several hundred pairs of Snowy Egrets, Little Blue Herons, Great Egrets, Tricolored Herons, and Black-crowned Night-Herons. When he returned there in 1891, he could see that plume hunters had raided the colony a year or two before: "Not a heron was visible" amid the shattered nests and crumbling bones of slaughtered birds.[21]

On a visit to a small swamp north of Waldo, in Alachua County's northeast corner, he found a heron colony that plume hunters had raided a day or two earlier. Here and there around their still-smouldering campfire lay dead herons, their backs raw and bloody where plumes had been torn away. Starving baby birds called from their nests for food. Larger young birds perched uncertainly on limbs. Now and then one of them, too weak to hold on any longer, fell to the earth with a thud. All the young were dying. Under tall grass was the body of an adult that had hidden after being shot. Before dying, it had beaten the ground smooth with its wings, trying to rise.[22] In later years, whenever Pearson wanted to drama-tize the cruelties of plume hunting, he drew upon his memories of the scene at Waldo.

During the spring and summer of 1891, while studying birds and writing notes and articles for the *Oologist* and the *Ornithologist and Oologist*, Pearson considered his future. The idea of making a living as a naturalist-merchant seemed plausible, as advertisements from taxidermists, naturalists, and natural history stores appeared regularly in the two ornithological publications, but Pearson learned quickly that his income would be small and uncertain. Moreover, his ignorance about most subjects other than birds and his lack of social poise concerned him. He had admired both Chapman, with his easy, cultivated manner, and one teacher who had exhibited notable grace and learning and had also been "very kind" to him. When the teacher left Archer, Pearson, with tears in his eyes, gave him several sets of his choicest bird eggs and a photograph of himself. He resolved to "learn to speak, walk, and act like that perfect gentleman," who "tactfully" had thanked Pearson for his strange gifts.[23]

Although Pearson and his friend Quaintance occasionally still hunted together, Quaintance had entered the Florida Agricultural College in Lake City in 1889, a separation Pearson later viewed as the "first real bereavement" of his life. "I now suffered from the lack of companionship. There was no one with whom I could talk about birds.[24]

Pearson now saw himself as the community's conspicuously bad example, the boy "who wasted his time and who was utterly worthless as a pupil or as a field-hand," the son whose parents were "pitied." In the summer of 1891 he wrote to several colleges to offer his museum for a term's enrollment. Quaker schools seemed especially attractive to him. He wrote to Earlham College, in Richmond, Indiana, which his mother and brother had attended, and to Guilford College, near Greensboro, North Carolina.[25] An acceptance came from Lewis Lyndon Hobbs, Guilford president, who wanted to strengthen the natural history cabinet, or museum, begun by a faculty member who had resigned. Hobbs offered Pearson tuition, board, and room for two years in exchange for his collection and his services as a curator of the college cabinet.

Pearson was excited by Hobbs's letter. That evening, he "rocked and rocked" for a long time in a squeaking hammock on the veranda of the Pearson home. His mother and father, who usually demanded evening silence, indulged him; the "squeaking brought no parental reproof."[26] Their peculiar son seemed to have found his own way to respectability.

# 3

# "Oh fashion! how many crimes are done in thy name!"
## (1891–1893)

IF PEARSON COULD HAVE CHOSEN any college in the nation, he probably could not have made a better choice than Guilford. Academically, he was unprepared for college, and Guilford had a two-year preparatory program. He was socially awkward and unaccustomed to being away from home except out-of-doors. He needed the nurturing intimacy of a small school where his poverty would not be an embarrassment, as well as a familiar religious setting and an atmosphere of intellectual tolerance.

Guilford met his needs. Founded in 1837 as the New Garden Boarding School, the college occupied 260 acres six miles west of Greensboro and one mile north of New Garden Station on the Salem and Winston Railroad. The North Carolina Yearly Meeting of Friends had selected a neighborhood "as free as possible from immoral influences," one safely away from "allurements to idleness and vice." Tobacco use was prohibited as "injurious to both bodily and mental powers." The "reading of pernicious literature, the use of intoxicating drinks, indulgence in profane language, carrying pistols or other dangerous weapons" were regarded as "grave offences."[1]

Pearson arrived by train a few days late for the 1891 fall term. With him, or in boxes shipped separately, was his museum. After his qualifications had been examined and his academic weaknesses noted, he was placed in the first year of the two-year preparatory program, a decision that probably did not surprise him.[2]

The natural history cabinet consisted of one room and its contents. Begun in 1875 by geology professor Joseph Moore, the collection included birds, plants, skeletons, anatomical models, and several thousand mineral and fossil specimens and was acclaimed at Guilford as being the "finest College Collection in the State."[3] It may have been the best natural history collection of any kind in the state. The North Carolina State Museum had been founded in 1879, but in 1891 it had not yet acquired a curator.

The college magazine, the *Guilford Collegian*, reported that new cases were built for the specimens Pearson brought from Florida, the bird eggs alone requiring an entire case. Representing more than two hundred species, the approximately eleven hundred eggs consisted largely of specimens he had taken from nests in Florida. By exchange, he had acquired a few eggs from foreign countries. Initially appraised as being "probably the largest" in the state, two years later Pearson's enhanced collection was described as the "largest scientific collection of bird-eggs in the South."[4]

The cabinet was located in King Hall, which also housed the president's office, a science laboratory, the college library, classrooms, and rooms for the four literary societies, each of which had a library and which together published the monthly *Guilford Collegian*. Nearby Founders' Hall housed an assembly room, the dining room, social parlors, and dormitory rooms for women. Dormitory rooms for men were in Archdale Hall. The YMCA Building was under construction. A farm supplied milk, butter, meat, and vegetables for the slightly more than two hundred students.[5]

Adapting readily to his new intellectual and religious environment, Pearson joined the Websterian Literary Society and the YMCA and became a leader in both. He had more trouble accepting the physical environment and "yearned for the sight of live-oaks and their long gray moss, for the magnolias and the palmettoes." The red clay hills of Guilford County at first led to embarrassment. When wet from rain, the paths and roads were so slick that walking from the train station to the campus on his first day, he fell several times. His clumsiness became a standing joke. "Our good natured curator," a reporter wrote in the *Guilford Collegian* in January 1892, "fell down ten times one day last week. Quite an improvement."[6]

In New York in November of 1891, at the AOU meeting where Pearson's application for associate membership was accepted, Dutcher reported that the feeling of hopelessness about bird protection still prevailed. Although Brewster described the guarding of tern colonies on Muskeget Island, Massachusetts, Sennett confined his report as bird protection committee chairman to the simple statement that progress was being made.[7]

In 1891, when the fall leaves "turned to red and gold," Pearson reassessed his surroundings. The "broom sage in the abandoned fields," the "gray rail fences," and the "blue haze that in autumn lingers on the horizon" were "soothing" to his spirits. On Saturdays, carrying gun and notebook, he roamed the college farm and adjoining woods and fields. No flocks of water birds appeared, and gradually he realized that Guilford County had few large streams and no natural lakes or large ponds to attract waterfowl. Writing to the *Ornithologist and Oologist* about his new life, he reported seeing one Bald Eagle, an apparently rare species. Cooper's Hawks (*Accipiter cooperii*), Turkey Vultures (*Cathartes aura*), Hairy Woodpeckers (*Picoides villosus*), and Pileated Woodpeckers (*Dryocopus pileatus*) were reasonably common; song and garden birds were abundant.[8]

During the Christmas holidays of 1891, an "old hunter named Jessup" took Pearson Wild Turkey (*Meleagris gallopavo*) hunting.

Jessup's son Dan shot a turkey hen for Pearson, but he believed the bird's body to be the most important part and so aimed for the head and neck, which he damaged so severely the specimen was unsuitable for mounting. Many months later, on the day before Thanksgiving 1892, he brought to the college two Wild Turkeys, both in "handsome" condition. Pearson spent Thanksgiving and the next two days mounting them.[9]

In the spring, birds migrated from the south in large numbers. On March 29, 1892, Pearson collected the first Brown Thrasher (*Toxostoma rufum*) to appear. Then came Black-and-white Warblers (*Mniotilta varia*), Blue-gray Gnatcatchers (*Polioptila caerulea*), Louisiana Waterthrushes (*Seiurus motacilla*), Whip-poor-wills (*Caprimulgus vociferus*), and Northern Parulas (*Parula americana*). The Golden-crowned Kinglets (*Regulus satrapa*), present all winter, departed. On April 18, he saw a Chimney Swift (*Chaetura pelagica*); on April 23, Summer Tanagers (*Piranga rubra*) were singing in trees "on every side."[10]

By spring term's end, Pearson had added to the cabinet numerous birds, eggs, bugs, reptiles, and other animals. He had also become an informal teacher of natural history, inviting classmates, professors, college visitors, and local residents to the cabinet, where he identified specimens and discussed them. His casual conversations and classroom contributions were usually about birds.[11] His lifelong effort to encourage people to know and like them had begun in earnest.

Pearson's awareness of the need for bird protection grew from field observation. In March 1892, he contributed to the *Guilford Collegian* an article expressing, for the first time in print, his concern about the decline of a bird species. Although "The Wild Turkey" was largely a factual account of the bird's life cycle, Pearson warned that the "time is probably not far off when the wild turkey will have disappeared from the country unless laws are rigidly enforced protecting them during the nesting season." Tur-

keys could still be seen in the woods near Guilford, but by the
early 1900s, the species had disappeared from large sections of
North Carolina.[12]

A faculty member gave Pearson two circulars she believed she
had gotten from the Audubon Society before it failed, apparently
the AOU bird protection committee's bulletins. Pearson studied
them and in the Websterian Society's oratorical contests in May
1892, he spoke on bird destruction by plume hunters. Although his
first speech in a debate had been disrupted by laughter at his florid
language and loud delivery, by spring, after many hours' practice
in the woods, he had become one of the society's best performers.
In his contest oration, "The Destruction of Our American Birds,"
he said, "Man, it would seem, has almost lost sight of the fact that
he was placed upon this earth to use the things therein, and not
destroy them." Noting the disappearance of the Great Auk and the
decline of the Passenger Pigeon, Pearson predicted that many
species would soon be extinguished if feather wearing were not
curtailed. After describing the cruelties of plume hunting,
he stated, "It is bad enough for any cause, to see such sights; but
when we know all this is done that women—yes, *even Christian*
women,—may decorate themselves with plumes, it becomes in-
finitely worse." With high drama he concluded, "O fashion! how
many crimes are done in thy name!"[13]

In the contest, he competed as a preparatory student with an
unconventional topic against three upperclassmen orating on traditional subjects ("The Future of Africa," "The Rise of the Dutch
Republic," and "The College Man"). The prize, a Webster's un-
abridged dictionary, was awarded to a senior, Edwin M. Wilson,
who had scoffed loudly at Pearson's awkwardness the previous fall.
After the contest, Wilson delighted Pearson by saying, "Not so
bad for a prep." According to a reporter for the *Guilford Collegian*,
Pearson's appeal for bird protection was "listened to with strict
attention."[14] It was also published in full in the magazine.

At Pearson's request, Guilford's treasurer provided a "little money" for a summer collecting trip to the coast.[15] Pearson wanted especially to look for the Ivory-billed Woodpecker (*Campephilus principalis*), not recorded as having been seen in North Carolina since Alexander Wilson had captured an injured specimen near Wilmington about one hundred years earlier. Pearson hoped to find the bird in the Great Dismal Swamp. On May 31, with two companions, he travelled by cart along a sandy road through pine woods to a canal leading into the swamp. There the three transferred to a boat, which they paddled for several hours through the forest. They spent the night on a dry knoll above the surrounding soft peat. The next morning they paddled to the heart of the swamp, Lake Drummond, tied up to a cypress, and ate dinner. Pearson alone went swimming in the reddish water, which he estimated at about eight feet. Two hours later they were paddling along one of the outlet canals. Once more they landed near high ground, which Pearson explored. He left the "melancholy silence of this weird forest" after two days, having seen few birds and no evidence of Ivory-billed Woodpeckers. The trip had been "well worth the trouble," he concluded, but "more desirable and more profitable" places for seeing birds existed.[16]

Pearson explored the Gates County countryside for several weeks alone and then went to a small hotel on Cobb Island, Virginia. In earlier years, huge numbers of seabirds had nested on the island, but Pearson saw no Royal Terns (*Sterna maxima*), which had formerly been abundant, and only one Least Tern (*Sterna antillarum*), "that beautiful fairy. . . . It perceived me apparently at the same time and with a startled cry was off like a bullet." Island residents told Pearson the Least Terns had been killed by feather hunters and shipped to markets in New York. One man recalled a day on which he had shot three hundred Least Terns. Birds less in demand by milliners still nested on the island. Pearson walked five miles to the north end, used by American Oystercatchers (*Haema-*

*topus palliatus*), Black-bellied Plovers (*Pluvialis squatarola*), Black Skimmers (*Rynchops niger*), Common Terns (*Sterna hirundo*), and Forster's Terns (*Sterna forsteri*). On the west were Willets (*Catoptrophorus semipalmatus*), Clapper Rails (*Rallus longirostris*), and Laughing Gulls (*Larus atricilla*). Pearson studied nest structures and looked for complete sets of eggs, which were scarce because islanders gathered bird eggs for food. At the hotel, boiled eggs of Laughing Gulls, American Oystercatchers, "terns," and Clapper Rails were served daily.[17]

For several hours Pearson watched and teased the gulls and terns. Lying in a boat, his face partly covered by his hat, he waited "to see what the birds would have to say." One tern noticed him, then another; a gull came, and within fifteen minutes more than one hundred terns and a dozen gulls were overhead, making a "great outcry." "Any movement on my part was a signal for a louder outburst of sounds as the birds rose higher or hurried away only to return a minute later to hover and stare and scream as before. Not until I arose and walked away were they satisfied to leave the spot where had lain the strange creature which had excited them so much."[18]

At the end of his visit, he packed eggs and the skins of two American Oystercatchers and several Black-bellied Plovers in a telescope valise and, with ten dollars borrowed from a friendly woman, took a boat to Washington, D.C. He rented a room for a dollar, lived chiefly on bananas and crackers, and spent two days at the Smithsonian Institution looking at exhibits and talking with bird curator Robert Ridgway, one of America's foremost ornithologists. Ridgway let him see the famous egg collection of Charles E. Bendire, who had studied birds during long periods of military service in the West. Then Pearson returned by train to Guilford, sitting up all night on a day coach.[19]

During his second year at Guilford, Pearson added to the natural history cabinet the shells, bird eggs, and skins collected in the summer of 1892, 120 Indian arrowheads and spear points found in Guilford County, and some foreign bird eggs. He also mounted a Beaver (*Castor canadensis*) taken in Caswell County and a Great Blue Heron (*Ardea herodias*), a Red-throated Loon (*Gavia stellatta*), and "ten beautiful and valuable species of duck." When the World's Columbian Exposition opened in Chicago in May 1893, he had on display eggs of ten bird species in a natural history exhibit mounted by Frank H. Lattin, who had invited readers of the *Oologist* to participate. Pearson provided eggs of the Barred Owl (*Strix varia*), Common Grackle, Laughing Gull, Wood Duck, Little Blue Heron, Chuck-will's-widow (*Caprimulgus carolinensis*), Fish Crow, Loggerhead Shrike (*Lanius ludovicianus*), Brown-headed Nuthatch (*Sitta pusilla*), and Northern Mockingbird.[20]

Absorbed in his work as natural history curator and unofficial teacher, Pearson was a poor student. Perhaps the courses seemed elementary. He later recalled having merely passed most subjects and having failed English grammar because of a "hopeless inability to comprehend" the rules. Preparatory Department principal Lydia N. Blair, pleased by his success in writing about birds, permitted him to graduate without having passed the grammar course. Pearson learned rudiments of English by example—reading books, memorizing striking passages, and trying to discern how good writers built stories or developed themes.[21]

Gradually he acquired some of the social skills he had wanted. The confidence he felt in the museum and in conversations about natural history began to appear in other situations. He was chosen Websterian Society marshal, YMCA recording secretary, and college representative at the New Berne Fish and Oyster Fair.[22] He made friends outside Guilford, usually among persons interested in nature. Often he visited the State Normal and Industrial School for women, a new institution that opened in Greensboro in the fall of 1892. Faculty members interested in natural history included President Charles D. McIver; Edwin A. Alderman, professor of history and English literature; Philander P. Claxton, professor of pedagogics; James Y. Joyner, who soon succeeded Alderman; and Dixie Lee Bryant, professor of natural history. Pearson invited his new friends to his museum and donated materials for the school laboratory.[23]

Instrumental music at society programs was traditionally forbidden at Guilford, where singing and making music with instruments had been regarded as lapses from grace. When Pearson enrolled in 1891, singing exercises and private piano and organ lessons were permitted, but instrumental music at college functions was still forbidden. Defying the rules, Pearson and several other Websterians carried a borrowed organ into the society room. President Hobbs, noted for appearing whenever mischief was being made, arrived as the organ was being put in place and ordered its return to the owner. Although in later years Pearson regarded himself as fortunate in not having been expelled, he probably had been in no jeopardy. The prank may have merely encouraged the president to relax the rules the following year.

Elsie Weatherly of Greensboro, a seventeen-year-old freshman at State Normal, played the violin at the Guilford Websterian Society's commencement oratorical contest in 1893. That same night, Pearson took second place in the oratorical contest with an oration on "The Vanished Race," possibly about the Great Auk or another extinct species. Watching Elsie perform, he was impressed by "her art, her grace, and her beauty." Soon thereafter he visited her in Greensboro.[24]

Guilford's modest budget uncovered a talent Pearson ultimately developed to a degree unique in the wildlife protection effort. In order to collect museum specimens in places beyond walking distance, he needed more funds than the college could provide. On his own initiative, he solicited donations of money. "From experience I learned that one may secure contributions for a worthy cause if one profoundly believes in its merits and if one looks a man directly in the eye and asks for help," he wrote later. Voluntary money raising for the college by a student in the Preparatory Department may have seemed presumptuous, but no evidence suggests the administration was anything but pleased. Pearson gave the donations to the college treasurer, wrote drafts that were submitted to the board of trustees for approval, and made reports to the board on how the money was spent.[25]

President Hobbs was proud of the natural history museum. In the college catalog containing announcements for the academic year 1893–94, the description of the museum ("one of the most interesting features of the Institution") was three times as long as the description of the libraries.[26]

Most male students at Guilford belonged to the YMCA, which opened its own building in January 1892. Pearson went there regularly to attend Bible classes (in addition to the Bible study classes required by the school), weekly prayer meetings, and monthly business meetings. In the spring of 1893, he and James Peale Parker were chosen to attend the World's Conference of Young Men at Northfield, Massachusetts, in July. Leaving Guilford well before the conference, Pearson went to Baltimore, where he solicited donations from sympathetic Quakers to finance travel for the museum, and went on to visit Frank Chapman and the American Museum of Natural History in New York.[27]

The Northfield conference was an annual gathering of college students sponsored by evangelist Dwight L. Moody. For almost two weeks (July 1–12), as one of approximately five hundred students from 125 colleges in Europe and America, Pearson attended Bible classes, discussion groups, and prayer meetings in the mornings and evenings and played ball in the afternoons. Among his teachers were Moody himself and Henry Drummond, the Scottish minister who wrote lectures and books reconciling science and religion.[28] In *Natural Law in the Spiritual World*, Drummond reconciled the theory of evolution and Biblical revelation. For Pearson, the experience amplified and strengthened what he already believed.

Pearson's next major stop was the World's Columbian Exposition in Chicago, where his bird eggs were arrayed with others in Lattin's large natural history exhibit. Turning back toward Guilford, Pearson visited Joseph Moore at Earlham College. Moore's former teacher, Louis Agassiz, considered him the "best scientist west of the Allegheny Mountains." God was the "Great First Cause" in the process of creation, Moore had taught his Guilford students, and "human affections" were the highest point of evolution. In the struggle for existence, the follower of the Christian life is the fittest to survive. Moore received Pearson kindly and gave him, for the Guilford museum, a mounted Passenger Pigeon, a species already almost extinct.[29]

Between June and the opening of Guilford's fall term in 1893, Pearson visited more than twenty natural history museums.[30]

# 4

# "The Birds Our Friends"

## *(1893–1897)*

A RECOGNIZED ORNITHOLOGIST at age nineteen, Pearson was invited by the World's Columbian Exposition Auxiliary to participate in an October 1893 congress on birds.[1] AOU President Elliott Coues was president of the congress and chaired the program committee; ministers and humane society leaders were asked to join ornithologists in contributing papers. The major themes were the science of bird study, the usefulness of birds to mankind, and the need for laws to protect them. An advisory council member, Pearson submitted a paper, but commitments at Guilford College prevented his attending the congress. Sometime during the four-day program, his paper was read by proxy. More exposition visitors came to the bird lectures than even the sponsors had expected, in part because what the lecturers had to say interested the general public. The "degree of civilization which the human race has reached would have been difficult if not impossible," Coues said in his presidential address, "without the assistance of our feathered freinds."[2] Chapman discussed birds seen on Columbus's voyage to America. Pearson, after portraying the beauty of herons, described the brutality of plume hunting. "Unless something is done to stop this awful slaughter, it is only a question of a few years before the herons, not only of Florida, but of the whole

44

South, will be exterminated." Women could stop the killing, he said, which went on "merely to gratify fashionable women's vanity"; it would cease as soon as women ceased wearing feathers.[3] His paper appears to have attracted the most attention at the time and three years later when the papers were published.[4] He was the only contributor who described the cruelties of plume hunting and who bluntly told women they were responsible.

At the end of Pearson's two-year agreement with President Hobbs, the college trustees voted to continue him as curator at fifty dollars a year plus room, board, and tuition. He was listed in a college advertisement as a faculty member, though he did not receive a full salary or participate in faculty meetings. It is unlikely any full faculty member worked harder than Pearson. He spent the Christmas holidays gathering specimens in rock quarries in nearby Davidson County.[5]

Each literary society at Guilford had an editor and an associate editor on the *Guilford Collegian* staff. Pearson represented the Websterian Society in one capacity or the other every year he participated in the college curriculum. As a freshman, he was associate editor for exchanges. He encouraged students to read *Our Dumb Animals*, published by the Massachusetts Society for the Prevention of Cruelty to Animals, and *Our Animal Friends*, organ of the American Society for the Prevention of Cruelty to Animals. Although the two humane societies supported the AOU's efforts to protect birds, their interest in bird protection continued to be subordinate to their interest in protecting domestic animals. They contributed to but rarely initiated direct efforts to protect birds. In 1894, the ASPCA president's annual message contained a protest against cruelty to horses and cattle but no mention of birds.[6] Nonetheless, appreciative articles on birds and other wild animals often appeared in humane society journals.

Pearson spent the summer of 1894 collecting specimens in Florida. His base was the home of his parents, whom he had not visited since leaving for college three years earlier. Among his expeditions was one to Cedar Key on the Gulf coast, primarily to collect Brown Pelicans (*Pelecanus occidentalis*), "large, grotesque looking birds" that in Pearson's opinion never appeared "to advantage unless in flocks on the wing or buoyantly riding the waves." In the fall, Pearson added to the Guilford museum twenty-seven mounted birds, a ten-pound Gopher tortoise (*Gopherus polyphemus*), an Eastern diamondback rattlesnake (*Crotalus adamanteus*) mounted in an attitude of readiness to strike, minerals, fossils, and bottles of marine life in alcohol.[7]

Darwin's scientific view of life, in company with a fresh examination of mankind's responsibilities to other creatures on earth, was welcomed at Guilford as long as it did not exclude God. Pearson was an enthusiastic Darwinian who looked to the future with hope. His address at a symposium was characterized in the *Guilford Collegian* as offering a "very optimistic" outlook, one "which if not agreed with by all, was nevertheless well worth the close attention paid to it." Another speech, "The Development of Modern Science," won first place in a Websterian oratorical contest. He also spoke at YMCA meetings on such topics as the "Personality of Christ" and "How Shall We Reach Our Fellow Students for Christ."[8]

The counterpart to the YMCA at Guilford was the YWCTU, the Young Women's Christian Temperance Union. A YWCA had been organized at about the same time as the YMCA, but its membership was almost identical with the already existing YWCTU and the two groups merged under the YWCTU's name. Although YWCTU members were interested largely in the "liquor curse," they saw the organization as an expression of their desire for "spiritual, mental and physical" well-being. Guilford graduates were expected to be missionaries, laboring in their local communities.[9] YWCTU leader Eula L. Dixon, like Pearson, saw kindness to animals as a Christian obligation. In the summer of 1895, while serving as North Carolina superintendent of the WCTU's Department of Mercy, she collaborated with him in publishing a leaflet, *Echoes From Bird Land. An Appeal to Women.* Pearson composed the appeal; Dixon provided a brief commentary and issued the leaflet in her organization's name. Birds were mankind's friends, "feathery tenants of field and river" who protected fruits and vegetables against grubs and insects, Pearson wrote, but because women liked hats adorned with feathers and bodies, millions of birds were killed in cruel ways each year. Dixon assured readers Pearson's statements were accurate and invited requests for further information. "Literature and pledges" could be supplied.

Pearson sent a copy of the leaflet to Frank Chapman. A thousand were being distributed, he wrote, and pledges not to wear birds or feathers were being issued. He had been invited to talk on birds in several communities and had just come from the University of North Carolina summer school, where he had instructed a natural history class. He asked Chapman for fresh details on the need for bird protection. "I want all the information I can get. Statistics, facts, etc. in regard to the destruction of species."[10]

His enthusiasm for campaigning to protect birds temporarily exceeded that of most AOU leaders. Some were complacent, partly because bird study was becoming popular, especially in public schools. C. A. Babcock, superintendent of schools in Oil City, Pennsylvania, established "Bird Day," which was soon adopted elsewhere. Some ornithologists were too involved in research and writing to think about bird protection. Chapman, AOU bird protection committee chairman in 1894, was preoccupied with his *Handbook of Birds of Eastern North America*, which was published in 1895 and recognized immediately as a work "marked for a career of extended usefulness."[11] He began at once to prepare a new edition in response to suggestions for revision.

Other AOU leaders did not know what to do. The growing popularity of bird study had not reduced bird destruction or changed fashion sentiment. "The fashion journals just at the present time," wrote a contributor to the *Auk* in October 1894, "are not altogether pleasant reading to bird lovers or to persons of refined or humane instincts; for it is evident that the absurd craze for hat decorations composed of bird skins, either entire or in endless degrees of multilation and disfigurement is again rampant." A *Harper's Bazaar* article on new hats and bonnets described small bonnets, each with "blackbirds . . . poised in pairs, with beaks meeting lovingly," and large hats bearing four birds. Appointed bird protection committee chairman in November 1895, Dutcher later characterized 1895 as the year of the "low tide of bird protection." The committee was "discouraged and hopeless, feather-wearing was as rampant as ever, the legislatures of the states of New York and Pennsylvania, where the model law had been enacted, had amended or repealed the same."[12]

During Guilford's 1895 fall term, Pearson was chosen junior class president and football team manager. In the spring he managed the baseball team. He was the principal organizer of an athletic association, which he managed until he graduated. Perhaps his increased association with people nurtured a growing sentimentality about nature. In "A Peep in the Autumn Woods," published that fall in the *Guilford Collegian*, he called attention to what the campus birds were doing. The Spotted Sandpiper (*Actitis macularia*) feeding at the college pond with Killdeers (*Charadrius vociferus*) was "doubtless giving them, as they strolled along, some account of what had transpired the past summer on the shores of his northern stream." When other sandpipers arrived, the Scarlet Tanager (*Piranga olivacea*) "went scampering about the thickets, perhaps whispering to all he met that the Sandpipers had come and Autumn was here." After the leaves had fallen, an Eastern Screech-Owl (*Otus asio*), looking for shelter, would "fly up close to the buildings and ruffle his feathers and look in at the window and wish for an overcoat and shiver and moan for hours at a time." One Saturday morning Pearson went into the woods to collect a pair of Blue-gray Gnatcatchers. Following the sound of a singing bird, he found it on a lichen-covered nest in a white oak tree. The song was so beautiful and the bird seemed so happy, Pearson could not shoot it. "I could not raise my gun," he wrote later, "and as I walked home I reflected on the fact that never before had sentiment prevented me from killing a bird I felt was needed for educational purposes."[13]

Humankind's place in the evolving universe continued to interest Pearson. At a class entertainment, he orated on "Evolution in Its Relation to Man," concluding, "The creature God now looks upon is the object towards which all life has tended, it is the product and climax of the ages." On another occasion, he spoke on "The Birds Our Friends," describing the services birds perform and urging humans to reciprocate with acts of friendship.[14]

With solicited funds, Pearson returned to Florida to collect specimens in the summer of 1896. He spent several days as a guest in a hunter's one-room house near Palmetto, on the Manatee River, where the two men lived on "cornbread, jerked venison, dried grapes, and boiled buds of the cabbage palmetto." He walked to Terra Ceia Bay and boarded a fishing boat that took him to Bird Key (later Indian Key Bird Reservation), a small island in Tampa Bay. Double-crested Cormorants (*Phalacrocorax auritis*) and Brown Pelicans nested in the mangrove trees. Man-o-war birds (Magnificent Frigatebirds, *Fregata magnificens*), having nested further south, searched the Gulf of Mexico for food by day and at night congregated on Bird Key. Near Tampa Bay's mouth an hour before sunset on July 17, Pearson watched the frigatebirds come in. "Imagine a swallow with a long forked tail, and wings whose sweep is seven and a half feet!" He estimated the total number of birds to be at least ten thousand.[15]

Before leaving the vicinity of Bird Key, he collected a frigatebird, some Double-crested Cormorants and Brown Pelicans, and a clutch of Brown Pelican eggs. On the Tampa Bay shore, he visited heron colonies, examined Bald Eagle nests, and collected a Gray Kingbird (*Tyrannus dominicensis*), an American Black Duck (*Anas rubripes*), an American Swallow-tailed Kite (*Elanoides forficatus*), a pair of Roseate Spoonbills, several nests, and more than "fifty varieties of shells and other curiosities." There seemed to be, he reported in the *Auk* after returning to Guilford, a "falling off in the number of large waders." [16]

Pearson and Guilford art teacher Lillian J. Hill created an exhibit for the annual state fair in Raleigh. In front of two tall pyramids bearing Pearson's mounted birds and animals stood two large showcases, one containing six hundred specimens of bird eggs, minerals, fossils, shells, and Indian relics, the other displaying china made at the college. The natural history display won five prizes, the china four. [17]

Throughout the United States, at fairs and museums, in lectures, articles, and books, natural history increased in popularity. Urban residents, historian Peter J. Schmitt has concluded, wanted to go "back to nature." Government agencies and private organizations responded to the interest. At Dutcher's request, the U.S. Treasury Department's Lighthouse Board forbade taking bird eggs for the market from nests on the South Farallon Islands, California. In New York, the Linnaean Society, the ASPCA, and the West Side Natural History Society jointly paid the salary of a state guard for a tern colony on Great Gull Island. The United Ornithologists of Maine was organized to "encourage a systematic study" of birds. Under the editorship of E. Irene Rood, chairman of the woman's committee of the World's Columbian Exposition Auxiliary, a volume of papers presented at the Congress on Ornithology appeared, including Pearson's graphic account of the cruelties of plume hunting. [18]

Harriet Hemenway, whose husband Augustus had inherited both money and a philanthrophic tradition from his mother, Mary Tileston Hemenway, talked with her neighbor Minna B. Hall in

Boston about the need to change women's attitudes towards birds. "We had heard," Hall stated later, "that 'Snowy Egrets' in the 'Florida Everglades' were being exterminated by plume hunters who shot the old birds, leaving the young to starve on the nests." Perhaps they had read Pearson on plume hunters in the Congress on Ornithology article, publicized before Rood's book appeared: "Young herons had been left by scores in the nests, to perish from exposure and starvation." Hemenway and Hall invited Boston "ladies of fashion" and eminent men to join in creating "a society for the protection of birds." Among the founding members at the first formal meeting on February 19, 1896, were William Brewster, Charles Francis Adams, George F. Hoar, Sarah Orne Jewett, Mrs. Louis Agassiz, and Bradford Torrey. "A goodly representation of what has been called Proper Boston—which broadly includes Proper Brookline and Proper Milton—may be discovered in the list of founders," Robert H. Welker wrote later. The name, Massachusetts Audubon Society, carried on the symbolism of the defunct Audubon Society that George Bird Grinnell organized as an AOU bird protection committee auxiliary. Brewster, who had first chaired the bird protection committee, was elected president of the new society.[19]

The Massachusetts Audubon Society and the AOU bird protection committee encouraged the establishment of societies in other states. In Philadelphia in October 1896, Witmer Stone, Academy of Natural Sciences conservator of ornithology and AOU bird protection committee member, helped form the Pennsylvania Audubon Society, modeled after the society in Massachusetts. "During the year," he reported to Dutcher, "I have delivered a number of lectures in Philadelphia and vicinity before schools, societies, etc. on ornithology. . . . Mrs. Olive Thorne Miller's course of lectures in the city last spring was productive of good results." A branch of the Pennsylvania society was organized in Wheeling, West Virginia.[20]

Pearson's writings suggest he had read books by Miller—*In*

*Nesting Time*, perhaps, or *Little Brothers of the Air*, in both of which bird behavior, closely observed, was often portrayed in human terms. Probably he had also read Florence A. Merriam's *Birds through an Opera Glass* and *A-Birding on a Bronco*, as well as Mabel Osgood Wright's *Birdcraft* and *Tommy-Anne and the Three Hearts*. All three women produced widely popular works. Dutcher added Rood, Miller, and Merriam (C. Hart Merriam's sister) to the AOU bird protection committee in 1896.[21]

C. Hart Merriam's Division of Ornithology and Mammalogy in the U.S. Department of Agriculture gained status when it became the Biological Survey in July 1896. Studies in economic ornithology expanded. As defined by Theodore S. Palmer, survey assistant chief and AOU bird protection committee member, economic ornithology is "the study of birds from the standpoint of dollars and cents. . . . It is the practical application of the knowledge of birds in everyday life." The survey's Circular No. 17 encouraged school administrators to observe Bird Day and require lessons on birds. Dutcher maintained that no laws to protect birds would be enforced until public sympathies were aroused and urged AOU and Audubon members to distribute the circular widely. Children "should be taught in every grade, from the kindergarten to the college, not only the aesthetic but the economical value of our birds." The Massachusetts Audubon Society sent teachers and superintendents in the state suggested Bird Day programs.[22]

While collecting on the coast during the Christmas holidays of 1896, Pearson bought a "Brünnich's murre" (now Thick-billed Murre, *Uria lomvia*) from a New Bern woman who said it had been shot near the Neuse River mouth. A member of the auk family, oceanic birds of the north, the Thick-billed Murre rarely ventured south of New York, and Pearson's acquisition was the first recorded in North Carolina. When he brought it back to Guilford along with other specimens, he had no good place for it. The museum had become so crowded he often left newly collected specimens in packing boxes. A proposal to move the museum to a large room in the YMCA building had been considered but not adopted. In the spring, American Tobacco Company president James B. Duke and his brother, Benjamin N. Duke, both of whom had attended the New Garden Boarding School, donated ten thousand dollars for a science building. The donation was celebrated at a faculty and student "jollification meeting," with college yells, music, and speeches. Representing the senior class, Pearson read resolutions of thanks. Tentative plans allotted a large room, thirty-six by fifty-five feet, for the museum.[23]

Pearson wanted to continue his education at the best institution he could attend. No affirmative responses came from such well-established institutions as Harvard, Yale, and Princeton, to which he had applied for employment as a museum curator and for the privilege of attending lectures. He wrote to North Carolina state geologist Joseph A. Holmes in Chapel Hill, asking for part-time employment that would enable him to attend the University of North Carolina. When Holmes had lectured at Guilford the previous spring, he had impressed Pearson with his presentation and his stereopticon slides. Pearson felt close to this man whose life was spent largely outdoors and wrote him with great expectations. He was deeply disappointed when Holmes "replied with a polite note expressing his regret that the State Geological Survey was unable to avail itself of my services." Pearson was depressed by the prospect of giving up ornithology and the effort to save birds and of returning to a Florida farm that barely met his parents' basic needs.[24]

Politics, to which Pearson had paid little attention, unexpectedly opened a way for him. In the elections of 1896 in North Carolina, the Democratic party, which had controlled the state administration since the end of Reconstruction, lost to the Fusion party, a combination of Populists and Republicans. Republican

Daniel L. Russell was elected governor; Populist William H. Worth, a Guilford trustee, was elected state treasurer. Like many southern Quakers, Pearson thought of himself as a Republican. He asked Worth whether Herbert H. Brimley, State Museum of Natural History curator, would be replaced. When Worth said yes, Pearson decided to apply for the position. Worth agreed to recommend him, as did President Hobbs, President Edwin A. Alderman of the University of North Carolina, and Professor Dixie Lee Bryant of the State Normal and Industrial School. Bryant requested Holmes, as a favor to her, to offer Pearson advice and support. Then Pearson wrote to Holmes, asking him for a letter of recommendation.[25]

As Pearson remembered events forty years later, he talked in Raleigh with Worth, who took him to Governor Russell. After questioning Pearson briefly, Russell said he could have the curator's position. Pearson returned to the treasurer's office, where he waited while Worth conveyed Russell's wishes to the chairman of the State Board of Agriculture. Holmes, who was also in the capitol at the time, learned what was happening. Distressed, he went immediately to Pearson. Why was he displacing Brimley? When Pearson explained that what he desired most was a position enabling him to study at the university, Holmes offered him a job in his Chapel Hill office.[26]

Surviving records show some of these events occurred in correspondence. By letter, Holmes asked Pearson why he sought the curator's position. Pearson replied he had been encouraged to apply by Fusion leaders who said most persons appointed by the outgoing Democratic administration would be ousted. Brimley himself had told Pearson he expected to lose his job. "I had hoped to go to college next year but could see no opening in any direction," Pearson wrote to Holmes. "I am entirely on my own resources and naturally was on the lookout for anything which I could do." More conversation followed the letters. In the end,

Brimley kept the curator's position and Pearson was employed in Holmes's office. Beginning June 1897, Holmes stated, Pearson would work two years for the Geological Survey, giving not more than a third of his time, for two hundred dollars a year.[27]

By graduation time at Guilford, Pearson's life had taken on an aura of order and progress. The college museum would soon have enlarged quarters, a curator to succeed him had already been appointed, he himself had a new position and a chance to continue his education, and he had a girlfriend, Elsie Weatherly. Perhaps with a feeling of gratitude to the church that had made such things possible, he decided not to talk about birds in his final oratorical appearance. As one of four seniors chosen to perform on commencement day, he orated on "The Influence of Friends in America."[28]

Afterward, he went to Charlotte to retrieve a college exhibit he had set up earlier in an exposition. Meanwhile a student friend, unnamed in Pearson's correspondence, invited him to spend the summer with him and his family in Michigan. Pearson had not had a vacation since entering Guilford. He wrote Holmes that he was "nervous and pretty much worn out" and requested permission to report to his new job in the fall rather than in June. Holmes agreed, but he apparently asked Pearson to collect for the Geological Survey while he was away. He spent part of the summer at Earlham College in Indiana, making field trips under the guidance of Joseph Moore, who helped him identify fossils he collected along the Whitewater River and added to them duplicates from the Earlham collections.[29]

# 5

# "A thousand impressions"

## (1897–1898)

THE PEARSON WHO entered the University of North Carolina had advantages over the Pearson who had gone to Guilford six years earlier. When he enrolled in the junior class for laboratory courses that had been unavailable at Guilford, most of his classmates were younger and less experienced than he. By the end of October, he had been chosen for the junior class football team and the Dialectic Literary Society and had been elected corresponding secretary of the YMCA. He had also been chosen as an editor of the *North Carolina University Magazine*, judged to have given the best speech saying no to the proposal that trusts are detrimental to society's best interests, and selected by acclamation to represent the junior class in debates with the Philanthropic Literary Society.[1]

In his spare time Pearson continued to study birds and to teach others about them. From Chapel Hill he contributed notes and articles to the *Auk*, the *Journal of the Elisha Mitchell Scientific Society*, the *North Carolina Journal of Education*, and the *North Carolina University Magazine*, which also published two of his short stories, both with nature themes. "The Story of a Snow-Bird's [Dark-eyed Junco, *Junco hyemalis*] Nest," set in the North Carolina mountains, contained a poem, "To the Carolina Snow-Bird," which the *State*

*Normal Magazine* reprinted.[2] Simultaneously university staff member and student, he taught a noncredit course in ornithology that included lessons in taxidermy and collected specimens for the university's biological laboratory and the State Museum of Natural History. He also gathered information for a book on North Carolina birds. No one had yet written a monograph on the birds of any southern state, though articles and lists had been published.

In the university's libraries, Pearson had access to most publications on North Carolina birds. He could read about the birds seen by the members of Sir Walter Raleigh's expeditions and later by explorer and author John Lawson. Still later, Coues reported on birds, mammals, and reptiles at Fort Macon, on the coast; Brewster described birds he saw and collected on a trip into the mountains; John S. Cairns, superintendent of a small woolen mill near Weaverville, studied birds in the surrounding mountains and collected for Brewster.[3] George F. Atkinson, a botanist who taught for two years at the university, had in 1887 compiled a "preliminary catalogue" of 255 bird species recorded as having been seen in the state, but he missed a few important reports, including Coues's. In 1897, Pearson's first year at Chapel Hill, John W. P. Smithwick amended the catalogue, recording 303 species and subspecies.[4]

Clement S. Brimley, the most prolific writer of short articles on North Carolina birds, managed the natural history shop he and his brother H. H. Brimley had established in Raleigh soon after their arrival from England in 1880. Providing "First-class Bird and Mammal Skins and Eggs. Reptiles and Batrachians both alive and in alcohol," they traded often with amateur collectors throughout the South and abroad. In the North Carolina fields, woods, swamps, and lakes, they found specimens to sell and accumulated data they reported in periodicals. Between 1886 and 1894, C. S. Brimley contributed more than sixty reports to the *Ornithologist and Oologist* and collaborated with his brother on ten more. H. H. also wrote several articles on his own. By 1894 many advanced ornithologists were protesting against hobbyist collecting of bird skins and eggs, and the Brimleys were less often in the field gathering items to sell to hobbyists. Moreover, after H. H. became state museum curator in 1895, neither brother had much time for writing. One was busy with the museum, and the other had to run the shop. When Pearson met them, they had for the time being stopped writing about birds.[5]

In Chapel Hill, the university campus offered an attractive environment to which even normally shy birds occasionally came. On wet ground inside the east wall, Pearson flushed an American Woodcock (*Scolopax minor*); in the same spot on another day he found several Common Snipes (*Gallinago gallinago*). Pileated Woodpeckers at times looked for food in large trees close to the college buildings. A Wild Turkey flew across the campus and landed behind the Episcopal church. Where Kenan Stadium was later built, Pearson collected, in fall migration, the first Bay-breasted Warbler (*Dendroica castanea*) to be recorded in North Carolina. He made a special study of migrating warblers, going out to search for them on twenty-one days between September 15 and October 15, and collected sixteen species for the university laboratory.[6]

Often he was up early and out of doors searching for birds while most other people on campus were still asleep. He became familiar with individual birds in definable territories. A Northern Mockingbird and a female American Kestrel were subjects of "Neighbors of Mine," his first article on birds in the *North Carolina University Magazine*. The mockingbird lived near a small, vine-covered church and was as "fine a singer" as any mockingbird he had ever heard in Florida, one exception to the saying that the more northern the mockingbird the less beautiful the song. He named the kestrel Xantippe, for Socrates' wife, because she had a quarrelsome disposition. Living largely on beetles and mice, Xantippe swooped down in annoyance on House Sparrows (*Passer domes-*

*ticus*), Eastern Meadowlarks (*Sturnella magna*), and other birds that
came near her favorite perch on a football goalpost. Two students,
on separate occasions, had shot at her and missed.

In March 1898 Pearson wrote to Chapman about his new position: "In connection with my work on the Survey I am endeavoring
to gather all the information possible on the bird life of the state.
Am in communication with all the parties of the state who are
students of birds, also with most of our light-house keepers and
life-saving station masters along our coast." (Chapman's *Handbook*
had been so popular he had revised it swiftly and repeatedly. Two
years after the original work appeared, he put out a fourth edition,
which Pearson reviewed briefly in the *North Carolina University
Magazine*, saying "it has no equal.")[7]

Pearson and H. H. Brimley had become friends. For a few days
that March, they collected birds on the coast. At a fair in New
Bern, they made lists of birds exhibited as examples of the state's
game resources. Pearson counted thirty-one species, including
some he had not previously seen in North Carolina. For Brimley,
"one of the most clearly defined incidents" of the trip was his own
"uncertainty as to the propriety of suggesting to a Quaker" that
they watch trotting races when their "business for the day was
concluded."[8]

The following month, Pearson accompanied Joseph Holmes
and two other members of his Geological Survey staff, miner-
alogist Joseph Hyde Pratt and forester William W. Ashe, on a ten-
day trip to Pamlico and Albemarle Sounds. Pearson collected
water birds while the other men made field studies. They lived on
the State Shell Fish Commission's steamer, *Lilly*. After a day at
Cape Hatteras, they returned to their dinghy on Pamlico Sound's
marshy shore. The *Lilly* was anchored four miles out. Having
explored Florida lakes and bays, when Pearson saw whitecaps less
than a mile offshore he recognized the possibility of danger and
suggested the party stay ashore until dawn. Holmes and the other

men, none of whom were experienced boatmen, wanted to return
to the steamer's comforts. Pearson warned them that the dinghy
was too small to carry the entire party safely in the rough water.
Although they discounted his opinion, Holmes let Pearson stay
ashore and arrange for a fisherman to sail him to the *Lilly* at dawn.
While Pearson watched, the men rowed toward the *Lilly*'s faintly
visible lights. The next morning, they came ashore again, ex-
hausted, their hands lacerated. Before reaching the *Lilly*, they told
Pearson, the dinghy almost foundered in the heavy waves. All
night they had struggled, first unsuccessfully to get to the *Lilly*,
then to return to land. Holmes conceded that one more man's
weight would have swamped the boat. Previously he had been "a
little distant" in manner to Pearson, perhaps because he resented
having been manipulated into giving him a job. After the boating
adventure, "his attitude underwent a change." When Pearson,
stimulated by the expedition, asked permission to remain alone on
the coast and continue collecting, Holmes agreed to pay him thirty
dollars a month and expenses and left open the date for his return
to Chapel Hill.[9] The group spent a last day together at Fort
Macon, across Bogue Sound from Beaufort, where Pearson collected five Bonaparte's Gulls (*Larus philadelphia*). A winter visitor,
the Bonaparte's Gull was, in Pearson's words, the "smallest and
most dainty gull" to appear on the North Carolina coast and
somewhat shyer than in Florida.[10]

Pearson withdrew from class and began what turned out to be
an almost unbroken period of five months exploring the North
Carolina coast. "The experiences of that spring and summer left a
thousand impressions imprinted on my mind," he wrote later.[11]
(They also provided him with much data for his North Carolina
bird book.) Four days after leaving Holmes and Fort Macon, he
was more than fifty miles away at Wyesocking Bay in Pamlico
Sound. In cedar trees near Lake Landing, he found Green-backed
Heron nests so close together that they formed a colony, a rarity

for the species. At Lake Mattamuskeet, he watched Tree Swallows (*Tachycineta bicolor*), not known to nest in North Carolina, behaving as if they were looking for a nesting site. "Over and over, for half an hour, they busied themselves flying about a dead tree on which they repeatedly perched and engaged in examining an old wood-pecker's hole." Three days later, on Cape Hatteras, he saw more of the same behavior, but he never found evidence that any Tree Swallows remained to nest. (Many years later, in June 1979, a pair of Tree Swallows was recorded as nesting not on the coast but on the New River in the North Carolina mountains.) On Hatteras Island, a favorite nesting place for Bald Eagles, he collected two immature birds. At Roanoke Island, he was given a captive eaglet that he sent to Brimley, who kept it alive "for many months" in the state museum.[12]

Pearson crossed Albemarle Sound to Belvidere, on the Per-quimans River, returned to Lake Mattamuskeet, and from there went back to Cape Hatteras. Thousands of migrating shorebirds congregated on the wet, grassy beaches near the lighthouse. He explored the area for nearly three weeks, May 2 to 20, studying, and with one exception collecting, sixteen species: Short-billed Dowitcher (*Limnodromus griseus*); Sanderling (*Calidris alba*); Ruddy Turnstone (*Arenaria interpres*); Common Snipe; Long-billed Curlew (*Numenius americanus*); Lesser Yellowlegs (*Tringa flavipes*); Greater Yellowlegs (*Tringa melanoleuca*); Piping Plover (*Charadrius melodus*); Semipalmated Plover (*Charadrius semipalmatus*); Black-bellied Plover; Stilt Sandpiper (*Calidris himantopus*); Least Sand-piper (*Calidris minutilla*); Spotted Sandpiper; Semipalmated Sandpiper (*Calidris pusilla*); White-rumped Sandpiper (*Calidris fuscicollis*); and Dunlin (*Calidris alpina*). The Stilt Sandpiper, unre-corded in the state before, was flying alone with no other birds nearby.[13]

Among some rushes on Gull Shoal Island, a two-hundred-acre patch of salt marsh in the Pamlico Sound about twenty miles north of Cape Hatteras, Pearson found four fresh eggs in the new nest of a Virginia Rail (*Rallus limicola*), a bird not previously known to breed south of New Jersey. Thirty-eight years would pass before another Virginia Rail nest was recorded in North Carolina.[14]

On the Outer Banks in April and May, Pearson saw hundreds of Double-crested Cormorants, a species ornithologists had not noted as nesting in any southeastern state except Florida. When he found no nests, Pearson conjectured the birds must be using lakes on the mainland. At Havelock, on a Neuse River tributary in Pamlico County, he hired a mule and wagon, a light canoe, and a guide. Following a course suggested by numerous rumors, he drove through woods, swamps, and freshwater marshes for about ten miles until he came to what had been a plantation. He and the guide put the canoe in a drainage ditch and paddled through a cypress swamp to the shallow waters of Lake Ellis. No cormorants were to be seen. The guide carried the canoe inverted over his head as they pushed on another mile, first over a marsh, then through a tangled jungle of vines and trees to Great Lake, a "beautiful rippling sheet" of water Pearson estimated at seven miles long and five miles wide. Cypress trees and stumps stood in the water for distances of up to about two hundred yards from shore. The guide told Pearson they would surely find cormorant nests. "And we found them!"[15]

In eighteen cypress trees near the north shore, scattered for a distance of a mile and a half, Pearson counted 150 nests, all occupied. One tree held thirty-eight nests, some with eggs, others with young birds. "When first hatched the young are naked and look like little, animated, greasy rubber bags. In a few days they assume a thick growth of black down." Several young birds were old enough to climb about in the trees. "In doing this they would often lose their balance on the limbs . . . but instead of falling into the water the hook at the point of the long bill would invariably catch on the perch and by dint of much scratching the birds would soon regain their former position."[16] The cormorants fed largely on eels. There was eel slime on their heads, and the young birds, when excited, disgorged eel fragments. Pearson collected several adult cormorants and captured a few young ones for Brimley. The specimens varied so much in size he did not know what name to give them: Double-crested Cormorants or Florida Cormorants. Later, acting on Robert Ridgway's advice, he called them Florida Cormorants. Eventually, the name Florida Cormorant, except as a local term, was subsumed by Double-crested Cormorant.[17]

At Orton Plantation, on the Cape Fear River in Brunswick County, Pearson was taken to the upper reaches of a mile-long pond where Great Egrets, Little Blue Herons, Great Blue Herons, and Tricolored Herons were nesting. Camouflaged in a boat with gray moss and cypress branches, Pearson and a guide rowed under low trees bearing heron nests. The young birds, "possibly in their efforts to drive us away, or, perhaps, because of their great uneasiness, would disgorge large quantities of partially digested minnows. In fitful streams these would descend upon us, falling in the boat, in our laps, our pockets, or down our necks."[18]

Near a heron colony, Pearson flushed an Anhinga from its nest in a small cypress tree. An "odd-looking and weirdly acting bird," the Anhinga had not been known to nest in North Carolina. This specimen was a male in "magnificent plumage." The large, heavy nest, made of sticks and lined with gray moss and cedar twigs, contained four eggs. Before leaving the plantation, Pearson collected the bird, the eggs, and the nest, along with the section of the tree to which the nest was fastened, and shipped them to the state museum. They are still displayed there, mounted in a group. For more than three decades thereafter, Pearson wrote later, no Anhinga nest was found in the eastern United States north of this point.[19]

Fishermen, lighthouse keepers, and crews of life-saving stations often fed Pearson and gave him a place to sleep. Some who hunted birds for market told him stories about the large numbers of birds formerly inhabiting the coast. Years earlier, they had found enormous colonies of gulls and terns and had shot them by the tens of thousands, leaving the young to die. One hunter told him, "At such places I have often shot strikers [terns] so fast that I had to put my gun overboard to cool the barrels." Gulls and terns were shot for their feathers, shorebirds for food. "Curlews, willets, plovers, yellow-legs, and dowitchers" brought the highest prices, but "turnstones [Ruddy Turnstones, *Arenaria interpres*], sanderlings, sandpipers and other species of the beaches" were also marketable. In migration, shorebirds still came to feed at shallow pools along the beaches. Pearson watched the hunters work. Some with guns concealed themselves between feeding grounds; others drove the birds from one feeding ground to another, within the gunners' range. Often the birds flew in "such compact flocks that many could be killed at each shot. I counted more than forty that dropped at the single discharge of a gun."

When Pearson expressed his disapproval of the extensive slaughter, one hunter said to him, "Pore folks have as good a right to live as city people. The good Lord put us here and the Good Book says, 'man shall have dominion over all creatures.'" Another hunter understood Pearson's concern for the future. "We ought to have a law to protect them until they catch up their numbers again. If something like this ain't done the plume-bird business will sure come to an end." A. T. Piner, a taxidermist as well as a hunter, showed Pearson his collection of birds, which included two Razorbills (*Alca torda*) and a Parasitic Jaeger (*Stercorarius parasiticus*). Pearson bought the jaeger and sent it to Brimley for the state museum, where for several decades it was recorded as the only bird of the species to have come to North Carolina.[20]

Pearson spent ten days at the end of June 1898 in Chapel Hill and then was sent to Beaufort, where Professor Henry Van Peters Wilson, Geological Survey biologist, studied marine life. Until the end of July, Pearson assisted Wilson and collected specimens for Brimley. "Captured a Portuguese man-o-war this A.M. together with some fish, crabs, &c. washed in by the present prevaling [*sic*] gale of wind from the gulf stream," he wrote to Holmes. Brimley reported to Holmes that the more than one hundred species of "marine material" Pearson sent him were "very valuable." For two weeks in August, on Holmes's instructions, Pearson surveyed the coastal fish scrap and oil industry, which the State Board of Agriculture wished to enlarge. He went with fishermen to catch menhaden and visited factories in which the oil was pressed out of the fish and the remains were converted to fertilizer.[21]

When Pearson was scheduled to return to work in Chapel Hill in September and re-enter the university, he asked Holmes for leave to visit his parents in Archer. "I have not seen them for two years, they are old, and are hoping very much that I can come to see them soon." He requested leave for a month; Holmes consented to his going for two weeks at the end of August.[22]

# 6

# "Life on the Holiday Campus"

## *(1898–1899)*

PEARSON AND John Mabry Greenfield, a law student and former Guilford classmate who later practiced law in New York, shared New East dormitory room 24, with bird pictures on the walls and mounted birds on the bookcase and clothes closet. Pearson enrolled in the junior courses he had dropped the previous spring, added senior courses, and worked in the state geologist's office and the university laboratory. To Theodore S. Palmer, U.S. Biological Survey assistant chief, he sent reports on migrating birds elicited from lighthouse keepers. At the October meeting of the Elisha Mitchell Scientific Society, which he joined, he read a paper on eastern North Carolina's "colony breeding birds."[1]

He was elected YMCA president and joined President Alderman and three faculty members in addressing new students at a reception. He became involved in bi-weekly twenty-minute YMCA meetings, monthly meetings, Sunday morning lectures, Bible classes, meetings of a committee to help the sick, and a drive to raise money for a YMCA building. The Sunday morning lectures were offered by Professor Kemp Plummer Battle, former university president and longtime observer of Chapel Hill birds. Pearson questioned him about his observations and took notes.[2]

The September issue of the *North Carolina Journal of Education*, founded and edited by Philander P. Claxton, State Normal and Industrial College professor of pedagogy, carried the first of several contributions by Pearson. "The Study of Birds in the Public Schools" endorsed children's studying nature in general and birds in particular. Nature study "deals with objects untouched by man, and as the children go on in their work there is sure to be aroused in them a sense of reverence and a love for the Infinite—the Creator of all things." They learn to appreciate natural beauty: "instead of wandering through the world blindly, they go on, as Mr. Burroughs says, 'opening up eye after eye' for the beauty around them."[3]

Southern states, including North Carolina, lagged behind northern states in developing bird study programs and bird protection societies and laws. "The protection we give birds during the nesting season in the North is not wholly satisfactory if they are shot on migrating South," wrote Florence Merriam, "and, as is well known, many of our most valuable insectivorous birds are used for food in the South, and as soon as they begin migrating are subjected to a persistent fusillade." Pearson had gathered data on the destruction of gulls and terns by feather hunters on the North Carolina coast. More than thirty breeding places had existed as late as 1880, but by 1898 only seven remained, "aggregating in all probably not more than 5,000 birds."[4]

In Texas, E. Irene Rood organized Bands of Mercy she hoped would, to some extent, "cover the same ground" as Audubon societies. Bands of Mercy had been introduced into the United States from England by the Reverend Thomas Timmins of Portsmouth, England, and George T. Angell of Boston, president and founder of the Massachusetts Society for the Prevention of Cruelty to Animals. Anyone could join a Band of Mercy by pledging to "try to be kind to all harmless living creatures, and try to protect them from cruel usage." By 1884, 3,403 Bands of Mercy in the United States had 234,000 members, mostly children. They wore pins bearing such mottoes as "Kindness to all harmless living creatures." Monthly meetings featured addresses, readings, hymns, and "anecdotes of good and noble sayings and deeds done to both human and dumb creatures." Primary school teachers received Angell's "Ten Lessons on Kindness to Animals," with one lesson devoted to birds. Like societies for the prevention of cruelty to animals, Bands of Mercy were more interested in domestic than in wild animals.[5]

Dutcher meanwhile had been urging all AOU members to help form additional Audubon societies. In February 1897, the Audubon Society of the State of New York was organized, with Chapman as executive officer and board chairman. In May, the Audubon Society of the District of Columbia was organized explicitly "in cooperation with the American Ornithologists' Union." Dutcher reported state societies founded in New Hampshire, Wisconsin, Minnesota (reported as "partly organized"), New Jersey, Rhode Island, and Illinois. The Maine Audubon Society founded in 1902 may have been a revival of one organized in 1897. As AOU bird protection committee chairman, Dutcher assumed the role of unofficial Audubon national chairman, encouraging each society secretary and other society officials to write to him for guidance and send him regular progress reports. His circular letter to newspaper editors about the Audubon cause was distributed widely by the Audubon Society of the State of New York.[6]

By the end of 1897, the Massachusetts Audubon Society, with 110 local secretaries, had distributed thousands of leaflets, including Florence A. Merriam's "How Birds Affect the Farm and Garden," Chapman's "The Wearing of Herons' Plumes or Aigrettes," and several U.S. government publications. The Massachusetts legislature was persuaded to pass a law prohibiting the use of song birds in millinery, but local police officials did not enforce it. In New York, Merriam reported, signers of pledges to the old

Audubon Society no longer abided by them. The new movement must be different, she wrote to Dutcher. "We do not want it to be a passing enthusiasm, but a vital growth." Dutcher could not understand why intelligent women continued to wear bird feathers. "It certainly is a curious inconsistency to visit a church or a lecture room and listen to a discourse on some philanthropic subject and note the extreme sympathy displayed by scores of women, while at the same time their hats are decorated with plumes and feathers that could only have been obtained by acts of the extremest cruelty." His long list of suggested activities for AOU members included lecturing to farmers, women's clubs, and any other "gathering of people where the subject of bird protection and the value of birds" could be "urged"; lobbying for Bird Day; and discouraging skin and egg collecting except by scientists or for scientific purposes. AOU members should "be prepared to instruct and interest anyone with whom they are thrown in contact."[7]

Dutcher was asking ornithologists to sacrifice enormous amounts of time to bird protection. Not everyone could comply. Perhaps such work took Dutcher himself away too often from his business, or perhaps an unexplained crisis arose. For whatever reason, in the fall of 1897, he announced his resignation, at least temporarily, from the committee chairmanship. Witmer Stone succeeded him.[8]

By Dutcher's count, state Audubon societies were organized in four more states (Connecticut, Ohio, Indiana, and Iowa) in 1898. The California Audubon Society organized in 1904 may have been a revival of one created in 1898. Some of the early societies existed "in name only," Pearson wrote years later. A state society established in Texas in 1898 or 1899 apparently died and was reborn in 1903 or 1904. Audubon leaders who approached local milliners sometimes won their support. A joint exhibit of "birdless hats" by Philadelphia milliners was followed by displays of "Audubon

Millinery" at individual firms.[9] The Connecticut Audubon Society provided for loan texts of bird lectures, a stereopticon projector, and colored slides. In New York, in cooperation with the state's fourteen normal colleges, Chapman prepared a course in bird study for use in each college. Several state Audubon societies sponsored junior societies in the schools. In Wisconsin, the adult membership rose to more than five thousand, the school membership to more than four thousand.[10]

Sentiment against collecting birds and eggs as a hobby continued to grow. Even ornithologists were urged not to collect birds unless they had no alternative. "The collections of our large museums," wrote Witmer Stone, "placed cordially at the convenience of students, answer the needs of many who would otherwise have to possess a cabinet of their own, and many an ornithologist today—well deserving of the title—has pursued his studies without a gun." On Stone's initiative, a leaflet signed by a group of the AOU's best-known ornithologists (including Stone, Allen, Chapman, Ridgway, Merriam, Brewster, and Dutcher) was addressed to boys and girls who were encouraged by dealers to acquire large egg collections. "This is not science," Stone wrote in "Hints to Young Bird Students," "and the men who advocate this sort of collecting, and who have the largest collections of eggs, rarely contribute anything to our knowledge of birds, and are not advancing the science of ornithology."[11]

William T. Hornaday, director of the New York Zoological Society's zoological garden, sent a questionnaire to authorities in every state and territory inquiring about the status of bird life during the period 1883–98. From twenty-eight states, the District of Columbia, and the Indian Territory came replies indicating that bird life had decreased an average of 46 percent.[12] George O. Shields, editor of the outdoor magazine *Recreation*, was concerned about the large numbers of fish, birds, and other game his fellow hunters and fishermen killed. In the absence of adequate bag limits, he tried to build sentiment against excessive killing by ridiculing "fish hogs" and "game hogs," whom he identified by name in his magazine. In January 1898, at a meeting in New York attended by sportsmen from seventeen states, Shields organized the League of American Sportsmen, primarily to "enforce game-laws where such exist and to secure and enforce such laws which are not now existent." Other national sportsmen's associations had been created and had died; two (the National Game, Bird, and Fish Protective Association and the Interstate Game and Fish Protective Association) were still alive. Although the League of American Sportsmen, uniting hunters, fishermen, ornithologists, and amateur naturalists, flourished only a few years, it exerted considerable force in behalf of national wildlife legislation. [13]

Senator George F. Hoar, Massachusetts Audubon Society vice-president, introduced a bill to prohibit importing wild bird plumage into the United States for millinery purposes. Ornithologists at the AOU's annual meeting in November 1898 generally agreed that the bill should not be supported until laws protecting American birds had been strengthened. Under existing conditions, a ban on importing feathers might encourage even more killing of American birds to meet feather market demand. The bill failed, as did a revised version in 1900. Chapman attributed the failure partly to opposition from "prominent naturalists." [14]

The AOU bird protection committee in 1898 distributed many copies of its model state law, along with suggestions for modifying it wherever strong resistance was encountered. After hearing Ruthven Deane talk about the law at a meeting in Chicago, game wardens from Illinois, Michigan, Ohio, Wisconsin, Minnesota, and North Dakota agreed to present it to their respective legislatures. Special appeals were made to farmers, many of whom seemed receptive to arguments that birds protected their crops. Impressive statistics had been compiled. In the Biological Survey laboratory, F. E. L. Beal sat at his table day after day, examining the contents of birds' stomachs. Ultimately he studied 37,825 stomachs. His small monograph, "Some Common Birds in Their Relation to Agriculture," published in 1897 as Farmer's Bulletin No. 54, summarized the results of his studies in simple, direct language. The AOU bird protection committee and Audubon leaders circulated the bulletin quickly and widely. By 1933 more than two million copies had been distributed and Beal was credited with having done "more than any other man to reveal the basic facts that were needed to convince legislators of the value of bird protection." [15]

Pearson remained on the university campus during the Christmas holidays of 1898, concentrating on a reading program and taking occasional walks. He watched a Yellow-bellied Sapsucker (*Sphyrapicus varius*) that for weeks had been feeding on one tree. Eastern Meadowlarks patrolled the grounds daily. Some Northern Flickers became bold; twice he found one inside a building with an open window. The female American Kestrel he had named Xantippe still perched on the football goalpost, and her mate, whom Pearson called Socrates, claimed the top of a locust tree. "Sometimes they would both come and perch near the laboratory, high on the fourth floor, and nod to each other and look in at the wide windows. Then the boys would look up from their microscopes and call to each other that the little Hawks had come to look on again." [16] At night the kestrels roosted under the eaves of Pearson's dormitory. A sapsucker was needed for the university laboratory, but Pearson had grown so fond of the one he saw daily, he could not collect it or any of the other campus birds.

Several other students remained on campus for the holidays. Just before Christmas, one of them killed Socrates, the male kestrel, and left the body on the ground. Pearson found the dead bird and buried him "beneath the locust tree on which he had loved to sit." One sunny morning, several students went hunting off campus. They returned with a rabbit and three Northern Bob-whites and on campus shot nine pigeons (Rock Doves, *Columba livia*), two meadowlarks, one flicker, and the sapsucker. In the evening, they cooked the game in an iron pot on a box stove in a dormitory room. The next day, most of the surviving birds that usually fed about the campus went elsewhere, except for Xantippe, the female kestrel, who flew at dusk to her roosting place under the dormitory eaves. Once more a gun fired. Xantippe managed to fly over the campus wall to die in the woods.[17]

Pearson later recalled that he "brooded over the matter and wrote, for relief, a story of the hunt and the banquet which followed." "Life on the Holiday Campus," a protest, appeared in the February *North Carolina University Magazine.* As far as Pearson could tell, his article had little influence on student behavior. After the holidays, he again offered a noncredit ornithology course, in which a "dozen or more" students helped him compile records on Chapel Hill birds.[18]

AOU and Audubon leaders felt there was a need for a national journal of ornithology that would reach the general public. Witmer Stone had been able to include only a few reports submitted by the Audubon societies in the AOU bird protection committee annual report for 1898 published in the *Auk.* He recommended the creation of a magazine through which the state societies could communicate with each other and news could be disseminated among members. Chapman had noted a rapid increase in the number of observers of birds ("those who study 'birds through an opera-glass'") as differentiated from bird collectors. Bird observers bought books on ornithology, especially clearly written textbooks. In the six-year period ending in 1898, publishers sold more than seventy thousand copies of such books in New York and Boston, a statistic that seemed to suggest a strong potential market for a popular journal of ornithology. Chapman obtained the endorse-

ment of all the state Audubon societies and solicited manuscripts
from John Burroughs, Bradford Torrey, Olive Thorne Miller,
William Brewster, Florence A. Merriam, Ernest Thompson Se-
ton, Mabel Osgood Wright, and other well-known authors. In
February 1899 he issued the first number of *Bird-Lore, a Bi-Monthly
Magazine Devoted to the Study and Protection of Birds*, the "official
organ of the Audubon Societies," with "the best photographs of
wild birds which have as yet been published in this country." To
Mabel Osgood Wright, the Audubon societies department editor,
Stone gave all the Audubon societies' reports. She urged the
Audubon leaders to send her lists of their publications, describe
their past successes and failures ("even the record of discourage-
ments . . . may often prove full of suggestion to workers in the
same field"), and announce their plans for the future. By June,
Chapman had a motto for *Bird-Lore*: "A bird in the bush is worth
two in the hand."[19]

New York governor Theodore Roosevelt, whom Chapman
characterized as a "born bird-lover," joined the Audubon movement. At fourteen, Roosevelt had already acquired a "good working knowledge of America bird life." His first printed work was
*The Summer Birds of the Adirondacks*, a catalog of birds he studied on
three expeditions. He entered Harvard intending to become, he
wrote later, "a scientific man of the Audubon, or Wilson, or Baird,
or Coues type—a man like Hart Merriam, or Frank Chapman, or
Hornaday, to-day." But his experience in Harvard's science classes
changed his mind. His professors "treated biology as purely a
science of the laboratory and the microscope," and Roosevelt had
"no more desire or ability to be a microscopist and section-cutter
than to be a mathematician."[20] In 1888, inspired by Grinnell, he
founded the Boone and Crockett Club, in which he brought
together a group of men interested in hunting, camping, and
preserving forests "as nurseries and reservations for woodland
creatures which else would die out before the march of settle-
ment."[21]

Unable to attend the Audubon Society of the State of New York meeting in 1899, Roosevelt wrote Chapman that he "heartily" sympathized with the society's purposes. "The destruction of the Wild Pigeon [Passenger Pigeon] and the Carolina Paroquet has meant a loss as severe as if the Catskills or the Palisades were taken away. When I hear of the destruction of a species I feel just as if all the works of some great writer had perished; as if we had lost all instead of only part of Polybius or Livy."[22]

Through one medium or another, Pearson continued teaching people about birds. In the *North Carolina Journal of Education*, he published a four-part series on woodpeckers ("woodland carpenters," he called them, borrowing an expression from Chapman's *Bird-Life*). Written in a tone teachers might emulate, each article concluded with questions for children to answer.[23]

A cold wave in February 1899 brought freezing rain and sleet that iced over tree limbs and twigs, grass and weeds. Then came a heavy snow and temperatures near zero. One evening, a "snowbird" (Dark-eyed Junco) went into the wall of Pearson's dormitory through an opening between two bricks. The next day, Pearson sprinkled bread crumbs on the snow. The bird returned about sunset, seemed to examine the crumbs, possibly ate some, and slipped into the wall. The next morning from his room Pearson saw a junco being attacked by a hungry Blue Jay. He opened his window, waved a piece of paper, and shouted. The jay ignored him. Pearson ran outside and floundered toward the birds, shouting as he went. The weakened junco broke loose from the jay's grasp but flew only a short distance before it dropped to the snow again. The jay pecked it hard before Pearson reached the two birds. Then the jay retreated a few yards. Concentrating on the jay, Pearson did not see which way the junco went. Whether it survived the attack and whether it was the same junco that had roosted in the dormitory wall Pearson never knew, although no junco came to the roost again.[24]

When Ruthven Deane, Illinois Audubon Society president and AOU bird protection committee member, wrote Pearson in March to ask how many birds had died in the cold, he wrote on the bottom of Deane's letter, as if making notes for a reply, that he had counted the frozen bodies of two "doves" (Mourning Doves, *Zenaida macroura*), ten "bluebirds" (Eastern Bluebirds, *Sialia sialis*), two dozen White-throated Sparrows (*Zonotrichia albicollis*), and nearly two dozen "snowbirds." Also, he wrote, "Saw a jay trying to kill a snowbird."[25]

During the spring and summer, Pearson tried to arrange to stay in Chapel Hill, work on a master's degree, and continue studying birds. His two-year contract with Holmes would be up at summer's end. Holmes declined to extend the agreement, apparently not regarding ornithological work as a fully authorized part of the Geological Survey's responsibilities. Although he used Pearson's ornithological skills and permitted him in the summer of 1899 to display the title ornithologist on letterhead stationery, he entered him on his accounts as a clerical assistant. After the agreement terminated, Pearson was designated consultant.[26]

Pearson once again wrote to northern universities "making various propositions," all of which were rejected. Most academic institutions had little use for field naturalists, museum curators, or specialists in ornithology. Pearson lacked the qualifications to be a biology or zoology professor at a large university. Unexpectedly, he was offered the position of YMCA assistant secretary for North and South Carolina. Although the salary was "alluring," and his mother urged him to accept the offer, he declined, fearing that he would be expected to expound a largely literal interpretation of the Bible and still hoping to continue his bird studies. Perhaps he could return to Guilford. President Hobbs responded to his inquiry with an invitation to be professor of biology and geology. Pearson was pleased but postponed making a decision.[27]

At the University of North Carolina, every senior was required to write either a thesis or an oration. All who wrote orations delivered them before a faculty committee, which selected four to be commencement orators. Well trained in speech at Guilford, Pearson and Greenfield prepared orations, faced the committee, and were among the four chosen. Possibly once again out of gratitude to the religious faith that had so often been his benefactor, Pearson chose the topic "The Quaker, a Factor in Civilization."[28]

Immediately after commencement, Holmes sent Pearson to Beaufort, where Henry V. Wilson, who headed the U.S. Fish Commission's marine laboratory, assigned him to a laboratory table with scientists from Johns Hopkins University, Trinity College, and Baldwin University. Pearson divided his time between birds and mollusks, holothurians, and echinoderms. He collected several common seabirds, with nests and eggs, as well as an unexpected Magnificent Frigatebird. A "splendid young male" with a seven-foot, seven-inch wingspan, the bird was mounted at the state museum, where it was recorded for almost twenty years as the only Magnificent Frigatebird to have been seen in North Carolina.[29]

Elsie Weatherly, Pearson's girlfriend when he was at Guilford, had become a teacher in the Greensboro public schools. When Pearson learned she was vacationing at the Atlantic Hotel in Morehead City across the bay from Beaufort, he went by mail boat to see her. He went back again and again and sat with her in the moonlight on the hotel's veranda, talking and listening to mockingbirds. "When not with her," he wrote later, "miserably I paced my room, the dock, the veranda or the railroad track."[30] Having a good job and making money suddenly became important. He stopped trying to find a way to attend graduate school and agreed to take the Guilford teaching position, even though the salary of three hundred dollars per year plus room and board seemed too low to support a family. On the evening of Elsie's last day at Morehead City, while tying his tie before going into the hotel for dinner, Pearson made what he viewed later as a "sudden desperate decision." He would talk to Elsie about his love and his hopes, in short, as he put it, tell her his "story." Her response was encouraging. "She didn't say 'yes' but she didn't say 'no,' and my spirits rose tremendously." [31]

Hobbs instructed him to come to High Point, where the Guilford Board of Trustees would meet on August 10 in conjunction with the North Carolina Friends Yearly Meeting. There he should request money to equip a biological laboratory at the college. Pearson packed and shipped his equipment and specimens, returned to Chapel Hill, terminated his employment with the Geological Survey and his residence at the university, and prepared to meet the Guilford trustees. [32]

# 7

# "There are a great many things to know"

*(1899–1901)*

THE GUILFORD TRUSTEES appropriated, Pearson recalled later, seventy-five dollars for equipping the laboratory in Memorial Hall, the new science building. He spent half that sum on one microscope. As soon as he had drawn a salary payment, he solicited contributions from the prosperous Philadelphia Quaker community. Edwin M. Wilson, a Websterian friend and now a master at Haverford College, introduced him to the president, who gave Pearson letters of introduction to potential contributors. "Friendly Philadelphia!" Pearson was given money enough to buy several more microscopes, a dissecting kit for each student, and other equipment.[1]

Drawing on the natural history museum and what could be collected outdoors, Pearson offered a conventional course in biology. In his zoology course for preparatory students, a major objective was to "arouse a deeper interest in ornithological study." He displayed mounted birds in the classrooms; nearby woods and fields served as a laboratory. "There are a great many things to know," he had written in a recent article. "For instance, the number of kinds of birds in the world, in America, or in North

Carolina. Become familiar with the correct names (not necessarily
the Latin or Greek names) of the common birds around you. Learn
of their life histories, the kind of nest each species constructs,
number and color of eggs, length of period of incubation, and
manner in which birds feed their young. What is the food of birds?
Learn their various calls and songs. Are certain species on the
increase or decrease in your neighborhood, and what are the causes
for this? What are the natural enemies of birds? Notice the natural
protection afforded them by their colors. What of the migration of
birds?" [2]

Pearson published his notes on Chapel Hill birds in the *Journal
of the Elisha Mitchell Scientific Society,* acknowledging his list to be
incomplete and offering it as a basis for additional observations.
Given no opportunity to read the proof, he was embarrassed by
errors in the printed text, especially after Allen reviewed it in the
*Auk* as a "good list" but one "marred by careless proofreading." [3]
Nonetheless, it helped observers in central North Carolina know
what birds they could expect to see and added to what was known
about the distribution of species.

During his first year on the Guilford faculty, Pearson wrote six
articles on birds for the *North Carolina Journal of Education* and four
for the *Guilford Collegian* encouraging teachers and students to
know birds, recognize their importance to humankind, and help
perpetuate bird species. He recommended making records of arrivals and departures as an easy and interesting way for teachers
and pupils to learn about birds. At a regular time in class, children
could report on the birds they had seen; cooperative records could
be kept on charts or blackboards. If the teacher would send the
records to the *North Carolina Journal of Education*, Pearson would
combine them and try to discern bird migratory patterns. [4]

He addressed audiences wherever possible—in a Winston
courthouse, at the North Carolina Teacher's Assembly in Morehead City, in an auditorium at Guilford. On trips he displayed

bird skins, nests, and eggs. (Onstage at Guilford he arranged seventy-five mounted birds in a semicircle.) Everyone should learn something about birds, he maintained.[5]

In 1900 Frank Chapman placed Pearson on a *Bird-Lore* advisory council. His association with Allen and other advanced bird students when he was a beginning ornithologist had given Chapman the idea that "it would be an admirable scheme to form an 'advisory council' composed of leading ornithologists throughout the United States and Canada, who would consent to assist students by responding to their requests for information or advice, the student being thus brought into direct communication with an authority on the birds of his own region." It was a way of compensating for the lack of ornithologists in academic institutions. Pearson agreed to be the advisor on North Carolina birds. In *Bird-Lore* for February 1900, Chapman listed his name along with those of the more than fifty men who had agreed to serve, including Brewster for Massachusetts, Ridgway for southern Illinois, and Chapman himself for Florida and northern New Jersey. A year later, Chapman reported having "very gratifying assurances of the happy results" from advisors as well as students.[6] The arrangement continued for several years.

Pearson's inability to accept a literal interpretation of the Bible and his insistence on teaching evolution at Guilford did not seem to distress either students or faculty, but a committee of three trustees visiting the campus in the spring of 1900 questioned him. Was he unable to believe the Bible entirely? For example, did he doubt that the sun stood still at Joshua's command? Yes, Pearson answered. Yes to both questions. He was skeptical of the accuracy of many biblical stories. Nonetheless, he had an abiding faith in God. At the end of the interview, the trustees told Pearson his salary would be raised from $300 to $450. "Quakers have always been broader minded than some uninformed people believe," he wrote later.[7]

At Philander Claxton's request, Pearson agreed to serve for a

time as business manager for the *North Carolina Journal of Education*.
He was already faculty editor of the *Guilford Collegian* and had a
knack for management. Claxton was busy teaching at the State
Normal and Industrial College and because he preferred editing to
management had allowed subscribers to fall behind in payments.
The magazine was about to go under. During the summer of 1900,
Pearson collected delinquent accounts and promoted circulation.
When he returned to teaching in the fall without having made the
journal profitable, however, Claxton suspended publication. In
April 1901, he sold the journal to B. F. Johnson Publishing Company, which revived it as the *Atlantic Educational Journal*, kept
Claxton on as editor, and retained the basic format. Through
publication offices in Richmond, St. Louis, and Dallas, the company tried to increase circulation. Pearson continued to contribute
articles on birds and bird study.[8]

Artist and AOU bird protection committe member Abbott H.
Thayer, having learned a great deal about gulls and terns in studying protective coloration in wildlife, urged the AOU to hire wardens to protect them. No money for such expenditures was
available in the small AOU treasury, and Dutcher, the treasurer,
doubted it could be raised. Thayer was willing to try. On the
AOU's behalf, he wrote an appeal for contributions that was
cosigned by AOU officials, Brewster as Massachusetts Audubon
Society president, and Merriam as Biological Survey chief. Thayer
circularized the appeal and solicited the money; contributions
were sent to Dutcher, who answered questions about the fund and
managed expenditures. Six hundred dollars had been raised by
April 1900, thirteen hundred dollars by June. Five Atlantic Coast
states were selected to receive AOU wardens, who were instructed
to enforce any protective legislation that might be in effect and to
solicit cooperation from landowners. "Every colony of Gulls and
Terns that has been found from Virginia to Maine has been

provided with a protector," Dutcher reported in June, "and will receive all the protection that the laws of the various states in which they are located afford them."[9]

These actions seemed necessary despite congressional passage in May 1900 of the Lacey Act, which prohibited interstate shipment of wild birds or other wild animals taken in violation of state law and assigned enforcement responsibility to the Department of Agriculture. Introduced by Representative John F. Lacey of Iowa and supported by George O. Shields and AOU leaders Merriam, Palmer, Grinnell, Stone, and Dutcher, the act was a revised version of two bills previously introduced by Lacey, combined with elements of Senator Hoar's bill of 1898. Although many Audubon societies supported the act, *Bird-Lore* gave little space to it. Chapman was preoccupied with the Hallock bill in New York, which forbade the possession of the plumage of specified nongame birds. He and Dutcher lobbied in the bill's behalf and sent a letter to New York State Audubon Society members, urging them to ask their respective legislators to support it. Governor Roosevelt later wrote Chapman that signing the bill had given him the "greatest pleasure."[10]

Chapman considered a proposal from merchants of the Millinery Merchants' Protective Association offering not to kill or buy North American birds if the Audubon societies and the AOU would pledge to "do all in their power" to prevent an enactment of state or national laws against "selling of plumage or skins from barnyard fowl, edible birds and game birds killed in their season, and all birds which are not North American birds." After Chapman and Dutcher met with the milliners' representatives, they took a mail vote among AOU bird protection committee members and solicited the state Audubon societies for their views. A majority of the AOU committee voted for the proposal; most Audubon societies opposed it. In the absence of a consensus, the agreement was rejected. The Audubon societies maintained they could not oppose the killing of birds in North America while tacitly sanctioning such killing on other continents, an "unanswerable" argument in Chapman's opinion. The solution, according to Mabel Osgood Wright, was international bird protection: "The fact that international laws may be difficult of passage is no reason for ceasing to work for them." Ernest Thompson Seton, who liked to write humorous verse about birds, sent a message of encouragement from Paris that indicated progress abroad:

> The Dames of France no longer wear
>   the Plumes they used to prize:
> They find that Aigrettes in the hair
>   Brings crows' feet in the eyes.

Stone believed the Lacey Act might eventually stop the feather trade, but only if state game and bird laws were strengthened. Wright agreed. The "bird must be given a legal status to command . . . respect," she wrote. But by the end of 1900, only five states (Indiana, Vermont, Arkansas, Illinois, and Rhode Island) had legislation that Dutcher viewed as up to the standard of the model law.[11]

In *Bird-Lore* for December 1900, Chapman proposed a unique method for regulating hunting—for one day. He suggested that readers abandon hunting on Christmas Day in favor of taking a Christmas Bird Census. From a small beginning in twenty-five localities, the Christmas Bird Census would become a widespread ritual, stimulating interest in birds and providing information for ornithologists.

The number of state Audubon societies had increased by six (Kentucky, Florida, Maryland, Delaware, Tennessee, and South Carolina); counting the weak organizations in Maine and California, the total had reached twenty-three. A national conference of Audubon leaders seemed desirable. Wright suggested a gathering in Boston in November 1900 before the AOU Cambridge meeting, but the group accepted the Massachusetts Audubon Society's invitation to confer in conjunction with the AOU. The joint meeting was so successful that Chapman, on behalf of the New York State Audubon Society, invited the Audubon societies to send delegates to New York the following year to meet again with the AOU. A motion calling for the appointment of a committee to plan an Audubon federation was adopted.[12]

In October 1900, Pearson was the educational department's general manager as well as manager of Guilford's exhibit at Greensboro's Central Carolina Fair. He set out chairs for guests, encouraging them to linger and ask questions about his birds and eggs.[13] In December, he spoke to the elementary education department of the Southern Educational Association's Richmond meeting, where for the first time he had an audience of teachers from all over the South. "Bird Study in Elementary Schools" summarized his major beliefs about the interdependence of the "bird world and the human world." Human beings need birds and birds need our sufferance. The stage has been reached in the evolutionary process at which birds "must depend for their very existence upon the favors of the coming generations." Birds aid the human society by eating destructive vermin and insects, cleansing the cities of decaying matter, and furnishing a food supply. Game birds provide employment to hunters and opportunities for outdoor exercise and mental relaxation. (Pearson had virtually ceased to hunt as a sport—"I would get poor joy from such exercise"— but he thought regulated hunting posed no threat to the survival of game bird species.) "Pretty and graceful" nongame birds are good for the human spirit. "They brighten the gardens and woodlands with their presence and cheerful moods. Their singing brings joy and gladness into the dreary moments of our lives." Each child should be taught "to love and protect the birds as his best friends."

Claxton suggested that Pearson write a book on birds, combining published articles with new material. Pearson discussed the proposal with Elsie Weatherly, who volunteered to make drawings for illustrations. "We both went to work at once—she with her drawing materials and I with a borrowed typewriter," Pearson recalled later.[14] He selected some articles for use as originally published, revised others, and added new ones. Robert Ridgway read the manuscript and offered suggestions for revision. His brother, John L. Ridgway, an artist whose work was often used in the *Auk*, took charge of the illustrations, supervised Elsie's twenty-seven drawings, and contributed eight full-page plates and forty-five drawings. The B. F. Johnson Publishing Company accepted the manuscript.

Working closely with Elsie on the book, Pearson wanted more and more to marry her. In the spring of 1901, he asked the Guilford trustee employment committee for a raise in pay from $450 to $600, citing his publications, announcing that his book would be out in the fall (no other Guilford professor had written a book, he reminded them), and showing them the laboratory equipment purchased with money he had solicited. Although the committee chairman said the college had financial problems and needed to reduce salaries, he offered Pearson $550 for the coming year. Pearson "loved Guilford and had many dreams" about what could be accomplished there, but he also loved Elsie and wanted money to "establish a home." He told the committee chairman he would accept the offer unless he got a better one elsewhere. When Dixie Lee Bryant decided to take leave from the State Normal and Industrial College to study for a doctoral degree at the Bavarian University, Pearson applied for the temporary vacancy. The salary would be $1,000.[15]

North Carolina governor Charles B. Aycock, having pledged in his election campaign to build up the state's public schools, began a crusade in 1901. Pearson attended the Conference for Education in the South at Winston-Salem, where Aycock spoke, and felt challenged to play a part in the crusade. With a renewed sense of inspiration, he accepted an appointment to teach ornithology at the University of North Carolina's three-week summer session for teachers.[16]

While visiting his parents in Archer after Guilford's commencement, Pearson received two letters from President McIver of State Normal. If Pearson became a faculty member, McIver wrote in one, he would be expected to develop a museum of natural history. The other letter announced that the trustees had approved the appointment. Pearson replied he would collect whatever he could for the museum before leaving Archer and would resume collecting at Chapel Hill after the summer term ended.[17]

Elsie would marry him now, he thought, as he rode the train to North Carolina. But she said no, she was not ready; so he planned a full summer of work and study. McIver told him he would teach botany as well as biology, geology, and zoology. Having had no formal training in botany, Pearson finished the ornithology course at Chapel Hill as quickly as possible and went to the Harvard summer school, where he took an advanced course in plant morphology and ecology.[18]

# 8

# The Audubon Society
# of North Carolina

## *(1901–1902)*

THE STATE NORMAL AND INDUSTRIAL COLLEGE regarded itself as "a part of the public school system," with the special mission of preparing women "to work in and improve that system." Most students were residents of North Carolina and would teach there, and tuition was free to all who signed an agreement to teach in the state for at least two years.[1] Until Pearson arrived, the natural science courses were taught almost exclusively through lectures and laboratory exercises. One afternoon soon after classes began in September, Pearson instructed his students to turn from their microscopes, look out the windows, and tell him the names of the nearest trees. As best he could remember later, none of the girls could identify a tree. He asked them to name one of the birds they could hear singing. They could not.

After class he asked President McIver for permission to take the students now and then into the small, relatively wild college park and teach them about streams, flowers, trees, and birds. McIver replied, Pearson later wrote, that "he had asked me to come to the College in the belief that I could inspire the young women with a love for nature, and that he would leave to me the choice of the method I should employ." The revised catalog description of physical geography included "field exercises"; zoology would now include several weeks of ornithology. Enlarged by Pearson with "skins and mounted specimens of birds and quadrupeds," the natural history museum appeared in the catalog for the first time.[2]

Open farm lands lay to the north of the college; to the west the forest extended for miles. Pearson went out to observe and collect almost every morning and occasionally at night. In class, he took a few minutes to tell the students what he had seen. He was "young, eager, the sort of person to whom each day seemed fresh as if just created," wrote Virginia L. Brown, one of his students. In the afternoons, he often invited all who were interested to go for a walk. Many students "welcomed study in the woods and fields," Brown recalled. "Before long several members of the faculty joined us and shared our enthusiasm." Elsie Weatherly walked with them now and then.[3]

Pearson's influence at the college was buttressed by a growing public interest in nature and lasted well beyond his departure three years later. Because he soon became more involved in saving bird species than in collecting them, the museum never developed as McIver had hoped, and mention of it was dropped from the college catalog after Pearson resigned; but the interest in birds and nature remained strong at the school. His successor as professor of biology and geology, after reverting to the traditional methods of classroom lectures and laboratory exercises, soon sensed the need to reassure students that they would continue to take field trips and become "well prepared to make use of nature study as a means in their teaching."[4]

Pearson's book, *Stories of Bird Life*, was published in November 1901 and advertised as especially intended for use in the schools as a supplementary reader. It was reviewed favorably by Chapman in *Bird-Lore* and Allen in the *Auk*, and in newspapers in New York, Boston, Philadelphia, Chicago, and several North Carolina cities and towns. The superintendent of schools in Kansas City, Missouri, declared it better than Ernest Thompson Seton's *Wild Animals I Have Known* because it did not involve "the element of the improbable"; the board of supervisors of the Boston public schools adopted it for use.[5]

A month after the book appeared, Pearson received a letter from Dutcher asking him to organize an Audubon society that could persuade the North Carolina legislature to adopt the AOU model law. As AOU treasurer and director of the Thayer Fund the previous year, Dutcher had performed much of the bird protection committee's work, and he had resumed the chairmanship in November. He had increased the warden force and paid expenses of lobbyists at state legislatures. He had himself visited the legislatures of New Jersey, New York, Maine, Delaware, Florida, and Georgia; on behalf of the District of Columbia, he had called on members of Congress. Theodore Palmer of the Biological Survey joined him everywhere except in New York; former committee chairman Witmer Stone collaborated in Delaware. The visits were almost completely successful. With the help of the Maine Ornithological Society, New Jersey Audubon Society, Delaware Audubon Society, Game Protective Association of Delaware, District of Columbia Audubon Society, and, in Florida, AOU bird protection committee member Robert W. Williams, the AOU model law was adopted in six of the seven jurisdictions Dutcher visited (all but Georgia). Because of the work of other AOU members, Audubon society members, and sportsmen, New Hampshire, Massachusetts, Connecticut, Wisconsin, and Wyoming also adopted the law. Nongame birds were still unprotected on the long coastlines of North Carolina, South Carolina, and Georgia. In February 1901, John S. Henderson of Salisbury, North Carolina, had introduced a version of the model law in the state senate, but it died in committee.[6]

For ten years, Pearson had worked in the interest of birds by sharing his enthusiasm for them, in his vigorous and charming prose, rather than by asking for protective laws. If birds became extinct, he had written in the *Atlantic Educational Journal* the previous July, insects might "quickly strip the earth of every green plant." But the birds are there. "Like a vast army, they are spread over the earth, patrolling the meadow lands, flitting in and out among the shrubbery, and peering from every branch and twig of the forests and fruit trees." He had watched a "flycatcher" make "thirty-five apparently successful dashes after passing insects in ten minutes." A "young swallow," he noted, "will eat six or eight hundred flies in a day." In the August journal, he had stressed the pleasure of bird study with an opera glass and a copy of Chapman's *Handbook* or Florence Merriam's *Birds of Village and Field*. "Bird students are usually enthusiastic over their work, and it is but natural that they should be so. Of all wild creatures, birds appear to enjoy life most, and it is small wonder that they impart their joyousness to the person who lives much apart with them." [7]

When Dutcher's letter arrived, Pearson was faced with troublesome questions. Did he want to sacrifice the time necessary to found an organization, direct it, and lobby for weeks or months in Raleigh? If the answer was yes, did he want the organization to be an Audubon society? Dutcher sent him an assortment of Audubon leaflets that were pleasing. Pearson then turned for advice to friends and colleagues at Guilford and State Normal.

On February 10, 1902, his address to the State Normal faculty council proposed affirmative answers to both questions. "His most interesting talk," the council secretary wrote in the minute book, "was followed by discussion favorable to the movement. It was suggested that a mass meeting be held at some opportune time and that Mr. Pearson should there present the matter and organize an Audubon society if the way be clear." [8] President McIver appointed two persons to help Pearson plan the meeting.

They set the meeting for Tuesday afternoon, March 11. Meanwhile plans were under way to organize the North Carolina Academy of Science at a meeting in Raleigh on March 21. H. H. Brimley, who counted on Pearson to be a leader in the academy, did not write him about the organizational meeting until March 8; Pearson, who assumed Brimley would help him with the Audubon society, failed to tell him about the mass meeting until he replied to Brimley's letter on March 10. "As I am so confident that you will be with us in this movement," Pearson wrote to Brimley, "I am going to present your name tomorrow . . . as one who wishes to become a charter member of the organization." He apologized for having let the "excessive press of duties" prevent him from writing earlier. The organization formed at the mass meeting would be an Audubon society, he said. "However, the feature by which the Audubon Society is chiefly known in many states; namely, the crusade against wearing birds and bird feathers in hats, will not for the present be employed. Our efforts shall be directed mainly toward arousing interest in bird study especially by young people. We shall expect to push the organization chiefly in the public schools. Hon J. Y. Joyner will probably be made the president."9

Approximately 150 people, most from State Normal, Guilford, and the Greensboro schools, gathered in the State Normal chapel on March 11. Pearson's address was followed by supporting speeches. The Audubon Society of North Carolina was chartered with 147 members and James Y. Joyner as president, Pearson as vice-president, Annie F. Petty as secretary, and Walter Thompson as treasurer. All the officers worked in the state's educational system. Petty was librarian at State Normal, Thompson was principal of the South Greensboro Graded School, and Joyner had reluctantly resigned from the State Normal faculty to become state superintendent of public instruction at the request of his friend, Governor Aycock. "He was a hard man to resist when he had his head set on something," Joyner later said.10

The final form of the society's constitution reflected Pearson's views of the role the society should play. It defined three major objectives: to disseminate information about the value of birds, to promote bird study in the schools, and to build public sentiment against bird destruction. Membership was open to any adult for an entrance fee of twenty-five cents, junior members under fifteen, ten cents; there was no annual fee. A sustaining member contributed five dollars annually; an honorary life member made one payment of ten dollars. The bulk of members was expected to be adults and juniors paying a one-time entrance fee. Financial support would come from the sustaining members. Administrative power was largely vested in an executive committee, a self-perpetuating body that included the president, secretary, and treasurer and was presided over by the vice-president. Pearson as vice-president bore most of the responsibility for the society's work.[11]

"This is going to be a big organization and do a lot of good in the state, and you cannot afford not to be identified with it," Pearson wrote to a friend in Chapel Hill.[12] Almost immediate endorsement came from the North Carolina Academy of Science. As newly elected vice-president of the academy, Pearson addressed the other twelve charter members on the state Audubon Society's plans. Founded at the same time, the two organizations were linked by Pearson and by H. H. Brimley, who became a member of the Audubon Society's executive committee. By April 17, Audubon membership had risen to about six hundred. Pearson wanted more members quickly. "When the representatives of the Audubon Society go before the next General Assembly to ask for effective legislation for the protection of non-game birds," he wrote to Brimley, "it will be of great value to have as large a list as possible of North Carolinians backing the movement."[13]

During the first weeks after the Audubon Society's founding, Pearson visited six public schools and formed branch societies in each: one in Greensboro, one in Burlington, two in Durham, and two in Winston-Salem. He wrote articles for newspapers and farm and school journals. Bird identification blank-books were printed without charge by B. F. Johnson Publishing Company, which distributed them for a five-cent mailing fee. In addition to spaces for bird records, the blank-books contained a reading list, an introduction to the topography of a bird's body, suggestions as to what to watch for in field observation, and an invitation to send information about any unidentified bird to Pearson, who would "endeavor to name the species as well as to give other information regarding its distribution and habits."[14] Pearson had now invited letters of inquiry about North Carolina birds through four public channels: *Bird-Lore*, *Atlantic Educational Journal*, *Stories of Bird Life*, and the bird identification blank-books.

Following the example of established Audubon societies, Pearson published leaflets. He sent copies of the first, a four-page statement on the society's "purposes and plans," to newspaper editors in the state with a covering letter asking them to publish articles about the society. "I trust . . . you may feel like lending the Society your support," he added.[15] In the second leaflet, *The Value of North Carolina Birds*, Pearson stressed the importance of birds to agriculture, the casualness with which they were being destroyed, and the need for protective laws.

Printing costs for the two leaflets were met by the Thayer Fund. A generous contributor to the fund in 1902 was George W. Vanderbilt, who had begun the first large-scale practice of forestry in the United States on the Biltmore Estate near Asheville. To plan the work, he had hired Gifford Pinchot, who in 1892, at the age of twenty-six, had sought clients interested in his services in the new profession of forestry. On Pinchot's recommendation, Vanderbilt employed as his resident forester Carl Alwin Schenck, a German forester with a doctoral degree. Although Pinchot showed little concern for birds other than as game, Schenck was interested in the relationship between trees and birds and in almost any other subject bearing on the raising of trees for timber. In 1898, he opened the Biltmore Forest School on the estate grounds, the first forestry school in the United States. He wrote many of the textbooks, taught most of the courses, and brought in lecturers on special subjects, including ornithology. C. S. Brimley lectured there from time to time. Harry Church Oberholser, an ornithologist with the Biological Survey, lectured in the school for four weeks every summer for several years.[16]

The Audubon Society's founding seemed to inspire an increasingly lyrical quality in Pearson's writing for teachers. "Apparently no bird is more cheerful than the song sparrow [*Melospiza melodia*]," he wrote in the *Atlantic Educational Journal*. "There is not a month in which he fails to sing. . . . I have heard him on the most impossible days, whenever there would be a lull in the storm, singing away from the top of a swaying limb as if all the world were a blooming garden and he the song-master of it all." In March, Pearson urged his readers to walk through fields and meadows on a clear morning, noting birds in migration. But there was an experience for the bird watcher more meaningful than merely identifying migrant species. The attentive bird student goes about "with eyes and ears open, biting a bud here and nibbling a twig there, as most woodsmen do." Along the way "something of the rising sap of the forest will steal into his blood and brain, and he will feel growing strong upon him a belief in the brotherhood of all living creatures."[17]

One afternoon, a Black-billed Cuckoo (*Coccyzus erythropthalmus*), rarely seen in the state except in the mountains, flew through an open window into Pearson's biological laboratory. Although C. S. Brimley had collected one in Raleigh sixteen years earlier, Pearson had never encountered one in the Greensboro area. He caught the bird, examined it, and freed it, knowing he might never see another one in that vicinity. He never did. His enthusiasm for

museum building was waning, although in January he had collected a Short-eared Owl (*Asio flammeus*), a rare winter resident in
North Carolina, and in April he had taken a male Horned Grebe
(*Podiceps auritus*). A farmer brought him a Long-eared Owl (*Asio
otus*) trapped on a game preserve.[18]

As he considered the probable demands on his time in the year
ahead, Pearson could see little possibility of accomplishing all he
hoped and would be expected to do. To the college's four-year
program for a diploma had been added a fifth year of study leading
to a degree. Pearson anticipated having twenty-three to twenty-five
hours of classroom instruction each week: twelve hours of freshman geography and botany, four hours of senior zoology, and four
hours of geology, plus three to five hours of advanced zoology for
the fifth-year students. Dixie Lee Bryant, whom Pearson had
replaced, had worked with a teaching assistant. Pearson wrote to
McIver, asking for an assistant to teach the freshman courses.
Although the request was denied, Virginia L. Brown was assessed
as a potential candidate. A spirited senior whom President McIver
invited to continue for a fifth year and earn a degree, Brown lived at
her family's home in Greensboro and rode a horse to class. To
Pearson's laboratory she brought specimens collected on horseback rides in distant fields and woods. She attended the Audubon
Society's founding meeting and enrolled as a charter member.
Pearson accepted her as a friend as well as a student. She admired
him greatly, was stimulated by him to pursue her interest in
wildlife, and many years later, after his death, wrote warmly
appreciative articles about him.[19]

Organizational problems developed relatively soon in the Audubon Society. Walter Thompson moved away from Greensboro
and resigned as treasurer. Annie F. Petty resigned as secretary
when the rapidly increasing responsibilities of her position took
more time than she could spare from her duties as college librarian.
The resignations were announced in June, when the society met in
Morehead City in conjunction with the North Carolina Teachers

Assembly. Robert N. Wilson, one of Pearson's former colleagues at Guilford, replaced Thompson, and Pearson succeeded Petty, taking with him from the vice-presidency the powers of executive officer. William A. Blair, already a member of the executive committee, was elected vice-president. A former teacher and school administrator who had become president of the People's National Bank of Winston-Salem, Blair was well known for his interest in charities and public welfare. The executive committee was enlarged to include sportsman and Guilford County sheriff J. F. Jordan and Asheville physician Chase P. Ambler. A sportsman who liked wildlife and natural scenery, Ambler in 1899 had founded the Appalachian National Park Association with the objective of establishing a national park in western North Carolina.[20]

Pearson's schedule grew even tighter. He accepted an invitation from Philander Claxton to teach at the Summer School of the South, in Knoxville, Tennessee, in 1902. Claxton had left State Normal to become chief of the Southern Education Board's Bureau of Investigation and Information in Knoxville, and Charles W. Dabney, the president of the University of Tennessee, had persuaded him to organize and superintend a summer school for southern teachers comparable in quality to northern summer schools. The General Education Board, the Peabody Board, George Foster Peabody, Robert C. Ogden, Albert Shaw, "public-spirited citizens of Knoxville," and "a number of friends of the school throughout the country" contributed money. Claxton was told "the school should be as good as possible, and so cheap no teacher might be kept away because of expense." The fifty-two faculty members included seven college and university presidents, several former presidents, a number of school superintendents, and an array of scholars and educational leaders. Tuition was $5.00 for the six-week term, the charges for room and board were $3.50 to $4.50 per week, and round-trip, first-class railroad tickets were available for the one-way ticket price.[21]

Elsie Weatherly decided to marry Pearson and go with him to

the summer school. Perhaps Pearson's invitation had reassured her that he had achieved standing among educators and was on the path of a traditionally respectable career. "When Elsie Weatherly was in college," Pearson wrote later, "she had been a devoted pupil of Professor Claxton and I have always suspected that his seeming approval of me at this time influenced her in my behalf." A simple ceremony took place at six P.M. on June 17, 1902, at the home of Elsie's widowed mother, Nannie C. Weatherly, a milliner in Greensboro. Mrs. Weatherly had sent "dainty" invitations to a few selected guests, including Virginia Brown, who thought the groom admirable, the bride "beautiful," and the couple "radiantly happy." [22]

No evidence has come to light about the relationship between Gilbert Pearson and his mother-in-law, and little about his new wife's feelings. Perhaps Mrs. Weatherly used wild bird feathers in her millinery work and thus embarrassed him; possibly he annoyed her by lecturing and organizing in behalf of birds. Other than that Elsie helped Gilbert prepare his first book, little information exists from her point of view about marriage to a man who seemed always to be at work learning or writing or talking about birds. There was no time for a honeymoon. The summer school at Knoxville was scheduled to open on June 19, two days after the marriage. The Pearsons left Greensboro almost immediately following the ceremony. In Knoxville, at a general reception on June 21, Charles W. Dabney introduced Elsie as the "bride of the Summer School." [23]

The school was far more successful than even Claxton had anticipated or hoped. He had expected a first year's attendance of four or five hundred teachers. More than two thousand persons enrolled. Pearson was "very happy and very busy." More than 150 persons, nearly all teachers in the South, enrolled for his five-week ornithology course taught as three classes. He illustrated his lectures with mounted birds and stereopticon slides, emphasized the

"habits of nesting, feeding and migration" of southern birds, recommended Chapman's *Handbook* as the first bird book the teachers
should buy, and sold subscriptions to *Bird-Lore*. At night, he
delivered illustrated public lectures in an outdoor auditorium. As
soon as he was familiar with the grounds, he drew local residents as
well as students into bird walks. He also wrote articles for newspapers, urging the adoption of bird protection laws by the Tennessee legislature.[24]

Among the other faculty members were C. Hart Merriam,
McIver, UNC President Edwin A. Alderman, Claxton, *World's
Work* editor Walter Hines Page, and Clark University President G.
Stanley Hall. Pearson was gratified to associate with such men and
to have an opportunity to talk about birds with them and with
responsive audiences of teachers. "The leven [*sic*] is working," he
wrote hastily to H. H. Brimley, "this old southern country is going
to have a due appreciation of i[t]s bird life yet."[25]

# 9

# National Recognition

## *(1902)*

STATE NORMAL'S ADMINISTRATIVE SECRETARY Laura H.
Coit arranged for the Pearsons, before turning to Greensboro, to
spend nearly three weeks at the Asheville home of her friends,
Mr. and Mrs. Robert U. Garrett, who liked birds. Pearson saw a
Canada Warbler (*Wilsonia canadensis*), apparently summering at an
altitude more than a thousand feet below its usual summer residence in the mountains. He watched a Song Sparrow carry food to
a nest. In the 1880s and 1890s, Cairns and Brewster had failed to
find evidence of the Song Sparrow's nesting in the mountains. By
1902, the bird's breeding range appeared to have been extended.[1]

Brown Thrashers had a nest with young in a thorn bush near
enough to be studied from the veranda. Using binoculars, Pearson
noted that the adult birds' labors had already affected their appearance: their feathers, normally bright in the mating and early
nesting seasons, "had lost their luster and many were badly torn.
Duty had laid her hand strong upon the birds," who fed their
young large numbers of insect larvae from as early as six A.M. until
about eight P.M. In two weeks, Pearson estimated, the parent birds
made 5,180 trips to the nest. Allowing for an occasional feeding of
plant matter rather than insects, Pearson concluded that the young
birds consumed at least five thousand insects in the two-week
period.

One afternoon, a boy with a rifle, accompanied by his father, walked by the Garrett house. The boy was shooting at birds. Inside the house, Pearson heard a shot and hurried to the veranda, where he saw the boy take aim at one of the Brown Thrashers. Pearson ran out on the lawn and shouted at the boy to stop. The father, a "well-dressed man carrying a cane," turned to Pearson "with evident surprise and not without some heat" and asked, "What do you mean by telling my boy not to shoot that bird?" Pearson explained how the thrashers protected gardens from insects, that their presence in the yard gave the Garretts great pleasure, and how much a state bird protection law was needed. He urged the man to talk to his friends about the value of birds. Father and son listened, and although the son did not shoot the thrasher, they went away with the rifle still loaded, having made no promises.[2]

Pearson talked with other Asheville residents about birds and the need for bird protection. Audubon executive committee member Chase Ambler was one of several sportsmen who wanted the society to work for laws to prohibit the export of game birds from the state and require nonresident hunters to buy licenses. Although such measures would greatly reduce game bird destruction, Pearson was unprepared to say the Audubon Society should sponsor them. The controversy aroused by a campaign for game bird protection might jeopardize the chances for getting a law protecting nongame birds.

He wrote to H. H. Brimley for advice. "Do you think all this will be too much to labour for this winter? And do you approve of these suggestions?" Although Brimley refrained from committing himself on the sportsmen's proposals, he advocated modernizing the state's game laws. "I am inclined to think that the time may be ripe for something reasonable in game laws and with proper help something a little more in keeping with modern ideas on the subject might now take the place of the awful collection we stagger under," he wrote. He cautioned Pearson against aligning himself with sportsmen and against other hunters of game birds. "It is an intricate problem and there are a good many interests to consider. . . . The Currituck market gunner has his point of view and must be considered and the poor man who shoots robins as game is at least entitled to a hearing."[3]

Pearson went from Asheville to a two-week teachers' institute in Atlanta. "I am gathering strength for Atlanta," he wrote to President McIver, "and am looking forward with much pleasure to the trip there with you." Each morning before class, all the teachers met in an assembly hall, where McIver addressed them for forty-five minutes on educational problems and methods of teaching. For an equal time period, Pearson talked about nature. "I urged them to study birds, teach birds, and preach the need of bird-protective laws." In the afternoons, he visited prominent residents who might be willing to work for bird protection. Emboldened by the conversations in Asheville, he advocated new laws for Georgia and a statewide warden system to enforce them.[4]

An inspiring speaker, McIver was one of the most popular educators traveling the South in behalf of education and Pearson began to feel himself drawn into the effort to improve school systems and teach everyone to read and write. In summer, he was teaching teachers; in winter, he was teaching women who were going to be teachers. "To me it was a glorious responsibility. I hailed with joy the approach of every day. I had found my place in life and here I would live and work and do my best to help raise the standard of literacy in North Carolina—the State of my adoption."[5]

In October, he arranged for the Audubon Society's incorporation as a nonprofit organization with the power to buy, hold, and convey property, anticipating that the society might need to play a larger role than had been at first envisioned. The "Audubon Society of North Carolina for the Study and Protection of Birds" became the "Audubon Society of North Carolina Company." One of the company's objectives was "to create a sentiment that will insure the enactment and enforcement of proper and necessary laws for the protection and the preservation of birds and game of the State." Adding game protection to nongame bird protection strengthened Pearson's position in appealing for support. Visits to business and professional men and government officials in Raleigh brought in a hundred dollars in membership fees. Governor Aycock accepted an Audubon Society honorary vice presidency. (He had already demonstrated his interest in natural resources by welcoming long letters from Holmes, the state geologist, by strengthening the Geological Survey, and by nurturing the Department of Agriculture.) Pearson wrote to the society's executive committee members, "It will interest you . . . to know that the Governor is one of the strongest supporters of this movement, and will render us valuable aid in regard to the legislation this winter."[6]

The *Atlantic Educational Journal* became a medium for spreading information about the Audubon cause. An unsigned article in the October issue, apparently by Pearson, called attention to the establishment of Audubon societies in seven states regarded as southern for the journal's purposes: Maryland, Virginia, North Carolina, South Carolina, Florida, Kentucky, and Tennessee. School teachers were encouraged to write for information to society secretaries, whose names and addresses were supplied. North Carolina teachers were asked "to support the passage of a bill in the Legislature this winter for bird protection."[7]

In 1902, North Carolina law did little to protect birds. As codified in 1883, the law stated that if a landowner posted No Trespass signs at the county courthouse door and at two or more places on the land, anyone convicted of hunting on the land without permission had to pay ten dollars to the owner. Because relatively few landowners bothered to post, this law had little effect. Other laws forbade killing "wild fowl" on Sunday, and by the code of 1883 as amended in 1891, no "partridges, quail, doves, robins, lark, mockingbirds, or wild turkeys" could be killed between March 15 and November 1. Further protection was extended to mockingbirds in 1897 by a statute making it a misdemeanor to kill one at any time of year or to rob or destroy a mockingbird's nest. Some of the numerous local laws strengthened this statutory protection, and others weakened it with exceptions. By 1903, 226 statutes concerning birds and game had been enacted, but no enforcement system had been established. Sheriffs, policemen, and other local officials seldom had any knowledge of wildlife protection laws or any interest in enforcing them.[8]

The Audubon Society's executive committee appointed Pearson, H. H. Brimley, J. F. Jordan, and Richard H. Lewis, a prominent physician in Raleigh who liked birds and humanitarian causes, to write a bird protection bill. Before they met together, Pearson worked on a preliminary draft with Aubrey L. Brooks, a society member and rising young Greensboro attorney. Pearson completed the bill in rough form by mid-November 1902 in time to take it to Washington, D.C., for the annual combined meeting of the AOU and the National Committee of Audubon Societies, which had been organized in New York in April with William Dutcher as chairman.[9] Pearson had never attended a meeting of the AOU, which did not meet south of Washington and had not met there since 1898.

The movement to protect American birds was predominantly eastern in strength. Of the thirty-one state Audubon societies existing in November 1902, including the District of Columbia Society, all but nine (California, Nebraska, Oregon, Oklahoma, Minnesota, Iowa, Missouri, Louisiana, and Wyoming) were in states east of the Mississippi. Seventeen states had adopted the AOU model law; all but two (Wyoming and Arkansas) were east of the Mississippi. Bird protection appeared to follow and depend on ornithological study. In the states "where the American Ornithologists' Union has the largest membership," Dutcher wrote,

"Audubon societies have been established, and . . . where there are no working ornithologists, no Audubon societies exist, and none are likely to be founded."[10]

In Washington, Pearson was introduced into the society of AOU and Audubon leaders. Chapman was there to greet him, as was Ridgway. Also there were Dutcher, Palmer, Brewster, Allen, Stone, and C. Hart Merriam, along with Louis Agassiz Fuertes, Olive Thorne Miller, and Mabel Osgood Wright. At the AOU business session in Merriam's home on the evening of November 17, Pearson was moved from associate member to member. The next morning in the U.S. National Museum, Pearson's paper, "Summer Bird-Life of Eastern North Carolina," "provoked much discussion." Largely a description of heron colonies he had located on the North Carolina coast in 1898, it presented new ornithological data. Pearson's audience asked for additional information, especially about the possibility of saving the colonies from destruction. Dutcher suggested that proposed congressional bills might help. Palmer "told of the immense number of ducks annually taken to the northern markets from the North Carolina coast." When he added that the upland game birds also needed protection, Pearson illustrated his point by describing the killing and marketing of Northern Bobwhites.[11]

Pearson again provoked discussion at the Audubon Societies' public meeting on the evening of November 19 in the Columbian University lecture hall. Presiding was District of Columbia Audubon Society President George M. Sternberg, an eminent bacteriologist and former U.S. Army surgeon general. Palmer, Miller, Wright, and other scheduled speakers emphasized publications, traveling libraries, free lectures, and school programs. When Sternberg called for comments, Pearson later recalled, Chapman responded "that there was a young man present from North Carolina who had recently formed an Audubon Society and that perhaps he would have something to say." Invited to the platform,

Pearson delivered what Wright described in *Bird-Lore* as an "eloquent address." He stressed "the importance of scientific accuracy" in arguments for bird protection, the equal importance of
presenting the arguments with "force and insistence," and the
necessity of increasing the Audubon societies' size and financial
resources.[12]

At a joint session of the AOU and the societies, Dutcher delivered portions of his long report on bird protection. Published in the
*Auk* as the "Report of the A.O.U. Committee on the Protection of
North American Birds," it was his dual report as AOU bird
protection committee chairman and National Committee of Audubon Societies chairman. "The two great bodies of bird-lovers
should go hand in hand, one for the purpose of obtaining an
intelligent insight into bird life, and the other for the protection of
the life of the bird." Money must be raised from the general public,
he said. "Too few people realize their public social responsibilities.
If they have been good to a family they think their whole duty
performed, but there is a broader field—the civic duty of doing
good to their neighbors and the State. The protection of birds,
from the economic standpoint, is as much a civic duty as voting
honestly and intelligently. The A.O.U. and the Audubon Societies are the forces to do the work, but from the citizen who
realizes his civic obligations must come the means."[13] Pearson was
placed on the AOU bird protection committee and, as the Audubon Society of North Carolina's representative, on the National
Committee of Audubon Societies.

When Dutcher reported that he had given half his time to bird
protection in the past year and had paid all the costs of clerical
assistance for the National Committee, the members pledged four
hundred dollars for clerical help in the coming year. To keep
expenditures low, they agreed to limit the effort to get bird protection laws passed in state legislatures in 1903 to North Carolina,
Virginia, Tennessee, Missouri, California, Oregon, and Wash-

ington. Sometime during Pearson's stay at the meetings, Dutcher and Palmer spent an afternoon with him, discussing problems in North Carolina and making suggestions to improve his draft proposal for a bird protection law. If the law were adopted, Dutcher assured him, the Thayer Fund would provide money to employ wardens to protect water birds on the coast.[14]

Pearson returned to Greensboro with an enhanced understanding of the bird protection movement and the role he could play. He did not know as much about ornithology in general as the older, more experienced bird students or write as gracefully as the best popular authors. But he knew more about birds in North Carolina than anyone else and had extensive field experience. No one at the meetings seemed to have his talent for raising money; the ineffectiveness of the National Committee members from the "rich and highly educated North" surprised him. Moreover, he appeared to be the most talented speaker in the bird protection movement. Even at scientific meetings, such skill was useful. When Pearson spoke, audiences usually listened. Any doubts about the effectiveness of his performance in Washington were probably resolved when he read the reports on the meetings. The *Auk*'s terse account of the AOU meeting gave only Pearson's paper (along with the discussion provoked by it), out of the twenty presented, more than routine attention. *Bird-Lore*'s report on the Audubon Societies' general session listed the scheduled papers in one paragraph and devoted another paragraph to a summary of Pearson's contribution.[15]

# 10

# The Audubon Law:
# Good Birds,
# Bad Birds, Game Birds

## *(1902–1903)*

PEARSON PLANNED CAREFULLY for the North Carolina legislature's opening in January 1903, laying a foundation of support for an Audubon Society bill and simultaneously ascertaining what kind of bill legislators would support. He wrote to each one at his home or office, using names and addresses H. H. Brimley provided. Intended to inform and persuade, Pearson's letter contained no mention of statewide game protection, potentially a divisive issue. He emphasized the Audubon Society, its work, and the need for a law to protect "wild birds," many of which "are so extremely valuable to our agricultural interests." Implying that the legislators were already thinking about the problem, Pearson offered on the Audubon Society's behalf to unite "our efforts with yours." "You can see that what I have attempted to do is simply open up the matter with them," he wrote to Brimley, who replied that the letter "seems to me to fill the bill exactly, containing neither too much nor too little."[1]

Many political leaders advised Pearson that the legislature

would not appropriate funds for wardens, and because a bird protection law would be virtually useless without enforcement, the Audubon Society would have to undertake the task. Such an arrangement had precedent in northern states, where humane society officers had for several decades been authorized to arrest persons who abused domestic animals. The private Delaware Game Protective Association had enforced the game and bird laws of its state since 1879.[2]

Pearson assessed the chances of a bill that would authorize the Audubon Society to pay wardens from funds raised by requiring nonresidents to buy licenses to hunt in North Carolina. Raleigh *News and Observer* editor Josephus Daniels, whom Pearson approached in the hope he would write editorials supporting such a bill, was cautious. He declined to commit himself, expressing doubts about the constitutionality of making nonresidents pay a license fee not required of residents. Perhaps he was simply unprepared to accept the idea that wildlife needed protection. Other political leaders, including Governor Aycock, generally saw no reason to raise a constitutional question. State Chief Justice Walter Clark, who was present when Pearson talked with Daniels, told him to look at his opinion in *State* v. *Gallop* (1900). "I looked that up and it said in substance that such a thing could be done all right," Pearson said in a letter to Brimley. Following the 1896 U.S. Supreme Court decision in *Geer* v. *Connecticut*, Clark had reaffirmed an English common law principle: "The ownership of game is in the people of the State, and the legislature may withhold or grant to individuals the right to hunt and kill game, or qualify or restrain it, as in its opinion will best subserve the public welfare."[3]

Both Pearson and Brimley were so pressed for time they had difficulty doing things well. Pearson planned a trip to the coast to gather fresh information about bird destruction and to allay opposition to his bill among local hunters. In preparing a draft of the bill to send out for review, he worked so hastily he put one section of the bill in the wrong place. When he sent a copy to Brimley, he forgot to enclose a copy of his long covering letter and had to send it separately with a letter of explanation. Brimley, in his letter returning the bill, which he annotated heavily, indicated that he understood: "I am so awfully rushed that I hardly know which way to turn. I have got more on my hands than I can properly manage in trying to get the Museum in shape before the meeting of the Legislature."[4]

When State Normal's classes suspended for Christmas in 1902, Pearson rode by train to Norfolk, where he changed to a train that took him to the northern North Carolina coast. Walking and catching rides on horse carts and sailboats, he traveled south, visiting markets, storage houses, and hunting clubs. Occasionally he stopped to make notes on bird life or take pictures, having earlier in the year arranged for State Normal to buy stereopticon equipment. On New Year's Eve, thirty-one miles north of Cape Hatteras, he found a live Dovekie (*Alle alle*) lying on the beach. An arctic bird known to spend winters feeding off the Atlantic coast, the Dovekie seldom came near land in North Carolina except when blown there by heavy winds. The specimen Pearson found lacked one foot, possibly bitten off by a large fish while the bird rested on the water. Pearson picked up the emaciated bird and took it with him. It soon died. Pearson took the skin with him to State Normal, where he mounted it and added it to the museum.[5]

A major problem in drawing up the Audubon bill lay in deciding which bird species to class as game. Any bird was suitable for the sport of shooting at a moving target. In some circumstances, any bird seemed good enough for a stew. Overall, however, as Americans had become more sophisticated and more humane and as the supply of cultivated foods had become more plentiful, their sense of what was sporting to kill and most suitable to eat had grown more refined. The list of game birds in the AOU model law of 1886 was unchanged in the slightly revised law advocated in

1902, when Pearson drafted his bill. Game birds were edible birds: "swans, geese, brant and river and sea ducks"; "rails, coots, mudhens and gallinules"; "shore-birds, plovers, surf birds, snipe, woodcock, sandpipers, tatlers, and curlews"; and "wild turkeys, grouse, prairie chickens, pheasants, partridges, and quails." Audubon societies sponsoring legislation were encouraged by the AOU to accommodate local demands by adding species. Pearson put the entire list in his bill and added doves, robins, and meadowlarks, all of which were commonly hunted for food in North Carolina. No birds would be classed as game that served primarily as challenging targets, such as the swiftly maneuvering Common Nighthawks, or that were marketable for their feathers alone, such as herons, gulls, and terns.[6]

Should it be legal to kill any birds other than game birds? Were some birds pests rather than good neighbors, injurious to crops or a threat to poultry and small livestock? The AOU bird protection committee had decided that all bird species in the United States except the English (now House) Sparrow were generally helpful. House Sparrows, introduced chiefly from England and Germany in the 1850s and 1860s, had been expected to eat caterpillars, cankerworms, and other insect larvae. They were transported for that purpose to Texas, Utah, and California. Wherever they were taken, they adapted readily, multiplied rapidly, and showed an appetite for a wide variety of foods, particularly for the bits of grain in horse droppings. Finding so much of that food in American cities, the urban sparrows neglected their responsibility for eating insect larvae. Moreover, they crowded out robins, cardinals, bluebirds, native sparrows, and other well-liked American birds. Their fecundity was disturbing. According to a U.S. Department of Agriculture study, a single pair of House Sparrows could theoretically produce in ten years 275,716,983,698 birds. "The day is evidently near at hand, therefore," Chapman wrote, "when the English Sparrow will be in complete charge of the country."[7]

Ornithologists in 1902 could not know that automobiles would displace horses in the cities and that the disappearance of horse droppings, among other changes, would be followed by a decline in the urban House Sparrow population.

The European Starling (*Sturnus vulgaris*), another fecund import that prospered in cities, was not yet creating problems. A flock of sixty to eighty starlings set free in Central Park in 1890 had readily made themselves at home. The first nest was found that year in the eaves of the American Museum of Natural History. Although the birds spread rapidly, they were still not numerous enough in 1902 for the AOU bird protection committee to recommend their being classed as pests or for Pearson to ponder the question. Seventeen years would pass before starlings appeared in North Carolina. The Common Pigeon, or Rock Dove, a Eurasian species introduced in the American colonies during the seventeenth century as a domestic fowl, was viewed in 1902, like the chicken, as outside the coverage of laws to protect wild birds.[8]

American farmers' views about what birds should be classed as pests sometimes differed from one area to another, for example in regard to Ricebirds, or Bobolinks (*Dolichonyx oryzivorus*). Bobolinks nest largely in Canada and the northern states and winter in South America. In the North, the birds were generally regarded with affection; William Cullen Bryant and Wilson Flagg wrote poems about them. In the South they were dreaded. As late as the 1880s, when millions of Bobolinks annually passed through the rice fields of North Carolina, South Carolina, and Georgia on their way south in August and September, they settled on the maturing rice stalks to eat the grains. One South Carolina rice planter wrote that "sometimes the destruction is so complete it does not pay to cut what is left of the crop."[9] Although by 1902, the number of Boblinks had declined sharply, in migratory flocks they were still destructive to rice crops.

Pearson included the Bobolink with the House Sparrow in the

section of his bill naming birds not to be protected. Deferring to farmers in general, he added hawks and owls, some species of which occasionally prey on chickens, along with crows, blackbirds, and jackdaws (grackles), which sometimes pull young corn plants from the ground, pry open husks of maturing ears, eat grains of shocked corn, or (especially in the case of blackbirds) eat fruits and berries.[10]

No birds other than game birds and pests could be legally caught, killed, bought, or sold. Nests and eggs could not be "needlessly" taken or destroyed. A convicted transgressor would be fined one dollar (reduced, on H. H. Brimley's recommendation, from five dollars in the model law) for "each egg, nest or bird killed or taken" or imprisoned for five to thirty days "for each offense." Permits could be obtained to collect for scientific study. The original AOU model law required an applicant to be eighteen years of age; by 1902, the age had been reduced to fifteen. Pearson lowered it to twelve. There was still no academic training in ornithology; one became an ornithologist by observing, collecting, and reading. To prevent abuse of the collecting privilege by boys with frivolous interests, an applicant for a permit was required to present written testimonials from "two well known scientific men."[11] Any nongame bird could be captured and caged as a domestic pet but could not be shipped out of state. Market hunting of some declining game species was discouraged by a provision requiring a permit to ship them out of state. Permits could be obtained to ship such birds live to another state for propagation.

The Audubon Society would enforce the proposed regulations and all laws regulating the taking of game of any kind. Audubon wardens would be appointed by the governor upon the society's recommendation and paid by the society from funds raised largely by selling ten-dollar licenses to out-of-state hunters. The licenses would be issued by county clerks of court; the money would go to the state treasurer for the Audubon Society's Bird and Game

Fund, which would also receive proceeds from the public auction of illegally killed birds and game.[12]

Governor Aycock liked the bill. In his biennial message to the legislature on January 8, 1903, he recommended the Audubon Society's plans to protect birds "without expense to the State" be given "favorable consideration." "The governor did us O.K., didn't he?" Pearson wrote to H. H. Brimley. Representative Wescott Roberson, of Greensboro, an Audubon Society member, introduced the Audubon bill on January 23; it was referred to the committee on corporations, which he chaired. When the committee met on the afternoon of the same day, Pearson and others he later identified merely as "two or three friends" spoke in the bill's behalf. In Pearson's view, the time was too short for the speakers to rebut effectively the arguments of committee members who thought the bill too long and complicated and who resisted giving regulatory power to a private agency.[13]

*News and Observer* editor Josephus Daniels was supplied with a copy of the bill, along with evidence that a law requiring nonresidents to buy hunting licenses was constitutional in North Carolina and was already in effect in twenty-five states. He also received a copy of a letter from Henry L. Lee of New York, who leased land in North Carolina. Lee said out-of-state hunters regarded bird protection as "greatly to their advantage" and would "feel it no hardship" to buy licenses. On the day after the bill was introduced, an article supporting it, possibly written by Daniels, appeared in the *News and Observer*. It contained Lee's letter, sympathetic comments about the "heartless slaughter" of "the beautiful sea gulls and terns," and a favorable conclusion: "The Audubon Bill is a long step taken toward bird protection in the State, it is not radical or stringent, and already has many friends."[14]

On February 3, Representative Roberson reported the bill favorably to the house. When February 5 was designated the day it would be on special order for discussion, Pearson faced a dilemma.

He had been invited to speak on February 7 to the Tennessee legislature, where Senator J. M. Graham had introduced the AOU model law. Dutcher, who had sent Graham printed materials, had probably suggested inviting Pearson to speak. But if Pearson accepted the invitation, he would have to leave Raleigh on February 6, only one day after the North Carolina house took up his own bill. Arrangements were made, probably by Roberson, for discussion of the bill to be postponed, and Pearson went to Nashville.[15]

As he stood before the Tennessee legislators, Pearson represented the Audubon Society of North Carolina, the AOU bird protection committee (Dutcher had paid his way from the committee's Thayer Fund), and the National Committee of Audubon Societies.[16] But he did not mention them. Instead, he said he spoke for birds. "I regard it as no small honor to stand to-day before this body of Southern statesman and represent that great class of nature's creatures which in the opinion of many scholars is of greater value to humanity than any other group of animals; to represent that class of feathered life which at this moment in every field, by every stream and on a thousand hills is proving its friendship to the human race by destroying, like a mighty army, the vast hosts of injurious insects which are laying waste the products of those who attend the herds and till the soil." Through the ages, birds had been "man's most enduring friends," but they had been persecuted "in every forest and by every ocean," he asserted. "Ignorance of the laws of nature, gentlemen, costs the state of Tennessee more money annually than all the deliberate waste and luxury combined."[17]

The Tennessee legislators had probably never before been addressed by a scientist steeped in information about his subject who used the figures of speech and spoke in the cadences of a political orator. They adopted the bird protection bill early in March. A few days later, an editorial in a Nashville newspaper praised birds: "A birdless land is a dreary land; where the silence is unbroken by the song of birds there is loneliness that is oppressive. Imagine a farm without the cheering presence and music of birds. Think of the fields and woods barren of feathered songsters."[18]

When the North Carolina House called up Pearson's bill on February 11, Roberson requested a recess to hear Pearson "explain the provisions of the bill." Several members objected. "If we have nothing better to do than listen to a man talk about jaybirds and sparrows, we had better go home," Pearson later recalled one representative shouting. The motion was adopted, nonetheless. Pearson spoke about the "robins and mockingbirds" that sang in their yards, the "jays" that called in the trees outside the windows, and the "woodpeckers" that had built a nest in the ball on the capitol dome above their heads. He "talked of the great value of the birds to the State, and how they were being killed by an unthinking public."[19]

In the subsequent deliberations, the Rufous-sided Towhee (*Pipilo erythrophthalmus*) was incorrectly listed as a game bird. Rufus A. Doughton, of Alleghany County, asked Pearson for the correct name of the bird that mountain people called the "joree." They wanted to be free to kill it because it pulled up and ate newly planted corn. "Chewink or towhee," Pearson said. Doughton then offered an amendment designed to add the bird to the list of unprotected species, but it was misunderstood. The words "chewink or towhee" were inserted into the list of game birds between "yellow legs" and "curlews," where they remained through enactment of the bill into law and for years thereafter.[20] Perhaps Pearson did not try to correct the mistake because the towhee would be safer classed as game than as pest.

Before Pearson's bill passed, the prohibition against shipping live wild birds out of state was deleted. Apparently someone engaged in marketing caged birds in northern cities had influence in the legislature. Pearson's bill further allowed game birds that were in plentiful supply, such as ducks and geese, to be killed and shipped to out-of-state markets without restriction but required the purchase of permits for shipping out of state the less numerous "partridges, pheasants, quails, wild turkeys, snipe or woodcock." In some quarter, Pearson found support for strengthening the protection of the less numerous species. In the bill's final version, North Carolina residents were denied the right to ship them out of state, and shipments by nonresidents "holding a hunter's license" were limited to "fifty partridges or quail in a season." No one could ship "pheasants," apparently meaning Ruffed Grouse (*Bonasa umbellus*) and Ring-necked Pheasants (*Phasianus colchicus*), or "wild turkeys, snipe or woodcock." [21]

After routinely passing in the senate, the bill became law on March 6, 1903, and took effect immediately. "Thus was passed," Pearson wrote later, "the first law ever enacted in any South Atlantic or Gulf state to provide for a state game-warden system. There were still seventeen states in the Union where no warden system had been put into operation, and in thirty-one states the law did not protect song and insectivorous birds." Florida had adopted the AOU model law in 1901 but had not provided wardens to enforce it; Virginia adopted some model law provisions in 1903. Dutcher used Thayer Fund money to provide wardens for the gull and tern nesting colonies in both states. [22]

Almost simultaneously with the Audubon Act's adoption, H. H. Brimley's lobbying for the State Museum ended and he went to Cape Hatteras for a rest. Pearson wrote to him, "I have no means of telling how much I should enjoy being there, for just at this season of the year it must be magnificent, grand and glorious. I have been there in April and hea[r]d six mockingbirds sing at the same time and I know something about what is in store for you." In his published writings, Pearson rhapsodized over the Northern Mockingbird, who "revels in the glory of his vocal strength, and shouts his ringing challenge to the trees, the flowers, the very sky itself. . . . At times the very intensity of the music within his breast lifts him many feet into the air. With dangling legs and carelessly flopping wings he drops again to his perch, singing the while."[23]

Pearson, H. H. Brimley, Joyner, Lewis, Jordan, Wilson, P. D. Gold, Jr., and A. H. Boyden were named in the Audubon Act as the society's incorporators. Except for Brimley, who was still at Hatteras and who sent suggestions in writing, they met together for the first time at Greensboro's Benbow Hotel on Saturday, March 21. Joyner resigned as president, saying he could not devote adequate time to the position's responsibilities. Jordan was elected president; Joyner accepted the vice-presidency; and Pearson and Wilson continued as secretary and treasurer, respectively. Jordan, Pearson, and Wilson were ex officio members of the executive committee, which also included five members chosen to provide regional representation: in the east, S. M. Beasley, of Poplar Branch, Currituck County; in the west, Chase P. Ambler, of Asheville; in the south central, Henry E. Knox, of Charlotte; and in the north central, P. D. Gold, Jr., and Julius I. Foust, both of Greensboro. Enough members lived in Greensboro for a three-man quorum to meet quickly for emergencies. Knox was identified by Pearson, in a letter of explanation to Brimley, as a "Civil Engineer from Charlotte, a man of some means and one who has shown great interest in the welfare of the Society and who is now busying himself gathering sustaining members."[24]

# 11

# The South's First State
# Wildlife Commission
## *(1903–1904)*

THE AUDUBON SOCIETY of North Carolina, the first state wildlife commission in the South, began its work with a ninety-nine-cent deficit. The almost eight hundred dollars raised in membership and gifts had been spent to publicize the society, encourage bird study, and win support for the Audubon bill. Although no money would be available from hunting license sales until December 1, two tasks seemed immediately imperative: publicize the Audubon Act and guard the gull and tern colonies. From the Thayer Fund Dutcher paid for two thousand linen warning signs that named "gulls, terns, nighthawks, or bullbats" as representative protected birds, reminded the public that game birds could not be killed except during open seasons established by law, and summarized the Lacey Act's provisions that no birds killed in violation of state laws could be shipped out of state. Lawbreakers were to be reported to the Audubon Society.[1]

On terms suggested by H. H. Brimley, the society gave Pearson full power to direct its daily work. He was to be paid six hundred dollars a year; the position would be part-time, supplementary to his career as a college professor. With three hundred dollars from

the Thayer Fund, Pearson hired the first of three wardens to guard
the seabird colonies, N. F. Jennett of Buxton, whom Brimley
recommended. By mail Jennett agreed to work through May, June,
and July and to send Pearson daily reports in batches once or twice
a week. Governor Aycock sent Jennett's commission to the Dare
County clerk of court, and Pearson mailed Jennett shield number
one.[2]

Pearson hired J. W. Mason of Atlantic and W. J. Weeks of
Southport soon thereafter. He assigned each man to a cape, the
barrier beaches associated with it, and the nearby lumps—small
islands of sand and shell projecting a few feet above water in the
sounds. Jennett was in charge of Hatteras, the northernmost cape;
his territory included most of Pamlico Sound. Mason patrolled the
area of Cape Lookout, including Shackleford Banks, Core Banks,
Core Sound, and the southern end of Pamlico Sound. Weeks
guarded the southernmost cape, Cape Fear.[3]

Pearson instructed the wardens to alert the local people to their
presence and tell them about the laws they would be enforcing.
After State Normal's classes ended in May, he went to the coast to
talk with the wardens, to publicize the Audubon Society and the
new law, and to look for seabird colonies. At Wilmington, he
organized a branch Audubon Society composed "of the very best
people of the city, the Sprunts, Worth, Waddell, and such people."
The bird population at Cape Fear was disappointing. "On the
beaches near Southport I saw 35 Oyster Catchers, 3 Least Terns,
and 5 Royal Terns. I saw no skimmers at all. Five years ago, at the
same place I saw probably 100 Terns, and twice that many skimmers," he wrote H. H. Brimley.[4]

By the time Gilbert and Elsie went to Knoxville that summer,
where again he taught in the Summer School of the South, he had
written his last essay for the *Atlantic Educational Journal*, a pleasant
meditation on what it was like to be a bird in July, "the most
peaceful of all the months." With the July-August issue, possibly

the best educational journal "ever produced in the South" ceased publication for lack of subscribers. Its assets were sold to E. L. Kellogg and Company of New York, publisher of *Teachers' Institute* and *School Journal.* Philander Claxton, who was busy superintending the Summer School of the South and building the University of Tennessee's education department, found his magazine's suspension a "welcome relief," but southern teachers had lost a forum and Pearson had lost a channel of communication through which he could speak to them about birds.[5] The Kellogg editors showed little interest in natural history.

President McIver was pleased that the Audubon Society had originated on his campus and maintained its headquarters there. When State Normal's fall term opened, he relieved Pearson of some of his teaching duties by assigning Virginia Brown, who had completed the degree requirements, to be his teaching assistant. Under Pearson's influence Brown had developed a strong interest in birds, but like her mentor respected the interrelationships among living things. "Every plant and every animal that has ever lived has had its part to play in the ongoing of the earth's history," she wrote in "Interdependence in Wood Life," "for every creature in the living of its life, makes possible the existence of other forms of life, and offers a means whereby they may fulfill their destinies." Brown taught Pearson's freshman classes. As his assistant, she saw less of him than she had as his student; his classes and the Audubon Society kept him "busy day and night."[6] (Later Brown married Stephen A. Douglas's grandson Robert D. Douglas, a Greensboro attorney and a sustaining member of the Audubon Society. They built a home in the woods, where she continued to study birds and wildflowers.)

Money from Audubon memberships soon enabled Pearson to employ part-time wardens at two dollars a day and expenses. In December, the first hunting license receipts were available, and by March 1904 he had hired twenty-six wardens on daily wages. The total warden force now consisted of twenty-nine agents stationed in twenty-two counties. Although most of the agents served in the coastal counties (four in Currituck County), several were in the Piedmont (two each in Davidson County and Guilford), and one was in the mountains (Buncombe County).[7]

When Pearson and his wardens surveyed the coast, they found "only a remnant of the great flocks" of seabirds that once nested annually in North Carolina. During the previous fifteen years, in Pearson's "conservative estimate," five hundred thousand seabirds had been killed in the state. In 1903, they could locate no Least Tern nests and no colony of Laughing Gulls, the only gull species known to have bred in North Carolina. Pearson saw five Least Terns near Southport but could find no evidence of nesting. Five miles north, a colony of about eighty Black Skimmers, protected by Warden Weeks, successfully reared their young. On Whalebone Beach in Carteret County, Warden Mason counted more than three hundred eggs of the Black Skimmer and the "Wilson's tern" (Common Tern), but just as the eggs were hatching a tidal wave "swept over the island and the eggs and young were totally destroyed." The parent birds then apparently went to Royal Shoal Island in Pamlico Sound. There and on several small lumps in the sound, guarded by Warden Jennett, skimmers and terns (possibly including Forster's Terns and Royal Terns as well as Common Terns) successfully reared their young. Altogether, Pearson reported to the Audubon Society, "about two thousand young terns and skimmers are known to have been reared during the past summer." Although he later revised the figure to seventeen hundred birds reared, he was pleased and optimistic. "If properly protected, there seems to be little reason why our coast should not again be populated with sea birds in their former numbers although the remnant is so small today."[8]

The first Audubon arrests were made at Greensboro on September 9, 1903. Two young men were seen shooting at Common

Nighthawks, flocking for migration south. A warden, following Pearson's instructions to all wardens, told the men about the new law, giving them a chance to stop before they were arrested. When they continued shooting, he arrested them, and the local magistrate fined them the required one dollar for each bird killed, a total of four dollars (the equivalent of two days' pay for a warden). The Greensboro arrest was noted as the first police action ever taken in a southern state against the traditional sport of nighthawk shooting. It "marks the beginning of a new epoch of bird protection," Mabel Wright proclaimed in *Bird-Lore*; she saw it also as "evidence of the effective activity of the North Carolina Audubon Society under Professor Pearson's leadership." She wondered whether other states could follow his example and wrote to Chapman, "The topic of the greatest interest to me at present is—How can Audubon Societies have the law enforced?"[9]

A few days after the arrests for nighthawk shooting, a Burlington homeowner was arrested for killing Chimney Swifts. Like the nighthawks, Chimney Swifts were gathering in flocks for the migration to their winter homes in South America. A large flock roosted in the chimney of G. W. Anthony, "one of the most wealthy and influential citizens" of Burlington. He regarded them as a nuisance, especially when they caused soot and mortar to fall into the fireplace and onto a nearby carpet. Although he could have kept the birds out by putting a screen on top of the chimney when they were on wing during the day, he chose to screen the chimney one night, trapping the birds inside. Then he stuffed the fireplace and lower chimney with straw and set it on fire. Several hundred birds were killed. An Audubon warden was told what Anthony had done and arrested him. Because of the possible size of the fine—several hundred dollars—the local magistrate referred the case to Superior Court. Anthony expressed regret for his actions. A friend of his, in a letter to the Raleigh *News and Observer*, berated "the Honorable T. Gilbert Pearson" and criticized the Audubon

Act as "a very foolish law." The *Burlington News* editor hoped the Audubon Society would "enter a plea of mercy" in Anthony's behalf. Pearson declined to do this, but a lenient judge accepted Anthony's plea of guilty and excused him from the fine.[10]

Changing the views of most North Carolinians toward birds would not be easy. Pearson wanted them to share his conviction that birds had as much a place in the divine scheme of things as human beings, and that by killing birds human beings were destroying natural allies. "It is no small service that a pair of robins render when they honor you by living a summer in your garden, and each day eating more than their own weight of worms and insects," he wrote in a society leaflet, *Protect the Insect-Eating Birds*. "It is no little thing to have a pair of pewees [Eastern Wood-Pewee, *Contopus virens*] nest in a tree near your house, and every day for weeks and weeks rid the air of hundreds of harmful insects which seek to destroy the foliage or sting the fruit of your trees."[11]

By Pearson's reckoning, the Audubon Society in its first year under the Audubon Act distributed more than seventy-six thousand items of printed information: copies of the Audubon Act, posters listing game laws, and society leaflets, as well as the first seven in a series of "Educational Leaflets" written by Dutcher and published by the National Committee of Audubon Societies. Each National Committee leaflet was devoted to a bird species that Dutcher viewed as being in particular need of human friends. His first choices were the Common Nighthawk, Mourning Dove, Eastern Meadowlark, American Robin (*Turdus migratorius*), Northern Flicker, Passenger Pigeon, and Snowy Egret. The leaflets were so popular that many more were written. Pearson would eventually edit one hundred of them, forty of which he had written or rewritten, for publication in the two-volume work, *Portraits and Habits of Our Birds*.[12]

Pearson created a North Carolina Audubon Junior Department with its own secretary, Mrs. W. A. C. Hammel, who worked under his direction. Adult volunteers served as local secretaries and organized local branches. Pearson selected a library of ten natural history books for the public schools, assembled fifty sets, and offered them with one subscription to *Bird-Lore* per set to county school superintendents. A superintendent who accepted a set was required to contribute five dollars to the society, keep the library in his office, and lend books to teachers, who were expected to study them and pass knowledge on to their pupils. The library was designed primarily for rural schools, few of which had a library of any kind in 1901. By 1903, some communities had taken advantage of the Rural School Library Act of 1901, which provided matching funds from the state and the county to any rural community raising as much as ten dollars for a school library.[13] Pearson probably reached some rural teachers with books sooner than Governor Aycock did in his effort to raise the level of literacy in North Carolina.

Pearson was following examples set by older Audubon societies, especially those in Massachusetts and Connecticut, that had pioneered in providing nature libraries for the public schools. They had also prepared circulating lectures, with texts, lanterns, and slides, that could be delivered by any good performer. Pearson's fifty libraries almost tripled in number the eighteen in Connecticut, but he had not yet developed a circulating lecture. He had, however, prepared illustrated lectures he delivered as he went about the state speaking in the Audubon Society's behalf.[14]

In seven months of operation, the society arrested only four transgressors against the law protecting nongame birds. Many more offenders could have been arrested if the society had not chosen to give them a lecture instead. Once they had been told about the Audubon Act, they were generally willing to obey it. As the fall hunting season for game neared, the wardens observed men following their previously accepted practice of killing turkeys, squirrels, and deer before the season opened. The same cautious enforcement guidelines were followed: they warned first offenders and arrested second offenders. Nineteen were convicted in 1903. Covert hunting out of season could not be completely prevented, but news of the laws was spreading and compliance was widespread.[15]

Warden W. John Weatherly of Greensboro (of no known relationship to Elsie Weatherly Pearson) was unusually successful in detecting shipments of Wild Turkeys, Ruffed Grouse, and Northern Bobwhites. Accompanied by his small black dog, Weatherly regularly examined freight in railroad stations. Pearson was with him at the Southern Railway depot in Greensboro when the first illegal shipment was discovered. Pearson had received an anonymously written letter about a package being shipped from Siler City to Wallestine Brothers, Washington, D.C., and he brought along several signed search warrants. The first train from Siler City carried a crate addressed to Wallestine Brothers packed with bobwhites covered by a layer of eggs. Two newspaper reporters asked how Weatherly and Pearson knew the crate contained bobwhites and a myth was created. The dog, Weatherly said, patting his pet's head, "pointed the box for us." "Within twenty-four hours," Pearson later recalled, "the whole State had been advised that it was a perilous undertaking to try to smuggle quail through Greensboro, because a dog of unusual powers and sagacity was on constant watch." On subsequent occasions, Weatherly nevertheless found birds packed beneath layers of rabbits, in the bottom of butter firkins, in boxes labeled "persimmons," and inside the bodies of large domestic geese and turkeys. Identifying shippers was difficult, sometimes impossible, and so was prosecuting them; only three were convicted. Persons of high community standing were sometimes implicated, and the crime was lightly regarded by most local magistrates.[16]

On the coast, ducks and geese were vulnerable to "fire lighting," an illegal practice often carried on openly by market hunters. At night, a lantern or a burning torch with a reflector behind it was placed on the prow of a boat, which was pushed about in the shallow waters where the birds slept in flocks. Blinded and confused, the awakening birds allowed the boat to come very close before fleeing. The gunners were able to kill a great many birds swiftly and easily, sometimes dispatching several with one shot.

Pearson directed his wardens to stop the fire lighting "at all hazards." In this effort, in contrast to the effort to end illegal shipping of inland game birds, influential people sided with the Audubon Society, seeing fire lighting as unsportsmanlike and unbusinesslike. It frightened the birds more than the usual kinds of shooting, causing them to shun the areas where it occurred, so that legitimate hunting was less successful. The combined weight of public disapproval, warden vigilance, the influence of the Audubon Society's Currituck branch, and the arrest and conviction of two hunters stopped the known fire lighting in Currituck County, which encompassed most of Currituck Sound. In Core Sound, Carteret County, Warden Mason encountered bold men reluctant to give up fire lighting; he was "unable to cope with the situation." Pearson sent three more wardens to help him. Two fire lighters were arrested and by season's end Pearson concluded that "only a few pot hunters" (men killing birds to eat rather than to sell) or "adventurous young men who wish for some unusual excitement" were still engaging in fire lighting.[17]

After a year's existence, the Audubon Society had 1,218 members and seven branches. Most of the 31 life members were wealthy men who lived ouside of North Carolina; 8 lived in New York. Overall, the geographical pattern of membership reflected the society's dependence on Pearson's personal soliciting efforts; most of the life and sustaining members hunted or lived in the counties he could visit most frequently. A third of the 341 sustaining members lived in Guilford County; all but 11 lived in a nine-county area.[18]

Except for Mrs. Hammel, Junior Department secretary, all the officers of the Audubon Society of North Carolina and of the seven branches were men. All but 3 of the 341 sustaining members were men. The society's law-enforcement power came from the state legislature, made up entirely of men. Women and children were urged to join the Audubon Society, but when they joined they usually chose regular or junior memberships.[19] In other Audubon societies, none of which were law-enforcement agencies, women played a larger role.

Mabel Wright was the most influential woman in the Audubon movement—Connecticut Audubon Society president, National Committee of Audubon Societies member, and Audubon Department editor of *Bird-Lore*. She understood the demands of ornithological field study and was aware that ornithologists of either sex needed spouses who shared, or at least tolerated, their interests. "Fuertes' wedding announcement, just received," she wrote to Chapman, "makes me hope that he will have a wife that will fit into his aims and ambitions as yours does and not 'spoil the crowd' and take the fun out of him." In the realm of ideas, she gave no quarter. She boldly suggested to Chapman that he surrender *Bird-Lore* to the National Committee of Audubon Societies (many years later he sold it to the National Audubon Society). After a dispute with Dutcher, she wrote Chapman that Dutcher's "only excuse has busticated & Wright & Dutcher has closed in favor of Wright."[20]

Several women, including Mrs. Garrett of Asheville, joined the North Carolina Academy of Science, which Pearson addressed twice about birds at the annual meeting in November 1903.[21] Later that month, women who (like many of the men) were members of both groups attended the coinciding meetings of the AOU and the National Committee of Audubon Societies in Philadelphia.

Dutcher's comparatively brief talks to the National Committee and the AOU were taken from his full AOU bird protection committee report, which occupied 110 pages in the *Auk*. His year spent working to save birds had been spiritually uplifting. "When we rise above the sordidness that so often hinders spiritual work, and learn to believe that it is better sometimes to invest in deeds of mercy to God's helpless creatures than it is to invest in the best of securities, we will find that our works of love are better paying investments and will bring us something far higher and nobler." Campaign successes had outnumbered failures. Audubon societies had been formed in four additional states (Michigan, Georgia, North Dakota, and Colorado) and apparently revived in two more (California and Texas); the AOU model law had been adopted in nine (North Carolina, Virginia, Tennessee, Georgia, Texas, Minnesota, Colorado, Oregon, and Washington). In only five states (California, Kansas, Michigan, Missouri, and the Oklahoma Territory) had efforts to strengthen nongame bird protection failed. Dutcher commended Pearson, without naming him, for his fund raising in North Carolina: the "work of the North Carolina Society . . . is an object lesson of the greatest force to other societies who complain of the difficulty in securing funds for their work. If in a State that is comparatively poor, 331 sustaining members can be secured for the asking, what would be the result of the same effort in the more wealthy and thickly populated States?"[22]

Dutcher was paying from the AOU Thayer Fund the wages of thirty-three wardens in eight states, including three in North Carolina.[23] One warden was assigned to Pelican Island in Florida's Indian River, owned by the U.S. government and inhabited by Brown Pelicans vulnerable to illegal feather hunters' raids. From that routine protective effort came some extraordinary results. A fellow employee suggested to Frank Bond, chief of the General Land Office's drafting division, the idea of turning Pelican Island into a government bird reservation, the same way forest lands had been set aside as reservations by presidential orders. As a journalist in Cheyenne, Wyoming, Bond had built a large state Audubon society; in 1903, having moved to Washington, D.C., he was an

AOU bird protection committee member. Knowing Theodore Roosevelt to be a bird student and an Audubon supporter, Bond prepared an order for the president, who signed it on March 14 and made Pelican Island the nation's first bird reservation, "set apart for the use of the Department of Agriculture as a preserve and breeding ground for native birds." At the request of Secretary of Agriculture James Wilson, who had no funds to employ a warden, the AOU bird protection committee provided one.

Although Pearson played no personal role in creating the Pelican Island reservation, he was aware of the historic significance of Roosevelt's action. What had been done once might be done again—and again and again. The following year the AOU bird protection committee requested, on the Louisiana Audubon Society's behalf, a bird reservation on Louisiana's coastal islands where seabirds were shot for their feathers and their eggs were taken to make "delicate films on photographic plates." Roosevelt obliged once more, establishing the Breton Island Bird Reservation. For the many proposals that followed, Bond usually wrote letters to the president explaining them and composed the executive orders.[24]

Large millinery enterprises were having more and more trouble getting wild bird feathers. Some accused AOU wardens of exceeding their authority and interfering with the legitimate use of feathers. Whether or not the accusations were true, the ornithologists, their wardens, and their Audubon affiliates had to be dealt with. As in 1900, New York milliners asked for a truce. Their earlier proposal had been rejected largely because they had insisted on retaining the right to use foreign bird feathers. By 1903, they had become willing to agree not to trade in the bodies of a large number of bird species, no matter where they lived or were killed, and this time their offer was accepted. In the spring of 1903, the Millinery Merchants Protective Association of New York and the Audubon Society of the State of New York, under Chapman's leadership as executive committee chairman, signed a three-year agreement in which the milliners pledged to abide by bird protection laws and refrain from trading in the bodies of numerous species identified in the agreement, even if the birds were legally killed abroad. In return, the Audubon Society pledged to "endeavor to prevent all illegal interference on the part of game wardens with the millinery trade" and "to refrain from aiding the passage of any legislation" against trading in feathers of domestic fowl or foreign birds not on the list in the agreement. The Western Millinery Association, the AOU, and several additional Audubon societies concurred in the agreement.[25]

Even with the agreement, avenues remained open for working for international bird protection. An AOU committee on foreign relations, of which Dutcher and Biological Survey executive Theodore Palmer were members, promoted bird protection throughout the world. The U.S. War Department, Navy Department, and Department of the Interior were urged to protect birds in the Philippines and the Midway Islands. Palmer publicized the need for foreign bird protection in a series of articles in *Bird-Lore*. Introducing the first of these, Mabel Wright envisioned a worldwide "protective wall against which the shot of the plume- and pothunter" would "rattle in vain" and which would "rise in its might to be one of the grandest monuments of the best spirit of modern civilization."[26]

The Audubon Society of North Carolina was prospering. In its first year, the sale of licenses to nonresident hunters brought in almost $5,000; membership fees amounted to approximately $1,700. Counting the AOU's donation, the year's income totalled about $7,300, with more than $2,200 still on hand at the end of the year. Pearson drew $500 in pay ($100 less than had been agreed upon) and almost $400 in travel expenses. The wardens' combined wages came to $2,532. A deposit of $235 was made on a naptha

launch for Warden Jennett to use in patrolling the Cape Hatteras
area; too often weather conditions prevented him from moving
about with dispatch in his sailboat. An exemplary warden, Jennett
was singled out for praise by Pearson in his annual report. For fifty
miles north and south of Cape Hatteras, Jennett had patrolled both
sides of the Outer Banks in "all kinds of weather and exposed to the
many dangers which lurk for the sea-faring man" about the cape.
He had succeeded in "extending to the sea birds absolute protection from the millinery feather hunters." He was teacher as well
as law enforcer. "I believe most profoundly," Pearson wrote to
Dutcher, "that he is doing a grand work in educating public
sentiment in that coast country."[27]

Early on the morning of January 21, 1904, a fire destroyed the
main dormitory, kitchen, dining room, and laundry at State Normal College. President McIver suspended the college and sent the
girls home. During the suspension, compartments set up in the
Student's Building substituted for rooms; returning students who
could not be accommodated there took rooms in nearby boarding
houses. A temporary dining hall was built on the tennis courts
next to the woods, to the "surprise and delight" of the students,
who liked the feeling of "going to the country" where they could
"hear the birds sing."[28]

# 12

# The Money in Game

## *(1904)*

"OUR FIRE WAS quite a knock-out blow and as a result I am out of a job until the middle of February. However, the violators of the game laws are giving me something to think about," Pearson wrote to H. H. Brimley.[1] Progress was slower in protecting game, including game birds, than in protecting song birds, gulls, terns, and other nongame species that had been the most vulnerable forms of wildlife only a year earlier.

Pearson accepted George O. Shields's invitation to address the League of American Sportsmen's annual meeting at Columbus, Ohio, in February. Though the league had begun to falter after only six years' existence, its meetings were often attended by state game officials with whom Pearson could fruitfully converse. Furthermore, Shields and the league were trying to persuade state legislatures to establish limits on the number of a given game species one hunter could kill in a day or in a season, a goal Pearson viewed as eventually appropriate for North Carolina. During the convention, he talked with Theodore Palmer, a vice president, and with William F. Scott of Montana, who two years earlier had founded the already dormant National Association of Game and Fish Wardens and Commissioners. The three men revived the association by assembling all the state game officials present. Renamed the National Association of Game and Fish Commissioners, the organization survived and was ultimately expanded into the International Association of Fish and Wildlife Agencies.[2]

At Pearson's invitation, Palmer addressed the Audubon Society's annual meeting in Greensboro on March 12, 1904, as did Francis D. Winston of Windsor, attorney, judge, former legislator, close friend of Governor Aycock, and Audubon Society member. Winston's topic was the history of game protection in the state; Palmer's, "some possiblities" for future action. Winston traced the Audubon Act's "genesis" to a 1738 act that forbade killing deer on "unfenced ground" between February 15 and July 15. The "germ" of the resident hunting license lay in early laws that required anyone who killed a deer to produce a certificate showing himself to be a freeholder owning one hundred acres of land or tending ten thousand hills of corn five feet apart, in the county in which the deer was killed. These laws were aimed against "evil and disorderly persons" from adjoining colonies who killed deer at all seasons and left carcasses in the woods, a practice viewed as reprehensible because it provided food for "wolves and bears and other vermin."[3]

Palmer summarized the Audubon Society's accomplishments: "(1) It has shown that the protection of birds and game is something worth having—that it is worthwhile to preserve the birds. (2) It has shown that it is possible to enforce the game laws—a seemingly curious achievement perhaps, but nevertheless a real one in the light of past experience, for it is well known that few statutes are more difficult to enforce than those relating to game. (3) It has shown the residents of the coast counties that 'fire lighting' which has been prohibited by law for more than a century can be stopped. (4) It has shown the people in other parts of the State that the unlawful export of partridges or quail which has been going on for 20 years or more can be greatly restricted if not entirely stopped." Palmer discussed at length the "money value of game," mentioning the profits farmers in the central and western counties made by leasing hunting rights on their lands to wealthy sportsmen; the money spent by other sportsmen, generally from the North, who bought land on the coast and maintained hunting clubs; and the sums expended for "railroad fares, hire of teams and guides, for board and incidental expenses." In short, protecting game was good for the state.[4]

At the Audubon Society's business meeting, State Commissioner of Agriculture Samuel L. Patterson was elected to replace Henry Knox on the board of directors. Richard H. Lewis, secretary of the State Board of Health, succeeded Jordan as president, a position he held for the rest of the society's existence. Superintendent of Public Instruction J. Y. Joyner remained in the vice-presidency.[5] Pearson hoped that enlarging the role of state government officials in the society would increase its prestige and influence.

Palmer's presence at the society's meeting enhanced its importance. "I can never get through thanking you for coming," Pearson wrote. Having decided to publish Palmer's address with Winston's in a single pamphlet, Pearson sent Palmer a stenographic record of his speech and requested he make his "argument *twice as long*." "Put in anything that you think ought to be said, for this is the campaign document that we are going to rely upon extensively." Over the next year, Pearson distributed five thousand copies of the pamphlet.[6]

The *State Normal Magazine* for February 1904 published what appears to have been Pearson's last short story, a comic farce about a Harvard student who came to the North Carolina mountains one summer to study and collect flowers. The year before, Pearson had published in the same magazine a long, anthropomorphic story about a wise and brave Canada Goose (*Branta canadensis*). Several nature writers were creating fanciful tales of animals behaving like people, and presenting them as true accounts. William J. Long, one of the most popular writers of such tales, told of a muskrat that lost a foot in a steel trap and smeared the stump of its leg with pine pitch in order to prevent infection, of American Woodcocks that mended broken legs with casts made of clay and straw, and of beavers that raised young otters to be their slaves. Chapman viewed these writings as "unnatural history" that did more harm than good: "While the writers of this class no doubt awaken much interest in animal life, it is not a healthy interest. It is based on false premises and unwarranted assumptions."[7] Possibly to avoid being identified with the writers of "unnatural history," Pearson stopped writing fiction altogether.

Soon after State Normal's commencement exercises in May 1904, Pearson went to the coast to study breeding colonies. For the first time since 1898, he was free to spend a few weeks in field study. Equipped with field glasses and a camera rather than a gun, he took notes and made photographs.[8] The collector of bird bodies had become a collector of bird pictures, intent on building a library rather than a museum.

With a local guide to help carry a canoe, he went to Great Lake to check on the cormorant colony, where he found 121 nests, 36 of which were in one tree. When adult birds flew away, they often dropped so low they struck the water before gaining enough speed to "rush hurtling across the lake." The cormorant, Pearson's guide said, cannot fly "until it wets its tail." A young bird on a slender limb lost its balance, fell into the water, and was at once chased by a large alligator. "We immediately started in pursuit," Pearson wrote, "and, after an exciting chase, rescued the young Cormorant; but not until the alligator had made two unsuccessful snaps at his intended victim, which escaped only by diving with marvelous quickness just at the proper instant."[9]

On Pamlico Sound's barren beaches and islands, Pearson found evidence of the value of warden protection: Royal Terns, Common Terns, Least Terns, and a few pairs of Laughing Gulls were nesting. By summer's end, when all the wardens' reports were in,

Pearson estimated that twenty-seven hundred young skimmers, terns, and Laughing Gulls had been raised in 1904, about a thousand more than the year before. Especially gratifying was the increase in the number of Royal Terns, which in 1903 had laid at the most "10 or 12 eggs" on the entire North Carolina coast. Pamlico Sound fishermen were pleased by the enlarged seabird population. One had pointed to a flock gathered over the water and told Pearson a school of fish was probably below the birds.[10]

Pearson did not return to the Summer School of the South in 1904. Possibly he gave precedence to the field trip. Nonetheless, he taught a three-week course in ornithology at the South Carolina State Summer School at Rock Hill and lectured on birds at the summer schools of Davidson College and the University of North Carolina. In August, he addressed the Georgia State Horticultural Society at Tallulah Falls on the topic, "The Practical Enforcement of Game Laws." Along with Dutcher, he was disappointed by Georgia's slow progress in bird protection. In the previous year, a state Audubon society had been organized, the AOU model law had been adopted (Dutcher had paid for the printing and distribution of eight thousand copies of a bulletin advocating the law), and the seasons for hunting game birds had been shortened, but no adequate enforcement system had been established. The Audubon Society was weak; its secretary, H. N. Starnes of the State Agricultural Experiment Station, did not have enough time to develop the society's work and was unable to find anyone else to do so. No Thayer Fund warden was employed on the Georgia coast because there was no supervisory agency to which he could be assigned. Pearson's address was probably intended to encourage the emergence of strong leadership in the Audubon Society, but such leadership did not appear.[11]

Dixie Lee Bryant, for whom Pearson had been substituting on the State Normal faculty, returned with her doctorate in September 1904, but in her absence, the school had grown enough for

Pearson to be kept on the faculty. In November, Theodore Palmer came to Pearson seeking help in gathering information about the practice among farmers of leasing land to wealthy men interested in Northern Bobwhite hunting. The wealthiest sportsmen created large private hunting preserves by buying several hundred acres and leasing hunting rights on several thousand more. They built spacious lodges and employed guards to keep trespassing hunters away. Pearson took Palmer to the preserves of Pierre Lorillard, George J. Gould, Clarence H. Mackay, and Samuel Spencer, president of Southern Railway. Spencer talked with Pearson and Palmer in his sidetracked private car and later entertained them at dinner in his lodge. In four days with Pearson, Palmer compiled a list of more than forty men who leased farmland for hunting purposes in Guilford County and in several adjoining counties. More than half were New York residents. The farmers commonly charged a leasing fee equivalent to their land taxes, thereby in effect holding their land tax-free. They raised their usual crops and, during the bobwhite-hunting season, yielded to the lessees the responsibility of protecting the land against trespassers. Pearson liked the system because the lessees were usually respectful of the game laws and restrained in their hunting practices. Moreover, several joined the Audubon Society as patrons; others became life members and sustaining members.[12]

Along the coast, Pearson occasionally visited well-to-do sportsmen's hunting clubs. Near hunting season's end in the winter of 1904–5, he was a guest at a club where he was permitted to examine the records. The twenty-one members had killed a total of about four thousand ducks and geese during the five-month season. For each bird killed, he calculated, eleven to twelve dollars had been spent. Together during the season, therefore, the members had spent perhaps forty-eight thousand dollars.[13]

Although Pearson could only guess at the total amount spent each year in the state by nonresident hunters, the figure was clearly large. Additional money went to local market hunters, who in Currituck County alone, according to Pearson's reckoning, received about one hundred thousand dollars for waterfowl in the 1904–5 season. Pearson envisioned game becoming even more important to the state's economy through good management. "North Carolina is well suited by nature as the home of the most valuable birds and game animals of eastern North America," he wrote, "and we believe that by proper protection, large areas of our State can in time veritably be made vast game preserves, which will be a source of great wealth to the State." [14]

He was trying to maintain a delicate balance, encouraging people to be sensitive to the lives and feelings of birds while making a distinction between birds that should never be killed and birds that should be protected in order to be in good supply for killing and eating. The Audubon Society counted on its wardens, forty by November 1904, to be teachers, providing each with several natural history books, copies of state and national laws, and a subscription to *Bird-Lore*. Instructed to "travel through the country visiting the towns, country stores and farmhouses, handing out literature and talking with the people," the wardens distributed Audubon leaflets and U.S. Department of Agriculture publications. By Pearson's estimate, 180,000 copies of these items were mailed, handed out, or, in the case of game laws, posted along highways and at courthouses and country stores, "wherever the people gather." [15]

After raising almost thirteen hundred dollars in special contributions, Pearson bought a thirty-nine foot, naptha-powered boat with a large cabin in which the wardens could cook and sleep. He named it *The Dutcher*, in honor of William Dutcher, who "more than any other man in America," he said, was "responsible for the present widespread and deepening interest in practical methods for protecting the non-game birds of the country." [16]

Elliott Coues (facing page, top) Joel A. Allen (facing page, bottom), and William Brewster (above). In 1883, these three men called the meeting to form the American Ornithologists' Union (AOU). Brewster was the first chairman of the AOU's committee for the protection of North American birds and first president of the Massachusetts Audubon Society, the oldest Audubon organization in existence. Ruthven Deane Collection, courtesy of Library of Congress.

Frank M. Chapman, AOU and Audubon movement leader. In 1891, he sponsored eighteen-year-old T. Gilbert Pearson for associate membership in the AOU. Ruthven Deane Collection, courtesy of Library of Congress.

George Bird Grinnell, AOU bird protection committee member who in 1886 founded, as the committee's auxiliary, the first Audubon Society. Ruthven Deane Collection, courtesy of Library of Congress.

T. Gilbert Pearson (top) and John M. Greenfield (bottom) in their dormitory room at the University of North Carolina, 1899. Friends Historical Collection, courtesy of Guilford College.

William Dutcher, longtime AOU bird protection committee chairman and first president of the National Association of Audubon Societies for the Protection of Wild Birds and Animals, now the National Audubon Society. Ruthven Deane Collection, courtesy of Library of Congress.

H. H. Brimley, first curator of what is now the North Carolina State Museum of Natural Sciences. Pearson's closest friend, he was relied upon heavily for advice in the administration of the Audubon Society of North Carolina. Ruthven Deane Collection, courtesy of Library of Congress.

# WARNING

The Laws of North Carolina protect at all times **GULLS, TERNS, NIGHTHAWKS, or BULL-BATS**, and all other wild non-game birds, also their nests and eggs.

## PENALTY upon conviction, a fine or imprisonment.

EXCEPTIONS: Birds not protected, Hawks, Owls, Crows, Blackbirds, English Sparrows, Jackdaws and Ricebirds.

**GAME BIRDS** can only be killed during the open seasons established by law, and Pheasants, Partridges, Quails, Wild Turkeys, Snipe and Woodcock cannot be shipped out of the state.

Under the Federal Law a fine not exceeding $200 is also provided:

I. For the delivery of any birds killed in violation of the laws of North Carolina to any express, railroad or steamboat company, or to any other common carrier, for shipment out of the State.

II. For the transportation of such birds by any common carrier out of the State.

III. For shipment out of the State of any package containing game, birds or plumage, which does not bear the shipper's name and address, and a statement of the nature of the contents.

Agents of common carriers are cautioned against forwarding any package of birds or game which is improperly marked or supposed to contain birds or game killed contrary to law.

## AUDUBON SOCIETY OF NORTH CAROLINA
### GREENSBORO, N. C.

The public is requested to report violations of the law to the above Society or to local game wardens.

These linen posters were distributed after the Audubon Society of North Carolina began functioning as the state wildlife commission in 1903. Courtesy of National Audubon Society.

Mabel Osgood Wright, foremost woman leader in the Audubon movement. She was president of the Audubon Society of Connecticut, editor of *Bird-Lore*'s Audubon Societies department, and a member of the National Association of Audubon Societies board of directors. Ruthven Deane Collection, courtesy of Library of Congress.

Theodore S. Palmer, U.S. Biological Survey official and AOU and Audubon leader. Other than William Dutcher, he was Pearson's closest associate in the national Audubon movement. Ruthven Deane Collection, courtesy of Library of Congress.

T. Gilbert Pearson (center, in derby and light suit) and others at the National Association of Game and Fish Wardens and Commissioners meeting, in 1907. Theodore S. Palmer is second from right; William F. Scott, president, is sixth from right. At the organization's next meeting, in 1910, Pearson was elected president. Theodore S. Palmer Papers, courtesy of Library of Congress.

William T. Hornaday, director, New York Zoological Society's zoological garden. An ardent and highly independent protector of wild species, he sometimes criticized Audubon societies and other organizations for their methods. Ruthven Deane Collection, courtesy of Library of Congress.

# 13

# The National Association of Audubon Societies for the Protection of Wild Birds and Animals

*(1904–1905)*

LATE IN NOVEMBER 1904 William Dutcher asked Pearson to come to New York. The National Committee of Audubon Societies was in debt; it needed, in Dutcher's words, a "position of permanence"; and at least one potential benefactor had asked for its corporate name so he could bequeath money to it. Committee members had voted by mail to incorporate and to do so in New York, even though Dutcher had initially proposed incorporation in Washington to reflect the national character of the committee's work and interests. The name would be changed to the National Association of Audubon Societies.[1]

Pearson met with Dutcher on the morning of November 25. Albert Willcox, Dutcher explained, was interested in the Audubon movement and might give it money. An insurance broker in New York, Willcox at age fifty-seven was one of two bachelor sons of Albert Oliver Willcox, who had accumulated wealth as a merchant and insurance broker. The other son, David, was an attorney and Delaware and Hudson Coal Company president. Albert Willcox wanted to help an organization devoted to protecting wildlife. If he donated money to the National Committee, he had told Dutcher, he would do so anonymously and on the condition it be used to raise more money; it could not be spent for routine operating expenses. Dutcher had told Willcox about Pearson and his aptitude for soliciting memberships and contributions.[2]

At lunch with Willcox, Pearson listened and answered questions. Willcox "said that he was deeply concerned about two great evils which existed in our country; one, the terrible destruction of birds and game animals; the other, the abuses being heaped upon the Negroes of the Southern states. I did not talk much about the second point, but had something to say about bird and game protection," Pearson wrote. Willcox concluded the luncheon with the noncommittal words "Now, we will go and see Mr. Dutcher."[3]

In Dutcher's office, Willcox "made a brief and businesslike statement," Pearson later wrote, to the effect "that if we incorporated the Audubon Committee as a National Association, not merely for the protection of birds but also for the benefit of useful mammals, and if I would devote approximately one-half of my time to the Association, he would contribute $3,000 a year for at least two years and would provide in his will, for the Association, a legacy of $100,000." Dutcher and Pearson tentatively agreed to his terms. The decision had already been made to use "association" rather than "committee" in the organization's name, and broadening the stated interest to include animals other than birds had proven useful for the Audubon Society of North Carolina.

The next day, Dutcher and Pearson went to Cambridge, Massachusetts, where other National Committee members, gathering for the annual meeting, approved Willcox's proposal. Pearson's compensation was probably discussed, as well as Willcox's insistence on anonymity. A year later, in Dutcher's annual report,

Willcox's contribution of slightly more than three thousand dollars for the year was described as a "Special Fund, contributed by 'Benefactor' for salary and traveling expenses of Special Agent to secure endowment and members," and the special agent (Pearson was not named) was shown to have received fifteen hundred dollars in salary and more than four hundred dollars in traveling expenses. [4]

Pearson would have to resign from State Normal. The traveling he would do as special agent would not permit him to conduct daily classes. But he could retain his position with the Audubon Society, to which he had never given more than half time except in short periods when concentrated effort was necessary. The two roles, Audubon Society secretary and National Association special agent, would be compatible, even reciprocally beneficial. Moreover, although he could not predict exactly what his jobs would pay, he knew he would be well compensated. As matters worked out, for the year ending March 1905, the Audubon Society paid him slightly more than one thousand dollars, bringing his salary for the year to approximately twenty-five hundred dollars, plus traveling expenses. The opportunity to perform work he believed in and to be well paid for performing it, even though it would take him away from the college classroom and, to a large extent, from the field study of birds, appealed to him strongly. "I hurried to Greensboro and told Dr. McIver of my offer of new employment and asked him what he thought of it, and if he could permit me to resign at once from the College. After some days' thought he told me that he believed my duty lay in the direction which I had long been traveling. 'A man's feet should follow his heart,' he said." McIver also said that Pearson could be an unpaid faculty member and retain his office space. Pearson taught until the Christmas recess began, and Dixie Lee Bryant and an assistant took over his classes for the last of the semester. [5]

Pearson became editor of *Bird-Lore*'s Young Observer's Department, an irregularly published experimental column designed to attract readers fourteen and younger. He awarded first prize for the best letter on "Feeding Birds in Winter" to a Rhode Island girl who put out bread crumbs, suet, and a "great many flies" she caught in her attic. A twelve-year-old Illinois boy reported making a feeding shelf: "One day I felt like hammering nails, and I wondered what to make."6 The responses to another contest, this time for the best report on putting up a birdhouse and watching the birds' behavior until the young were on the wing, were apparently so disappointing that the experiment was discontinued.

The National Association of Audubon Societies for the Protection of Wild Birds and Animals was incorporated in New York on January 5, 1905. Its sponsors consisted of societies in thirty-four states, the District of Columbia, and the Territory of Oklahoma; its hopes lay in Pearson's skill at attracting individual members. Pearson's appointment as special agent "to awaken public interest and secure financial assistance" had already been announced. He was "eminently fitted" for the position, said a writer for the *Auk*, "by his energy and earnestness, and his well-known effectiveness as a public speaker."7

Dutcher asked Pearson to come at once to New York to help organize the board of thirty directors. Twenty seats were allotted to the member societies and seven to representatives at large, with three reserved for the AOU. Among the first directors, in addition to Dutcher and Pearson, were Ruthven Deane, Frank Chapman, Witmer Stone, Joel Allen, George Bird Grinnell, William Brewster, Theodore Palmer, Mabel Wright, Abbott Thayer, and John Thayer.8 Although the AOU bird protection committee became relatively inactive after being reduced in size and reorganized (without Dutcher and Pearson), the bond between the AOU and the National Association remained close and strong. The latter's foremost leaders, except for Pearson (whose energies were directed almost exclusively to bird protection and appreciation), continued also to be AOU leaders. Dutcher, Deane, and Stone were on the AOU council, Allen was editor of *Auk*, and Grinnell was an AOU fellow. Chapman was elected AOU vice president and appointed to the bird protection committee. Jonathan Dwight would serve for a time as treasurer of the AOU and of the National Association simultaneously.

Yet in terms of organizational responsibility, a notable transfer was taking place. The primary national leadership for protecting nongame birds was being formally shifted from the AOU bird protection committee to the National Association of Audubon Societies. Dutcher's annual report, hitherto published in *Auk* as the report of the AOU bird protection committee chairman, would henceforth appear in *Bird-Lore* as the report of the National Association president. The AOU Thayer Fund would become part of the National Association's treasury.

Pearson could not go to New York immediately. A new legislature had convened in Raleigh, and already there were bills to be opposed or supported, many of them local in coverage. The Audubon Society itself seemed to be in jeopardy. Governor Aycock, a supporter, was succeeded by Governor Robert B. Glenn, who in his campaign had criticized ("loudly and at great length," Pearson said later) the nonresident hunting license upon which the Audubon Society depended for money to enforce the bird and game laws. Propitiously, a heavy snow fell, followed by sleet and low temperatures. Birds in central and western North Carolina began to starve. Pearson telegraphed all his wardens to put out food and to encourage the general public to do the same. Many newspapers published his personal appeal to the people of the state. When those efforts appeared insufficient, he hired additional wardens to distribute food on farms and game preserves. In Guilford County alone, five men with teams of horses scattered many bushels of cracked corn and cowpeas purchased by the Audubon Society and donated by local residents. On the basis of reports he received,

Pearson concluded that "thousands of our citizens aided thus in keeping the birds alive." Articles complimentary to the society appeared in newspapers. A "well-known politician" said, "Pearson, the very elements of nature fight on your side. With the Legislature just meeting what could be more helpful for you than this very opportune sleet storm and the way you have capitalized it? They will not repeal your Audubon Law this year."[9]

By the middle of January, Pearson felt free to go to New York. Dutcher sent him at once to Boston to talk with National Association board member John Thayer. Thayer had inherited money from his father, Nathaniel Thayer, a financier who amassed "one of the largest fortunes acquired by any New Englander of his day," and he contributed generously to the AOU and to the Audubon cause. He made yearly donations to the Thayer Fund established by Abbott Thayer ($500 in 1904); and joined the Audubon Society of North Carolina as a patron for a fee of $100 and contributed $200 to help pay for *The Dutcher*, the society's launch. Dutcher wanted Pearson to persuade Thayer to chair the National Association's finance committee. "I did my best with Mr. Thayer," Pearson wrote later, "but my best was not good enough." Thayer was more willing to give his money than his time. He declined to become a life member of the National Association for a single fee of $100, choosing instead the less committed and more generous path of an annual membership and a $750 donation. In Cambridge, Brewster gave Pearson a check for $100 and was enrolled as the National Association's first life member.[10]

At the first meeting of the National Association's board of directors on January 30, 1905, Dutcher and Pearson were elected president and secretary, respectively. John Thayer accepted the position of first vice-president; Palmer, second vice-president; and Chapman, treasurer.[11] As the only full-time Audubon leader, Pearson simultaneously held three key positions: executive officer of the Audubon Society of North Carolina, special agent of the

National Association, and secretary of the National Association. As a state official he was independent of the National Association; in the other two positions he was responsible to Dutcher and to the National Association's board of directors.

Although the North Carolina Audubon Society's membership had reached 1,225 by March 1905 and expenditures were made with caution, in 1905 the financial accounts were temporarily unbalanced. Pearson had to solicit renewals from many society members who joined on an annual basis. In October he wrote to H. H. Brimley, "You know the sources of our income; yet perhaps you don't quite realize the amount of discouraging labor it requires to collect it, particularly our membership fees. The Society is now over a thousand dollars in debt, and for the last two months I have been paying from my personal account those bills which I could not possibly stave off any longer; and this is money which I have borrowed and am now paying 6% on, the interest of which will not be returned to me by the Society." The society resorted to modest economies. When *The Dutcher* was not needed for patrolling the sounds, it was rented to Brimley and other sportsmen to help offset the cost of using the boat for law enforcement. After the annual hunting license fees were received, all accounts were settled and the society's treasury had a slight surplus.[12]

Dissension arose in Asheville, where Buncombe County branch society members who disliked centralized control decided to seek legislation creating a Western North Carolina Audubon Society with jurisdiction over the western counties. Untrue stories about Pearson and the state society were circulated. The county society was alleged to have sent a regular contribution to the state society but to have received no credit for it, and the local warden was said to have quit because he had not been paid for several months. Pearson was alerted to the allegations as well as to a planned meeting in Asheville to discuss the proposed bill setting up an independent society. Only Pearson seems to have recorded what happened at the meeting. The host, whom Pearson did not name in his account, labored "under evident embarrassment" at Pearson's unexpected presence. Pearson proved the local warden had been paid regularly by the state society and had been on duty all the time, though no contributions had been received from the Buncombe County branch for several months. After "that group of men realized how they had been misled by one of their number," amends were swift. The group gave Pearson a check for the unpaid branch dues, dropped the proposal to present a bill to the legislature, and adopted a strong endorsement of Pearson and the state society. At a mass meeting the following night, a large, friendly audience came to hear Pearson speak. The Buncombe County branch, paralyzed by controversy, ceased to function for two years; then it was revived, with Pearson's friends Chase P. Ambler and Robert U. Garrett as president and vice-president.[13]

Almost 7,000 young terns, skimmers, and Laughing Gulls were reared on the North Carolina coast in 1905, compared to 2,700 in 1904. Among them were 577 young of the Least Tern. In only two years' time, a substantial Least Tern colony had developed, one of only five colonies on the entire Atlantic coast. In Hyde, Craven, and Brunswick counties, heron colonies were also growing rapidly under Audubon protection.[14]

Raising money for the National Association in northern cities was more difficult than Pearson had anticipated. Accustomed to success, he was puzzled and embarrassed. In April 1905, he spent several days in New York calling at business offices. "These efforts were amazingly barren of results," he wrote later. He went on to Boston, where the large audience at his lecture on "The Mission of the Audubon Society" was encouraging, but almost two weeks later he had solicited only one new membership. Six men whose names had been supplied by John Thayer could not, with one exception, be reached at home or office, and the one Pearson reached declined to contribute. "Several men whom I attempted to see were away and one turned me down in a very rude manner," Pearson wrote to Dutcher.[15]

The help he needed from influential local residents came first in the form of an offer of desk facilities in the Boston office of Charles W. Dimick, a U.S. Cartridge Company agent and Massachusetts Fish and Game Protective Association member. Dimick and Augustus Hemenway helped Pearson write a circular appeal that was mailed to six thousand persons and brought in one thousand dollars in gifts and memberhip fees and one promise of a bequest. Hemenway himself donated one hundred dollars. The canvass for money in the North was suddenly successful.[16]

North Carolina's unique law-enforcing Audubon Society functioned so well that Pearson, encouraged by Dutcher, decided to foster the establishment of similar societies in South Carolina and Georgia. In *Bird-Lore*, Dutcher praised Pearson's accomplishments in North Carolina as "an excellent object-lesson" that demonstrated the advantages of placing the "bird and game protection work of a commonwealth" in the hands of a "non-political organization" supported by the revenue from hunting license sales. Pearson's initial task in South Carolina and Georgia was to heighten interest in birds and reinvigorate the existing Audubon societies. In South Carolina, he offered classes in bird study at the Clemson College Summer School and gave public lectures there and around the state. He needed to find a counterpart to himself, an established ornithologist who was a persuasive speaker and a skilled organizer. No such person appeared. Arthur T. Wayne of Mt. Pleasant was a proficient ornithologist who contributed regularly to the *Auk* (after he died in 1930, Witmer Stone praised him as the "most eminent of the ornithologists of the South"), but he preferred to conduct his studies isolated "from kindred spirits" and "remote from the great scientific centers." The most Pearson could do in South Carolina was to persuade eminent government officials and educators to accept responsible roles in the Audubon Society. On July 10, 1905, the society was reorganized with Senator Benjamin R. Tillman as president and State Superintendent of Education Oscar B. Martin as secretary. Pearson helped the new officers by visiting several towns to solicit memberships. He also organized an educational department in the society in which he enrolled 225 teachers as members.[17]

Enforcing bird protection laws was possibly more difficult and more dangerous in the South, where fewer people believed such laws were needed, than in the North. Audubon Warden Guy M. Bradley, also a deputy sheriff, guarded colonies of nesting plume birds in the Florida Keys. Bradley told Dutcher in February 1905 that plume hunters had "sworn" to kill him. Five months later a plume hunter did kill him. Walter Smith, his three sons, and three other men sailed in a schooner to an egret colony about two miles across the water from Bradley's house near Key West. Two of the party, including one of Smith's sons, went ashore and began shooting egrets. Bradley heard the shots, looked across the water from his house, recognized the schooner, and put out in a small skiff. By the time he reached the schooner, the two plume hunters were climbing back into it with their birds. Bradley told Smith he intended to arrest the two men for killing egrets illegally.

The sequence of events that followed remains murky. Smith claimed he shot Bradley in self-defense. Although a coroner's jury charged Smith with murder, county and state officials showed little interest in the case, possibly because Bradley and Smith had had encounters before. Dutcher employed two men, one after the other, to represent the National Association and to press criminal charges, but the grand jury failed to return a bill of indictment. No charges were brought against the two men in Smith's party who Smith admitted had killed egrets illegally. "Every great cause must have its martyrs," Dutcher wrote, "and Guy M. Bradley is the first martyr in the cause of bird protection." For the aid of the destitute widow and her two small children, Dutcher opened a special fund.[18]

An incident in North Carolina evoked strong emotions but no

violence. In August 1905, thousands of Purple Martins (*Progne subis*) gathered for the migratory flight to South America in a grove of trees near a Wrightsville Beach hotel. In spring and summer for generations, Purple Martins were welcomed everywhere. Indians had hung gourds for martins to nest in; white settlers put boxes on poles. "Martins defend their nests with great tenacity," Pearson wrote, "and drive from the neighborhood any Crow or Hawk that comes within sight; they are, therefore, cherished as important guardians of the poultry yard." But when the birds collect at roosts in late summer, they can be nuisances. They are messy and noisy. Harsh hissing replaces their pleasant springtime twittering. The hotel at Wrightsville Beach began to lose business. In an effort to get rid of the birds, the proprietor invited local men to shoot them. Late one evening, at least twelve men armed with shotguns gathered at the grove and killed an estimated ten to twelve thousand birds and wounded a great many more. Dying birds fluttered about the fields and roadsides for several days afterwards.

It was "one of those wholesale, useless slaughters of birds which always make my blood boil," Pearson wrote later. As soon as he learned about it, he sent a warden to identify the men involved and to charge them with violating the Audubon Act. "Some of the hunters claimed that they did not know that they were violating any law, and probably this was the case," he conceded. But the law had been in force for more than two years, and during that time he had been urging the public to come to the Audubon Society with problems about birds. There are harmless ways of persuading unwanted flocks of birds to choose another roosting site. Although such methods are not always successful, they often are, and Pearson succeeded at Wrightsville Beach. "We drove the offending martins from the neighborhood with burning tar barrels, placed in such a position that the dense smoke drifted through the trees the birds were occupying."[19]

Twelve men were tried and convicted for shooting the martins.

The token fines were admonitory rather than punitive. Nonetheless, strong grievances were expressed against Pearson and the Audubon Society. Always a little uneasy about enforcing the Audubon Act against respectable citizens, H. H. Brimley wrote to Pearson, "I hope you came safely and satisfactorily out of the trouble at Wrightsville over the martins. It looked to me to be a rather complicated case, judging from the newspaper reports, but I have no doubt you managed to adjust matters satisfactorily." [20]

Pearson and Brimley wrote to each other with increasing frequency. Although Brimley liked wild things, he never fully shared Pearson's sympathy for birds and remained generally detached about what happened among wild species. When he visited the Lake Ellis cormorant colony and saw an alligator pursuing a young bird, he did not rescue it as Pearson had on a similar occasion. Instead he watched nature's course, admiring the alligator's skill, and wrote to Pearson, "Saw a gator take down a young cormorant in good style, holding his head well out of the water while taking the bird down." He respected Pearson's conversion from collection builder to photographer. "I wish you could have been on Royal Shoal when I was but I am almost afraid you would have had a fit, by reason of the . . . dull clouds and a fine rain, making photography out of the question." [21]

Pearson persuaded H. H. Brimley and his brother C. S. to collaborate with him in writing the North Carolina bird book, having concluded that alone he would be unlikely to complete the necessary field study. "I'm working away on our book as I have time," he wrote to H. H. Brimley in February 1906. [22] Because he could rarely go on solitary excursions to study birds, he had to gain what new knowledge and experience he could as he performed his Audubon duties.

For ten years or more, he had not hunted for recreation, killing wildlife only for museum collections; but in constant association with sportsmen, including H. H. Brimley and Dutcher, he was drawn into their sport. After a trip to the Outer Banks at Christmas 1905, he wrote to Brimley about the "good luck" he had had. "The wild fowl came to me fine, and a native gunner would have killed twice the number I did, I have no doubt." Warden Jennett took him "possum hunting," a venture he "enjoyed very much."[23]

# 14

# Pearson Labors, Willcox Bequeaths

## *(1905–1906)*

PEARSON'S AUDUBON ORGANIZATIONS were becoming self-sustaining. By fall 1905, he had moved the North Carolina society office from State Normal to 109½ West Market Street, with a full-time stenographer. In October Dutcher moved the National Association headquarters out of his home at 525 Manhattan Avenue to 141 Broadway, where two full-time clerks were kept busy. Already there were almost six hundred national members. Pearson subscribed to $100 life memberships for himself and for the North Carolina Audubon Society. By the end of his first year as special agent, he had sold twenty life memberships, bringing in $2,000, which the finance committee invested in 4-percent bonds. "This is a beginning on which can be built a great structure of consecrated wealth," Dutcher wrote.[1] It was also the foundation for a dual role for the National Association, which by admitting individuals as members became an Audubon society on its own as well as a federation of societies.

Five more states (California, Missouri, Michigan, Pennsylvania, and South Carolina) adopted the model law, leaving Alabama the one coastal state without it. At the National Association's request,

President Roosevelt had set aside six areas as bird refuges, and the association guarded them with a warden force of fifty. State societies also had begun to establish reservations. The Louisiana Audubon Society leased twenty-two islands used for nesting by gulls, terns, and skimmers; they were protected by the National Association warden who guarded the national Breton Island Reservation.[2]

Dutcher pushed the Audubon cause abroad. To the German Embassy he presented a "complete history of the Audubon movement and its method of working," which was forwarded to the German government in the hope that bird protection laws would be adopted. The Japanese government agreed to try to stop Japanese plume hunters from raiding bird colonies on American islands in the Pacific. A plume hunter's request to kill up to 20,000 birds a year in Hawaii, reported to Dutcher by a National Association member, was denied after Dutcher wrote to Secretary of State John Hay, who referred the letter to the territorial governor.[3]

Pearson tried to get bills like the North Carolina Audubon Act through the legislatures of South Carolina and Georgia. In the absence of an enforcement system, the AOU model law, already adopted in both states, had little value. Pearson's address before the South Carolina legislature in January 1906 failed to win the necessary support. "I worked like a beaver, in Columbia," he wrote later, "exhausting every device I could think of to get our Audubon bill considered, but the Legislature adjourned without its having been brought to a vote." In Georgia he almost succeeded. His bill was reported favorably out of committee but was confronted with another bill allocating the money from the sale of nonresident hunting licenses to the schools rather than to the Audubon Society. Without that income, the society would be unable to employ wardens. "This rival bill brought on a fight that split the legislature and a Kilkenny cat episode ensued. We killed the bill of our opponents but did not have enough support left to pass our own bill, and the Georgia Legislature adjourned with nothing gained for bird protection."[4]

In April 1906 Pearson took his cameras to Florida on a mission with a four-fold purpose: to visit bird reservations in Tampa Bay, to look for bird colonies on government islands that could be made reservations, to investigate egret plume trade, and to buy a house in Key West for Mrs. Guy Bradley, the martyred warden's widow. Arriving at Indian Key Reservation near St. Petersburg on April 11, he was too early in the season to learn much about nesting there. At Passage Key, near the mouth of Tampa Bay, he found a colony of about fifteen hundred Tricolored Herons. Continuing south to Gasparilla Sound and then to the Ten Thousand Islands, he found more herons and five Brown Pelican colonies.[5]

Plume birds had almost disappeared in some parts of Florida. "Egrets and Snowy Herons are now so scarce in the sections visited that not over a dozen individuals were seen during the six weeks of field observations." Convincing people that egrets merited a chance to live was more difficult than demonstrating the value of birds useful to farmers. "Egrets are not regarded as of very great economic value as destroyers of obnoxious insects. This, however, is no reason why they do not deserve our protection," Pearson wrote after his return. "The pure glossy whiteness of their plumage and the elegance of their form and movement are sufficient reasons for preserving these living objects of statuary of the southern marshes, even as civilized man preserves in the home and in the forum the marble statues, carved by the hands of inspired artists."[6]

Pearson traveled from one site to another on a chartered two-masted sailing vessel with a superstitious captain who blamed Pearson's white cap for troubles on the voyage. Jumping from a launch to the dock, Pearson fell into the water. After he had been pulled out, the captain said to him, "Don't you know that in shallow-water cruising it is bad luck to wear a white cap?" Dis-

regarding the warning, Pearson wore the white cap when they left
Marco for Key West. The boat had gone only a mile or two before
it grounded on a sand bar. Soon after it was freed, a heavy storm
struck. Sheets running to the end of the main boom were torn from
their fastenings; the rudder jammed. The captain shouted at Pearson, "Why the h— did you bring that d—d white cap aboard this
boat?" Two days later as the boat docked at Key West, Pearson in
his white cap stepped into the bight of a hawser, was thrown
against the shrouds, and was jerked overboard. Back on the boat,
he was examined by a doctor who found a dislocated shoulder and
two broken ribs. Pearson noticed his cap was not with him. The
doctor smiled. "Your Captain said to tell you that he did not sal-
vage it."[7]

In spite of his injuries, Pearson escorted Mrs. Bradley on a tour
of houses for sale in Key West and bought one she liked for fifteen
hundred dollars. The remaining four hundred that Dutcher had
raised for her was set aside for her children's education.[8]

At home in Greensboro, Pearson developed whooping cough,
which compounded his discomfort. Coughing, with one arm
bound to his side and adhesive tape over his chest, he dictated to his
secretary an account of his trip. Three of the government-owned
islands he had visited were soon made bird reservations.[9]

The sudden death from apoplexy of Charles D. McIver at forty-
six in September 1906 was a severe shock to Pearson and a "keen
personal loss." From the beginning, the president of State Normal
had encouraged and supported Pearson's efforts to teach people
about birds. Even after Pearson left the college faculty, the two
men traveled and spoke together at meetings of teachers and school
administrators, McIver on children and teachers and the need to
educate them, Pearson on birds and other wildlife and the importance of teaching children to appreciate them. At the time McIver
died, he and Pearson were scheduled to address a high school
principals' convention in Ohio.[10]

Pearson could still call upon State Normal faculty members to help the Audubon Society. Julius I. Foust, head of the department of pedagogy and dean of the college faculty, was a charter Audubon board of directors member, and he retained that position after succeeding McIver as president. Eugene W. Gudger, Dixie Lee Bryant's successor as professor of biology, replaced Robert N. Wilson as Audubon treasurer.[11]

Pearson's lectures on birds were increasingly popular. At schools, colleges, teachers' institutes, and teachers' meetings, he displayed selections from his growing collection of photographic slides. The pictures of large birds—eagles, hawks, owls, gulls, cormorants, egrets—seemed to impress his audiences most, but he also enthralled them with descriptions of small birds' dramatic feats. "Some of the smallest birds make the longest journeys," he said to teachers meeting in Raleigh. "Some little birds not over five inches long breed within the Arctic circle and go to the Argentine Republic to spend the winter, making the journey of 7,000 or 8,000 miles twice each year." Sitting near him was State Superintendent of Public Instruction Joyner. "Young robins in captivity have been known to eat of worms their own weight and 46 per cent over, between daylight and sundown," Pearson said. "That is equal to Superintendent Joyner here eating about 120 pounds of beefsteak and drinking eight gallons of coffee in a day!"[12]

Articles that Pearson offered to the *News and Observer*, the *Charlotte Observer*, and other newspapers were usually welcomed. "The press," he wrote, "has been uniformly friendly and many editorial comments of an encouraging and commending character have appeared." A writer in the *Charlotte Chronicle* said, "Professor Pearson is doing a great work. His heart is devoted to God and nature." A contributor to the *Wilmington Star*, after reading Pearson's report as Audubon Society secretary for the year ending March 9, 1906, urged every land owner in North Carolina to join the society. In the *Greensboro Record*, the suggestion that Pearson might some day be memoralized with a monument was dismissed with the conclusion that his work in protecting birds would "erect a monument of itself." Pearson "cares little" about being honored, the writer added. "What he is after is protection to the birds and he is getting there very fast."[13]

Despite the praise, discontent with the Audubon Society had not disappeared. There was no painless way to change the behavior of people who until 1903 had been free to capture or kill songbirds or destroy their nests at any time for any reason. In the year ending March 1906, fourteen men (including the twelve at Wrightsville Beach) were penalized for killing Purple Martins, two for killing Common Hawkhawks, and two for killing Eastern Bluebirds. One man was convicted for trapping Northern Cardinals (*Cardinalis cardinalis*), another for killing them, and a third for killing Northern Flickers. Two persons were convicted for destroying bird nests.[14]

The trouble at Asheville, the first of its kind to appear, represented discontent of another sort, more complicated and more troublesome than simple resentment toward regulation. It had arisen in part from hostility toward centralized, statewide authority as opposed to local control; in part from resentment toward Pearson, the authoritarian figure who had created the Audubon Society and imposed the protective system; and in part from suspicion and jealousy of a private organization functioning as a public agency. Pearson suggested to Brimley the names of men who would be likely to know about plans to change or repeal the Audubon Act and who might talk freely to Brimley if he approached them. "Be sure to let me know if anything should ever get to brooding down your way." In Currituck County, where hunters chafed under the restrictions on shooting waterfowl, Pierce Hampton, backed by a Gunner's League, won the Democratic nomination for a seat in the North Carolina House of Representatives by the "largest vote ever polled" in the county. The league made plans to put through a bill that would either remove Currituck County from the Audubon Society's jurisdiction or abolish the society altogether.[15]

Pearson also had to deal with discontent arising from the National Association's protection of birds on refuges created by President Roosevelt. Bird hunters and gatherers of bird eggs questioned the power of wardens commissioned by the secretary of agriculture and paid by the National Association. Congress had enacted no protective legislation for the refuges, and state laws, it was argued, could not be applied to lands owned by the U.S. government. The National Association appealed for help to Representative John F. Lacey, chairman of the Public Lands Committee, who introduced a bill making it unlawful to kill or disturb birds on government lands reserved as breeding grounds for birds by law, proclamation, or executive order. On the bill's final reading, Lacey was subjected to teasing questions. Would a person attacked by a bird on a refuge have a right to self defense? Lacey joked with his colleagues but reminded them that the rapid extermination of birds was a serious problem. The House approved the bill and referred it to the Senate Committee on Forest Reservations and Game Protection, which held it from February to June 1906. Meanwhile, the bird breeding seasons on most refuges had begun, and the wardens needed explicit legal authority. Dutcher appealed to Senator John F. Dryden, of New Jersey; Frank Bond, to Senator Francis E. Warren of Wyoming.[16]

Pearson went to Washington to see Senator Lee S. Overman of North Carolina, a Forest Reservations and Game Protection Committee member. Having left North Carolina without enough money to cover his expenses, Pearson borrowed twenty-five dollars from Theodore Palmer. Immediately upon his return to Greensboro, he wrote to Palmer, enclosing payment of his debt and reporting on the success of his trip. "I saw Senator Overman. He at once went to work on the members of the committee and at 3 o'clock told me he had permission from everybody except the South Dakota Senator who would not agree unless the 'Black Hills Forest Reservation' was excepted from its provisions. I told him to accept the amendment and he said he would thus report the bill at once,—this morning." The "South Dakota Senator" was Alfred B. Kittredge. Overman reported the bill to the Senate on June 11. When the bill was still stalled on June 23, Overman asked for unanimous consent to call up the bird refuge bill, probably after a reminder from Pearson. Consent was granted, the bill was approved, and Roosevelt signed it five days later.[17]

National Association benefactor Albert Willcox invited Pearson to call on him in New York. Impressed by Pearson's achievements, he had decided to bequeath more money to the National Association than the $100,000 originally promised. Soon thereafter, on August 13, 1906, he died of a heart attack at Seabright. "He had just returned from a 300-mile automobile trip," the *New York Times* reported, "had luncheon, played a little tennis, and went bathing. After an hour in the surf he came out on the beach and dropped dead." He had kept his promises to Pearson and Dutcher and had bequeathed $100,000 outright to the National Association. Most of his remaining money was put in trust for his brother David, but upon David's death half the residuary estate would go to the National Association. Not suspecting that he would live only another year, David Willcox let the National Association take its share in advance. The total legacy amounted to $331,072, a sum large enough, Dutcher said, to transform the National Association from "a weak and struggling Society to a permanent and strong organization."[18]

# 15

# Defending the Audubon Society and Saving the Biological Survey

## (1907)

ANTICIPATING A VARIETY of bills to ease hunting restrictions, Pearson planned for the North Carolina legislative session of 1907 well in advance. Representative Pierce Hampton had promised to try to reduce or abolish the Audubon Society's authority in Currituck County. Residents of several other coastal counties, Pearson had been told, might also try to free themselves from the society's jurisdiction. "It is the same old question," Dutcher commented in *Bird-Lore*, "whether the assets of a commonwealth, that belong to all the people, shall be confiscated and used by a very limited class." What had happened that year in the Missouri legislature, which kept the model law but abolished the enforcing agency, could also happen in North Carolina. In Missouri, Pearson wrote, "The commercial interests had regained their 'rights' to exploit to the last fin, fur and feather of wild-life resources of the State."[1] He hoped not only to defeat such efforts in North Carolina but also to establish a statewide hunting season for game birds that would open November 15 and close March 1.

161

Governor Glenn, originally opposed to the Audubon Society, had become a supporter, possibly out of respect for the work he saw being accomplished, possibly under the influence of the society's many friends with whom he associated. In addition to J. Y. Joyner, H. H. Brimley, Samuel Patterson, and Richard Lewis, there was Francis D. Winston, who had been elected lieutenant governor in 1904. "The Audubon Society . . . is growing in favor every day, and should be encouraged in its efforts to stop the wholesale slaughter of birds," Glenn said in his biennial message to the 1907 legislature. "The only thing the Society asks of the Legislature is a uniform law in regard to the time during which game birds should be hunted. . . . I approve the request." With the governor's open support, Pearson strengthened his position in the legislature by persuading the presiding officer of each house to create a committee on game. Lieutenant Governor Winston, senate presiding officer, named to the new committee the men Pearson recommended. "I succeeded in getting a bird and game committee established in the senate to handle all game laws," Pearson wrote to Dutcher. "This had never been done in North Carolina before. I named all the members of this committee, as the president of the Senate is friendly to our cause." A few days later, at Pearson's request, House Speaker Edward J. Justice of Guilford County also created a game committee.[2] Although Pierce Hampton was appointed to the committee, most other appointees were Audubon Society supporters.

Hampton proved to be a man of mild disposition who declined to introduce his expected bills in the face of organized Audubon resistance. He "is one of the least of my troubles," Pearson wrote to Dutcher on January 19. "He will hardly be able to do anything serious." Shortly thereafter, however, a Currituck County delegation arrived unexpectedly in Raleigh and demanded a hearing before a joint meeting of the game committees. "Things are getting hot in Raleigh in many ways," Pearson wrote to Dutcher. "It is a very uncertain body for game protection. I have not dared to introduce any Bills yet. Don't repeat any of these things in print or by letter." [3]

Sentiment in Currituck County was divided. Several shooting clubs wanted to tighten restrictions on hunting and prohibit the shipping of ducks from the state. Opposing them were Hampton's constituents, local residents who asked for more freedom in duck hunting and a continuation of the right to market ducks out of state. At a hearing before the game committees in February, Pearson was called upon to open the discussion. He took a compromise position in which he favored Hampton's proposal for easing the restrictions on hunting from bush blinds or boats, as well as the shooting clubs' stand against using power boats and sailboats to flush birds from the water so they could be killed more easily. He said it would be unwise at that time to impose a law on local hunters forbidding them to ship ducks to out-of-state markets. Busbee and Busbee, attorneys for the hunting clubs, introduced a letter from Dutcher stating that as a hunter he believed the time had come to "prohibit the sale of wild fowl." Pearson, though sharing Dutcher's desire to restrict commercial waterfowl hunting, anticipated that if the market hunters lost on the issue they would demand and probably receive complete freedom from the Audubon Society's jurisdiction. He did not want that to happen. After all preferences had been expressed, Pearson's views prevailed. "We finished up with a sort of love feast there yesterday morning," he reported to Dutcher. [4]

Pearson tried to keep abreast of everything happening in the legislature in regard to birds and game and to act promptly against undesirable measures. From the game committee chairmen, he collected copies of recently introduced bills, and he discussed any that looked harmful to wildlife's welfare with the legislator who had introduced it. "If the legislator persisted in pushing his measure, I would get from him the names of his constituents wanting this law, go to his county, and try to induce them to drop the matter. Sometimes when there was much local sentiment to be overcome, I would call a public meeting in the court-house or a church, or a school building, give a talk on bird protection, and explain why the Audubon Society was trying to preserve the birds. Usually this settled the matter. When a bill could not be handled in this manner, I would ask the Game Committee of the House or the Senate to wield the big stick." From Greensboro on January 19, 1907, he reported to Dutcher, "I have this week succeeded in killing several harmful bills." One such bill would have permitted killing Blue Jays and Northern Flickers in Chatham County, another would have allowed night-herons to be killed in Craven County, and a third would have permitted fire lighting in Carteret County. The numerous local laws adopted "almost without exception" tightened regulations rather than loosened them. In seventeen counties, including Guilford, killing deer, "grouse," and "pheasants" was prohibited for several years; in Davidson County, bird netting was forbidden permanently. Nonetheless, local views of hunting privileges were so much stronger than Pearson had realized when the legislature convened that he decided not to ask for a bill creating a statewide game-bird hunting season.[5]

He was unprepared for the hostility of Beverly S. Royster, representative from Granville County, and Archibald A. Hicks, senator from Granville and Person Counties. "Opposition to our Audubon work has developed in an unexpected quarter by very influential Members," Pearson wrote to Dutcher upon discovering that Royster and Hicks planned to introduce a bill exempting Granville County from the Audubon Act. At Pearson's request several prominent Audubon Society members visited Raleigh and talked with the two men but failed to dissuade them. Pearson then went to Granville County, where he found that many "sportsmen and bird lovers" had united behind Royster and Hicks. "I found a great deal of adverse sentiment to the Audubon Society throughout the county which has been centralized and intensified at Oxford, the county seat." When at last he discovered the animosity's cause, he was reminded again of the extreme care that always needed to be exercised in enforcing the Audubon Act. "Oddly enough," he wrote to Dutcher, "the whole disturbance arose from the prosecution by one of our game wardens of a man who killed a robin out of season."[6] Having learned this, Pearson was able to soothe the feelings of the aggrieved man and his friends and to persuade them to withdraw their request for a change in the Audubon Act.

In Currituck County, illegal night hunting of waterfowl, which Pearson had believed to be declining, appeared inexplicably to increase. He hired a professional detective, Milford W. Haynes, at twice the usual warden's wages ($5.00 a day rather than $2.50), and put five local wardens under his direction. Haynes's forcefulness soon became known. "A number of the natives of the county, whom I met in Raleigh this week told me that he was the bravest man they had ever seen and that he had arrested, single handed, three of the most desperate characters in the county," Pearson wrote to Dutcher. By season's end, Haynes and his wardens had made five more arrests. Local sentiment was not strong enough for the arrests to be more than admonitory. Three of the hunters were acquitted by a local magistrate; the remaining five were bound over to superior court, where four were freed by the grand jury. The remaining violator was convicted and lightly fined. Five wardens on Core Sound had an experience similar to that of the wardens on Currituck Sound: two men they arrested for fire lighting were acquitted for lack of evidence. Pearson wrote a bill "regarding fire lighting and night shooting" and persuaded a legislator from an inland county to introduce it. "If that Bill becomes a law," Pearson told Dutcher, "it will be much easier in the future, I think, to get sufficient evidence to convict."[7] The bill died in the house game committee, and Pearson made no further attempt to obtain legislative assistance to stop illegal night hunting. The wardens continued to patrol, their presence a reasonably effective deterrent.

The National Association's growing income enabled Dutcher to enlarge the field worker staff. Edward Howe Forbush, Massachusetts Division of Ornithology director, became the association's New England agent. Following Pearson's pattern of action, he wrote bills, lobbied, and lectured. "All proposed bills inimical to bird protection were defeated," he reported at year's end. The Connecticut legislature adopted laws limiting the hunting season and requiring hunters to buy licenses. Harry H. Kopman, "one of the leading ornithologists of the Gulf States," and William L. Finley, author, bird photographer, and Audubon Society of Oregon president, were also employed as field workers.[8]

Another new employee, Mary T. Moore, a former school teacher who liked birds and public speaking, worked half-time for the Audubon Society of North Carolina and half-time for the National Association. After studying under Pearson's tutelage for several weeks, she joined a North Carolina Department of Agriculture team conducting summer institutes for farmers. At each of twenty-five institutes, the mornings were devoted to separate programs for men and women; in the afternoons, the men and women met together. Moore spoke at the joint meetings, explaining the value of birds on the farm. "In most instances I found the people interested in what I had to say, but the idea that birds are of real use seemed to be a new one to the majority of my hearers," she reported. Birds seemed generally to be regarded as destructive pests; occasionally, a listener "openly scoffed" at something Moore said. Nonetheless, she made an impression. Approximately three thousand of the forty-six hundred people she addressed on the six-week tour gave her their names and addresses so she could send them leaflets about birds, the Audubon Society, and the North Carolina bird and game laws.[9]

In the fall, Moore promoted bird and nature study in the public schools. To interested teachers whose names were submitted by superintendents, she mailed leaflets, soon amounting to "many thousands." She took over the Audubon junior membership program and sent the nature study library to each person in charge of a junior chapter. Pearson's leaflet *Protect the Insect-Eating Birds* was popular. Mrs. Garrett, one of the society's "most faithful and indefatigable workers," at whose Asheville home approximately twenty teachers regularly prepared lessons on nature, wrote of the pamphlet, "Some of the teachers make the higher grades learn the text and recite from it." [10]

Early in 1907, the U.S. House of Representatives Committee on Agriculture suddenly decided to abolish the Biological Survey merely by omitting provisions for it in the agricultural appropriations bill. Its chairman, James W. Wadsworth of Geneseo, New York, had frequently questioned agency chief C. Hart Merriam's policies. In the committee's opinion, Representative William W. Cocks of Long Island explained to AOU and Audubon leader Joel Allen, the survey's scientific work could be transferred to the Smithsonian Institution and the Lacey Act could be enforced by food and drug agents. Overall, Cocks said, "there seemed to be no commercial agricultural advantage to be gained from the retention of this Bureau." Dutcher, who knew Cocks well, wrote to Pearson, "Confidentially I say to you that . . . he is just about as fit to be a member of Congress as your kid is," a "man of absolutely no weight." [11]

The "friends of bird protection stood aghast" at the committee's action, Pearson recalled later. None of the Biological Survey's work seemed likely to be carried on by any other agency. In Pearson's opinion, if the survey were abolished "there would come an end to all governmental effort for educating public sentiment to a better appreciation of wild birds; no further scientific investigation of the food habits of birds and mammals would be carried on and no more effort would be made to enforce the Lacey Act." [12]

The agriculture appropriations bill as originally introduced had increased the Biological Survey's budget. In an effort to save the agency and to have the provision for increased funding reinstated, Dutcher lobbied in New York and Forbush in New England. Meanwhile, Pearson went to Richmond, where he asked prominent men to send messages to Virginia's Representative John Lamb, ranking Democrat on the House Agriculture Committee. Virginia's governor, he learned, had already asked Lamb to support the Biological Survey. The lieutenant governor agreed to send a message, and the state superintendent of public instruction signed a telegram composed by Pearson and addressed to three more of Virginia's representatives. "Newspaper men were interviewed, and messages were sent to many prominent Virginians requesting them to communicate with their representatives in Washington and ask that they stand by the Biological Survey."[13]

From Richmond, Pearson went to Norfolk, where he persuaded the mayor, several members of the state legislature, and other prominent men to sign telegrams. "A number of these promised to follow the telegrams with letters in the evening," he wrote to Dutcher. At home again in Greensboro, Pearson sent messages to the congressional delegations from North and South Carolina. He also telegraphed South Carolina Audubon Society President B. F. Taylor, who in turn sent telegrams to the South Carolina delegation.[14]

In response to the many appeals, the House Agriculture Committee inserted in the agricultural appropriations bill a provision keeping on the Biological Survey's main staff but eliminating the clerk and the chief. The Senate committee reinstated the entire original appropriation. After the problem was referred to a conference committee, Pearson went to Washington and talked with members of the North Carolina delegation, including Senator Furnifold M. Simmons, a conference committee member. Other committee members were "buttonholed," as were their friends.

"Letters inspired by Dutcher were pouring into Congress by every mail." At 3:00 P.M. on February 28, Senator Simmons came out of the conference room and told Pearson, who was waiting, that the Biological Survey was safe for another year: it would receive the same appropriation it had received during the past year. Partly with the indirect help of President Roosevelt, the bill passed in the Senate.[15]

The conference committee added a paragraph to the appropriations bill, directing the secretary of agriculture to report to the next Congress on the extent to which the Biological Survey's work was being duplicated elsewhere and on its "practical value" to agriculture. During the next few months, while the report was being prepared, Pearson concentrated on generating additional expressions of support for the Biological Survey. There was sufficient time now for using his oratorical skill. After he and Chapman gave public lectures in Washington, Robert W. Williams of the agency's staff wrote to Dutcher, "Pearson's lecture here last night was the best bird lecture I ever listened to. He made a profound impression on his large and enthusiastic audience. I consider his lecture far and away above Chapman's. I was sorry his stay here was so short."[16]

Pearson introduced and pushed through to adoption resolutions endorsing the Biological Survey in meetings of the League of American Sportsmen, the National Association of State Game and Fish Wardens and Commissioners, and the International Conference of Cotton Manufacturers and Growers. During the game and fish wardens and commissioners meeting, at which he was elected vice-president, many speakers mentioned their indebtedness to state Audubon societies and to the National Association.[17]

Endorsements for the Biological Survey from organizations associated with agriculture were critical, and getting resolutions adopted at the International Conference of Cotton Manufacturers and Growers required more than usual ingenuity and boldness.

The story of what Pearson did there is his own report, but there seems little reason to doubt its accuracy. It comports well with what is known about him from other sources. The approximately five hundred conference delegates composed "the most influential body of agriculturists that would meet during the year." They assembled first in Washington and agreed upon an agenda; then they went for deliberations to Atlanta. Pearson joined them there. Informed that the agenda had already been adopted and that no new subjects could be considered, he went to the conference president, who suggested that a resolution from the floor might be given consideration. Pearson then asked a North Carolina delegate to introduce the resolution; the man declined, saying he had never heard of the Biological Survey. Another North Carolinian, more sympathetic, appointed Pearson a delegate from his own organization and assured him that the North Carolinians present would vote for the resolution if he succeeded in introducing it.

At the first session, Pearson stood up before anyone else and introduced his resolution, a North Carolinian seconded it, and the president referred it to the committee on growing and handling cotton. Pearson deliberately arrived at the committee meeting early and offered his services to the chairman as secretary. A little "briskly," the chairman said the secretary would be chosen by the committee as a whole. Pearson walked down an aisle until he found a North Carolinian, whom he asked to nominate him on the chairman's call. Nominated and elected, he was placed in charge of keeping minutes and producing, upon the chairman's request, resolutions introduced from the floor in the general session. Pearson's resolution had not been taken up when the chairman announced that it was time to adjourn and that no more resolutions could be considered. This was one of the possibilities Pearson had reckoned on and one of the reasons he had maneuvered himself into the secretary's position. Before the chairman could adjourn the meeting formally, Pearson rose with his resolution in hand. He said he was certain that the "leaders of the Congress" would expect the committee to report on it the next day. Assuring the committee members that the resolution would cause no debate, he read it quickly. A North Carolinian moved its adoption, the motion was seconded, and the resolution was adopted.

At the general meeting next morning, the resolutions sent forward by the committee on growing and handling cotton were considered one at a time. After the first three resolutions stirred such debate that each was referred back to the committee for further study, a motion was made and seconded that the entire report be returned to the committee. Pearson's resolution would die unless he acted quickly. Hurrying to the platform before the president could put the motion to a vote, he shouted, "Mr. Chairman, I am secretary of that Committee and I have here one resolution of the greatest importance that we are anxious to have passed. It will cause no discussion." Without waiting to be recognized, Pearson read the resolution, ignoring protests from the floor that he was out of order. Still shouting, he lectured the delegates briefly on the Biological Survey's studies of birds that ate boll weevils and other insects destructive to cotton. After he moved for the resolution's adoption, a North Carolinian seconded the motion.

The president, impressed and probably amused, ignored the pending motion to return the entire report to the committee. He put Pearson's motion to a vote, and it passed. "Down on the convention floor one minute later I reached under a seat for my derby hat, and leaving the room, wired Dutcher that the resolution he wanted had been adopted at twelve o'clock M. on October 8, 1907." The resolution required the conference secretary to send a copy to "every Senator and Representative in Congress from the cotton-growing states."[18]

In December, Secretary of Agriculture James Wilson's report on the Biological Survey was read to the Senate and printed. He

stressed the "great practical value" of the agency's work to agriculture and maintained "no part" of the work was duplicated
elsewhere. Two months later, a popular article on the Biological
Survey that referred to birds as "policemen of the air" appeared in
the *National Geographic Magazine*. Reviewing both publications in
the *Auk*, Allen concluded the Biological Survey had benefited by
the effort to abolish it. Before the controversy, "many of the lawmakers of the nation were in blissful ignorance" of the agency's role
"in behalf of the public welfare." "Now, however, there is no
longer excuse for such ignorance." [19]

# 16

# South Carolina
# and Georgia

## *(1907–1908)*

PEARSON HAD PERSUADED the South Carolina legislature to adopt his bill authorizing the Audubon Society to enforce the bird and game laws. "We had our hearing on the Audubon Bill this afternoon before the Corporation Committee and the House and got a favorable report," he had written Dutcher from Columbia in January 1907. He spent much of April helping the society organize to meet its responsibilities. President B. F. Taylor, who impressed Pearson as being a "splendid officer," lent money to the society, enabling Secretary James H. Rice to employ wardens without waiting for hunting license fees in the fall.[1]

At Winnsboro, near Columbia, Pearson talked with an egg collector, a newspaper editor, and an attorney who was a local ornithologist; they promised to organize a branch Audubon society. A "government official" in Georgetown, near the coast, introduced Pearson to many prominent people to whom he talked about the need to save birds. A visitor to Sumter reported seeing "wholesale slaughter" of American Robins. When flocks arrived in February 1907, "everyone, almost," began to kill them. "You can hardly look out on the streets that you do not see some one passing with a string of a dozen or more. . . . It is a wonder that there are any Robins left to continue the journey northward." Pearson decided a program of education in Sumter would be the most appropriate action. He spent an evening with the school superintendent, who promised to cooperate with the Audubon Society in an effort to teach students the value of robins and other birds.[2]

Dutcher asked Pearson to find the source of caged Painted Buntings (*Passerina ciris*) appearing in Philadelphia stores. The male bunting with its "lavish use of color" was a readily marketable captive bird.[3] In North and South Carolina Pearson found no evidence of buntings being trapped, but in Savannah he discovered "an old man named Adams" who had been trapping birds for thirty years, assisted by his wife, and who had no intention of stopping while the law was not enforced. During the 1907 season, Adams had caught and shipped to northern markets more than four hundred Painted Buntings for thirty-five dollars per hundred. In winter, Adams told Pearson, he trapped and shipped Northern Cardinals. Pearson found no local authorities willing to take action. "No one seemed to care anything about the case."[4]

For the Audubon Society of North Carolina, early in 1907 Pearson purchased four islands in Pamlico Sound used for nesting by seabirds. One island, a small, low, exposed bar of shells and sand about ten miles northeast of Ocracoke Inlet, was known locally as Royal Shoal; the other three were referred to collectively as the Legged Lumps. Laughing Gulls, Royal Terns, Common Terns, Least Terns, Black Skimmers, and American Oystercatchers bred there under Warden Jennett's protection. Brown Pelicans, not then known to breed on North Carolina's coast, used the islands as a "safe retreat" when visiting in summer.[5]

At laying season's peak in June, high storm tides swept completely over two of the four islands and partly over the other two. Visiting the islands to assess the damage, Pearson estimated that thirty-five hundred eggs (a figure he later reduced to fifteen hundred) had been washed from their nests. Laughing Gull eggs and young on a high part of Royal Shoal were not disturbed, but on June 20 a hailstorm killed all the young. "At times nature is certainly very unkind to her creatures," Pearson wrote Dutcher. The combined estimates by Audubon wardens on the Atlantic and Gulf coasts in the summer of 1907 indicated that storms destroyed nearly 40 percent of the approximately two hundred thousand eggs laid by Laughing Gulls, Herring Gulls (*Larus argentatus*), Black Skimmers, Common Terns, and Brown Pelicans.[6] All along the coast, however, the birds proved persistent and adaptable. A few days after North Carolina's hailstorm, Pearson found the birds nesting again on the Audubon islands. Royal Terns sitting on eggs were so close together their backs almost touched.

The birds seemed generally tame and unsuspicious of Pearson, a condition he attributed to Jennett's four-year stewardship. They permitted him to come with his camera as close as about fifteen feet. He noted the presence of a tern species he had never seen before. "It looked like a small Royal Tern except that the forehead was black instead of white, and it had a yellow-tipped black beak rather than a bright yellowish-red one." More than twenty such birds were on nests among the closely clustered Royal Terns. Pearson crawled cautiously over the sand toward one of them. When he advanced into the usual fifteen-foot space, the bird rose into the air and hovered over the nest, ready to flee. Pearson stopped. The bird settled on the nest again. Pearson moved slightly forward. The bird flew up again. Once more he stopped, and the bird dropped back down on the nest. These movements were repeated several times before Pearson stopped for good at a distance of about seven feet. Then for several minutes, man and bird observed each other at leisure. In writing hastily to Dutcher on his return to Greensboro, Pearson referred to the newly observed tern as a Roseate Tern (*Sterna dougallii*). That was a careless mistake. He knew the Roseate Tern only by name, and possibly its name was the first plausible one to come to mind. At any rate, he soon realized, as he reported in the *Auk*, he had seen Cabot's Terns (Sandwich Terns, *Sterna sandvicensis*), a subtropical species not previously known to nest as far north as North Carolina.[7]

Pearson's warden force for North Carolina had grown to seventy-nine. Hunting license sales brought in enough money for him to employ more wardens in the mountains, where comparatively little policing had occurred except in Asheville. He assigned men to Morganton, Boone, Jefferson, North Wilkesboro, and Brevard. On the coast, the warden force got a second boat, a gasoline launch named *Dovekie*, primarily to police duck and goose hunting on Currituck Sound. During the year ending March 1908, the Audubon Society successfully conducted 245 prosecutions in the courts, almost as many as the total number of convictions for the previous four years of enforcement work, a record Pearson attributed to "increased efficiency" rather than to increased crime.[8]

In South Carolina, neither Audubon Society President Taylor nor Secretary Rice was able to arouse adequate support for enforcing the Audubon Law. The society's membership remained low; the wardens were at first slow to make arrests and often unsuccessful in obtaining convictions. By November, one person had been convicted of killing a Great Blue Heron. Two months later, the number of convictions had risen to eleven, but many reports of uninvestigated violations were reaching Pearson. The society needed stimulation and public support. Pearson consulted with State Superintendent of Public Instruction Martin and arranged for Mary T. Moore to lecture in the schools for six weeks. By the tour's end, she had spoken sixty-eight times to an estimated total of fifteen thousand teachers and pupils.[9]

"Mr. Taylor and Secy. Rice are making considerable headway in South Carolina," Pearson reported to Dutcher, "but they have a big raw field to work in." Under the law, game birds could be killed for home consumption but could not be offered for sale. Nonetheless, Pearson found restaurant and hotel menus openly listing "doves" and "quail" (Northern Bobwhites). A large North Augusta tourist hotel employed hunters on salary to shoot bobwhites; local residents said the population had been "almost wiped out" for a radius of fifteen miles. In Charleston, a fruit merchant sold caged American Robins. On game preserves, nonresidents hunted without licenses. In a few more months' time, several hundred arrests were made by Audubon wardens, but overall the burden of law enforcement seemed to be greater than the society had anticipated or was prepared to bear.[10]

By examining the holdings of public and private libraries as he conducted his Audubon work, Pearson added considerably to his knowledge of ornithological writings, particularly those relating to North Carolina birds. From historian Stephen B. Weeks he borrowed *The Natural History of North Carolina*, by John Brickell. In the University of South Carolina library he leafed through Mark Catesby's *The Natural History of Carolina, Florida and the Bahama Islands*. His research was reflected in the presidential address he delivered to the North Carolina Academy of Science in May 1908. Entitled "Ornithological Work in North Carolina," it was a historical survey of studies beginning with sixteenth-century explorers' observations. Revised and renamed, it became an essay in *Birds of North Carolina*.[11]

Pearson traveled often to Georgia, seeking support for his bill to establish the Audubon Society as the state's game commission. From Atlanta a circular letter went out to all legislators and many prominent Georgia residents. On one day in Greensboro, Pearson sent out seven hundred copies and wrote individually to "about seventy-five" influential Georgians, urging them to ask their legislators to vote for the Audubon bill. By his arrangement, John H. Wallace, Alabama state game and fish commissioner, addressed the Georgia legislature as the National Association's representative. Receiving many compliments for his performance, Wallace became convinced the Audubon bill would be adopted. Pearson talked with several legislators over a period of several days following Wallace's address and reached the same conclusion. The bill was approved quickly and unanimously in the house of representatives and was sent to the senate.[12]

Confident of the bill's enactment, Pearson left Georgia for several weeks. At the University of Virginia's summer school for teachers, he delivered lectures on the Audubon program. Then he took Elsie and their child, Elizabeth, to Hendersonville, North Carolina, "for a rest," explaining to Dutcher that Elsie had been "in poor health" for some time. From there he went on to Knoxville, where he served on the Summer School of the South faculty for the first time since 1903. Afterward came a two-day stay at the Indiana Audubon Society's annual meeting in Fort Wayne, where he and Gene Stratton Porter were featured speakers. Porter took him to "Limberlost Cabin," her twelve-room log house on the edge of Limberlost Swamp near Geneva. Pearson remained several days, conversing about flowers, books, and birds, visiting Porter's friends, and seeing the locations of her nature studies. He read *Freckles* and at Porter's request examined the "dummy" for a book to be entitled *Birds of the Bible.* Asked for criticism, he remarked that she had selected pictures of American birds to illustrate some of the Asiatic birds mentioned in the Bible. After the book was published, she sent him a copy along with a letter in which she said, "You gave me small encouragement about writing this book; but I am sending you a copy just the same."[13]

When Pearson returned to Georgia in August 1908, he discovered that strong opposition to the Audubon bill had developed. Help in confronting the opposition was hard to find. The Audubon Society was small, and the state's sportsmen were unorganized. Unable to determine what had generated the opposition, Pearson did not know how to deal with it, and the bill was defeated in the senate by four votes. "I hope you will not think that I have lost what little ability I may ever have had in dealing with a Legislature, by our failure in Georgia," he wrote to Dutcher. "I have never been quite so upset by defeat as by this one."[14]

That fall Audubon wardens in both South and North Carolina were subjected to violence. In September near St. George, South Carolina, an Audubon warden was assassinated by a man whose mule was tracked by bloodhounds down a small branch to a public highway; there the scent was lost. Audubon Secretary Rice was convinced the assassin was one of two "notorious fish-pirates" who had been told by the warden they might be prosecuted. "The Audubon people are much stirred over this murder, and if the assassin is caught he will be hanged," Rice wrote. He nonetheless doubted that the murderer would be satisfactorily identified. A North Carolina warden was more fortunate. He was shot "in the face, hand, and body" by a "night shooter of ducks" on Currituck Sound but pursued the hunter and others with him until he could identify them. "The trial will be this week," Pearson wrote to Dutcher.[15]

In contrast to the South Carolina society, the North Carolina society appeared to be still gaining strength. Former Governor Aycock, whom Pearson regarded as the "most prominent lawyer in North Carolina to-day," replaced Joyner as vice-president. At a special legislative session in 1908, the house committee on game protection killed a bill, viewed by Pearson as "very dangerous," that would have permitted nonresident stockholders in corporations owning lands in North Carolina to hunt on those lands without buying licenses. Junior membership continued to grow, rising to nine hundred by March 1909. Pearson lectured to the juniors occasionally. "We hope to have another visit from Mr. Pearson," one junior secretary wrote, "for the children fell in love with him." Dutcher requested that a copy of the North Carolina society's sixth annual report be sent to all other Audubon societies so they might see in it examples they could follow.[16]

Pearson's role in the National Association grew more important. Dutcher's health deteriorated under the strain of administering the growing organization while keeping up his insurance business; he was moody and overly sensitive to criticism. When the National Association's board of directors objected to his spending money from capital funds, he said he was quitting as president. By the rules, he should have called a meeting and formally resigned. Instead, he wrote to a board member, asking him to present his resignation to the board. Under the organization's bylaws, only the president could call a meeting, but when asked to call it, Dutcher left New York on a trip to the Adirondacks. Nonetheless, he wrote Palmer, who was in California recovering from an illness, that he was resigning. Palmer wrote immediately to Chapman. "Is there no chance of getting him to reconsider, and, if not, who is to take his place? Would you be willing to take it in case Dutcher persists in his determination to retire? It seems to me that the President ought to be a resident of New York if possible." By the time Chapman replied in January 1908, Dutcher had returned to New York, an "armed truce" had been reached, and Chapman was able to assure Palmer that "things will continue to go on as they have before," at least for the time being, and that there was "no occasion for worry." He predicted, nonetheless, that "our over-wrought, nervously irresponsible friend, W. D.," determined to "have his own way," might create "some conflict of authority before the end of the year."[17]

Pearson wrote a solicitous letter to Dutcher expressing awareness of his "anxiety of mind" and offering to take an "inexpensive room in New York, live cheaply by economizing," and "share the burden" of the "heavy office work." He suggested he might also be able to raise more money for the National Association by staying in New York for a few months at a time than by making occasional visits. He could spend "the greater part of the remaining winter and spring months" with Dutcher, he added. Dutcher said no, for "it would be almost impossible to raise any money" in New York because of the depressed economy. Furthermore, he and the chief clerk could "get along" with the office work. Nonetheless, when Walter Hines Page agreed to publish an article on the National Association in *World's Work*, it was presumably Dutcher who decided the author should be Pearson. In "The Warden of Our Bird-Life," the term "warden" refers to the National Association and its member societies, and "Audubon Society" often means all Audubon organizations regarded as one. State societies were functioning in thirty-one states; the AOU model law, becoming known as the "Audubon law," had been adopted in thirty-seven states; and the Audubon Society made its "influence felt in every state in the Union" and in several foreign countries. "Wherever the interests of wild birds and game are threatened its agents appear to plead the cause of the wild creature," Pearson wrote. He praised Willcox, whose bequest had made much of the National Association's work possible, and Dutcher, who "has devoted the best years of his life to the cause so near to his heart without remuneration of any kind save what he derives from the consciousness of great results achieved."[18]

# 17

# Birds and the "Conservation Movement": Vainly Seeking Equal Status

## *(1908–1909)*

SINCE 1898, THE YEAR Gifford Pinchot stopped working for Vanderbilt at Biltmore, he had been head of the U.S. Department of Agriculture's forestry office. Known as the Division of Forestry when Pinchot was appointed, the office was renamed the Bureau of Forestry. In 1905, it became the Forest Service after President Roosevelt had transferred to its custody sixty-three million acres of forest reserves formerly under the Department of the Interior.[1] Pinchot's desire to maintain forests that could forever supply wood products for increasing numbers of people led him to consider saving other natural resources. With the collaboration of his associate forester Overton Price, who suggested the term "conservation," and of William J. McGee, ethnologist and geologist, who defined the term and a philosophy to go with it, as well as with Roosevelt's encouragement and support, Pinchot led what became known as the "conservation movement."

Partly at Pinchot's urging, Roosevelt withdrew millions of coal-rich acres from land available for purchase or lease. In 1907, he created the Inland Waterways Commission, which recommended that for maximum use every river be considered a unit, from its source to its mouth. The commission also suggested a conference to consider natural resources in general. In November 1907, Roosevelt invited the governor of each state and territory to a conference at the White House on May 13–15, 1908. Later, invitations went to selected members of Congress, judges, experts in and out of government, periodicals, and organizations. [2]

The president declined Dutcher's request that he invite the National Association to send a delegate to the White House conference. In envisioning a movement to save natural resources, neither Roosevelt nor Pinchot considered wild animals to be a significant part of those resources. Roosevelt treasured beautiful birds as he did great works of art and literature, but he wanted the conservation movement to concentrate on economic efficiency and America's need to be efficient in order to compete with other nations. "The underlying principle of conservation has been described as the application of common sense to common problems for the common good," he wrote, drawing on Pinchot's language. "If this description is correct, then conservation is the great fundamental basis for national efficiency. In this stage of the world's history, to be fearless, to be just, and to be efficient are the three great requirements of national life." [3]

No wildlife agencies, organizations, or periodicals were invited to send delegates to the conference. Among the forty-eight "general guests" were Smithsonian Institution Secretary Charles D. Walcott, U.S. Commissioner of Fisheries George M. Bowers, and Biological Survey Chief C. Hart Merriam, none of whom were on the program of speakers. In the entire array of persons selected to address the conference, only George F. Kunz, president of the American Scenic and Historic Preservation Society, explicitly advocated the conservation of wild animals, which he defended merely as needed "to give color and movement to the landscape." [4]

Although the conference delegates limited their natural resources list to land, water, forests, and minerals, they agreed that
"the beauty, healthfulness, and habitability of our country should
be preserved and increased"—thus leaving room for expansion of
the list—and recommended that all states establish conservation
commissions to cooperate with each other and "with any similar
commission of the Federal Government." In response to this recommendation, Roosevelt in June created the National Conservation Commission, to which he appointed forty-eight men
interested in natural resources, including members of Congress
and heads of national government resource agencies. The commission's work was planned by an executive committee that included
Pinchot (as chairman), William J. McGee, Overton Price, and
Julian A. Holmes, who had left the North Carolina Geological
Survey to become chief of the U.S. Geological Survey's tech-
nological branch. The executive committee met on June 19 and
began to inventory the nation's natural resources.[5]

Pearson and Dutcher, meanwhile, recognized the Audubon
societies' increasing need to build strength by cooperating with
other wildlife organizations. At the Fourth International Fishery
Congress in Washington, D.C., in September 1908, they infor-
mally dispensed information about birds and the Audubon cause
in talks with other delegates. Dutcher concentrated on meeting
foreign delegates, to whom he stressed the need for an "International Bird Protection Society." The Chinese and Japanese delegates, in particular, seemed interested. At their request, Dutcher
later sent them bundles of National Association publications. Pearson spent his time largely with American delegates, including
Pinchot and Theodore Palmer. Palmer's formal manner caused
him to be remembered years later by French ornithologist Jean
Delacour as a "stuffed shirt," but Pearson liked him. In correspondence, he addressed him as "Dr. Palmer" and treated him with a
deferential but teasing affection. Upon returning to Greensboro

after the fishery congress, he wrote to Palmer. "I enjoyed you more than ever this last trip! If I were an unattached girl I would marry you if I could get you!" He said he was spending the entire day writing letters of solicitation for the National Association and drew a picture of himself holding out "The Itching Palm" to a well-dressed man and saying "A little for the birds!"[6]

Before he left Washington, Pearson had written to Dutcher, "I have just been up to the office of Mr. Gifford Pinchot, where I had a conference with him about the Audubon Society being recognized in the work of the Conservation Commission. He took your address and said he would write to you shortly and invite the National Association to appoint a committee to work on the Commission."[7]

Dutcher had received Pinchot's letter by the time the National Association held its annual meeting in October in New York, and Forbush (chairman), Dutcher, Pearson, Palmer, and Chapman were appointed a committee to cooperate with the National Conservation Commission. Even in declining health, Dutcher was expanding his vision of the National Association's future. In his presidential address, he asked for a much enlarged endowment and more newspaper articles, educational leaflets, lecture kits, and field agents, "at least one for each state, and, where the commonwealth is very large and populous, there should be two or three." "If we permit the heritage of wild birds that still exist to be wasted and destroyed, we are robbing our children. We are simply trustees, and should seek to enlarge the estate in our care rather than squander it."[8]

Pearson, reporting as secretary, reviewed the major gains and losses in laws enacted in the sixteen states where legislatures met. The one "actual backward step" had been taken in Virginia, where the Audubon Act was amended to permit the killing, at any time, of "Hawks, Owls, Eagles, Blackbirds, Ricebirds, Bobolinks, Doves, Wilson's Snipe and Robin Snipe [Red Knot, *Calidris canu-*

*tus*]." The most important forward step had been taken in Louisiana, where a state board of commissioners was established to direct a warden force supported by a tax on all hunters, resident as well as nonresident, and Audubon Society President Frank M. Miller was appointed commission chairman and executive officer. National Association wardens had been stationed in fourteen states across the country, including Michigan, Minnesota, and North Dakota as well as states on both coasts. Their combined reports showed that among the nearly 700,000 gulls, terns, pelicans, grebes, cormorants, and other birds that they guarded (forty-seven species altogether), more than 227,000 young were raised. A proposal for reducing the size of the National Association's board of directors from thirty to eleven in order to gather a quorum with relative ease was adopted at the annual meeting. In addition to Dutcher and Pearson, the new board included Allen, Grinnell, Chapman, Brewster, Dwight, and Palmer, thus maintaining the organization's close bond with the AOU.[9] Because of the board's composition, it functioned much like an AOU committee.

A Joint Conservation Conference called by the National Conservation Commission met in Washington on December 8–10, 1908. Chosen as the National Association's representative, Pearson was advised by Dutcher to "get acquainted with as many of the delegates to the Convention as possible and talk about the National Association" but not to solicit memberships. "If you can get a list of the members present from the register, with their addresses, we can approach them a couple of months from now without having it appear that we are 'working them.'" Fifty-nine organizations were represented; Pearson was the only delegate from an organization devoted to protecting wild animal species. He could take some comfort in the presence of Hugh M. Smith of the Bureau of Fisheries and C. Hart Merriam. Thirty-one states and territories were represented by their governors, governors-elect, or persons chosen to act in their stead; many state conservation commissions had also sent delegates. The rest of the conference consisted of the National Conservation Commission and delegates-at-large. Discounting Pearson and Senator Lee S. Overman of the National Conservation Commission, North Carolina was unrepresented as a state, even though at the earlier White House conference, Governor Glenn's enthusiastic speech on forest conservation had drawn "great and prolonged applause."[10]

The Joint Conservation Conference offered possibilities for beginning far-reaching programs, but hostility to it and the National Conservation Commission was evident at the opening ceremony. Pinchot chaired the conference. The temporary chairman for the opening session, at which Roosevelt welcomed the delegates, was William Howard Taft, who a month earlier had won the popular vote for the nation's presidency. According to Pinchot's subsequent account, he, Roosevelt, and Taft had spent an evening together in Roosevelt's study a few weeks before the conference. "Then and there Taft pledged himself to T. R., and incidentally to me, to stand by and carry on the conservation fight." Taft was given the manuscript of a speech "which took the T. R. position on Conservation." But Taft surprised them. Introduced by Pinchot as the "President-elect,"a title that would not be technically accurate until the presidential electors had voted in January, Taft used the inaccuracy to express misgivings about the conservation movement. "Mr. President, ladies and gentlemen, there is one difficulty about the conservation of natural resources. It is that the imagination of those who are pressing it may outrun the practical facts. I have been introduced as the President-elect. I am not the President-elect, except in the imagination of Mr. Pinchot."[11]

Along with other delegates, Pearson may not have understood the full implications of Taft's remarks. "This is a wonderful meeting!" he wrote to Dutcher. He talked about birds, game, and the Audubon program with many influential men, including Robert C. Ogden, Walter Hines Page, and the governors of Louisiana,

Mississippi, Georgia, South Carolina, and Minnesota. At the conference secretary's request, he prepared a brief speech, but he was never called upon to deliver it. The delegates from private organizations were not allowed an opportunity to speak until near the conference's end. By the time four of them had appeared on the platform, the conference ended without the well-being of wild animals ever having been brought up for discussion. Nonetheless, the delegates received copies of inventories and reports prepared earlier for the National Conservation Commission, including C. Hart Merriam's "Relations of Birds and Mammals to the National Resources" in which birds were described as being more useful than any other broad category of wild animals. "So important are birds as conservators of the forest and as protectors of farm crops that neither forestry nor agriculture could be successfully practiced without their aid," Merriam maintained.[12] All bird species contribute, he said, and all should be preserved.

The National Association and other organizations represented at the conference were asked to submit for the published proceedings reports on how they could assist the National Conservation Commission. Pearson gave Pinchot a five-thousand word report on "Bird and Game Protection in America." Except for what he possibly gained from performing the task, his time was wasted. None of the reports were included in the published conference proceedings.[13]

During the conference, Pearson talked with Pinchot about the preliminary natural resources inventories prepared for the National Conservation Commission and suggested the National Association could produce a rough census of the "amount of wild bird and animal life to-day" as compared with "that formerly existing in the United States," an analysis of the causes of wildlife's decline, and some objectives for the future. Pinchot "seemed very much pleased" with the plan, Pearson wrote to Dutcher. "He not only stated that it was 'splendid,' but went so far as to say 'this is the best and most practicable thing that has been submitted during the entire Conference.'"[14]

Pearson's plan was endorsed by the National Association and announced in *Bird-Lore*. "Report blanks" were to be sent "broadcast" throughout the nation to National Association members, *Bird-Lore* subscribers, sportsmen, and "all others interested in wild birds and animals." Before the plan could be implemented, however, the National Conservation Commission died. Roosevelt had initially asked for a congressional appropriation of fifty thousand dollars to support the commission's work. When his request was denied, he authorized the preliminary inventories made, the joint conference held, and the reports published with the use of existing staff and budgets. Congressional supporters of the conservation movement were outnumbered by those who opposed spending money for it, resented Roosevelt's expansion of executive power, or objected to Pinchot's influence. Moreover, Roosevelt's tenure as president was almost over, and although Taft would later support conservation proposals, the incoming president had already publicly ridiculed the "conservation movement" and its leaders. Congress adopted a measure forbidding the use of funds to pay the expenses of any commission it had not specifically authorized. As a consequence, no employee of the national government, including Pinchot himself, could any longer give official time to the National Conservation Commission or allow it the use of space or supplies. It ceased to function without ever having acknowledged wildlife to be a major natural resource.[15]

Another effort to enlarge the national government's role in protecting wildlife also failed for the time being. It had begun in December 1904, when Representative George Shiras III of Pennsylvania introduced a bill to protect migratory game birds. An attorney, Shiras was also a naturalist, an Audubon movement supporter, and a wildlife photographer (earlier in 1904 he had accompanied Frank Chapman on a field outing in Mexico). The reluctance of state and territorial governments to provide adequate protection for birds, especially game birds, distressed him. In the Lacey Act, Congress had demonstrated its willingness to assist in enforcing state bird protective laws, but it had not yet challenged the prevailing concept that birds and other wild species were the exclusive property of the states in which they resided. Shiras believed the concept inherent in the Lacey Act—that birds shipped from one state to another are in the stream of interstate commerce and therefore subject to national government regulation—might be taken a step further. Under his bill, game birds moving voluntarily from one state to another were "deemed to be within the custody and protection of the Government of the United States," and the secretary of agriculture was authorized to set the dates of hunting seasons for migratory game birds. Deliberately limiting himself to one term in Congress, 1903–5, Shiras did not expect his bill to pass; he merely wanted it printed, circulated, and discussed to prepare the way for passage of some such bill in the future.[16]

When Representative John W. Weeks, of Massachusetts, reintroduced Shiras's bill with slight revisions in December 1908, Dutcher asked him to extend its coverage from migratory game birds to "all migratory birds." Weeks said he would do so if he could "get the bill up in Committee." Although Dutcher urged all Audubon supporters to write to their congressmen in behalf of the bill, it failed in committee. Nonetheless, like Shiras, Dutcher had come to see national government action as a necessary component of migratory bird protection. "After years of effort by the National Association, it is found practically impossible to obtain uniform legislation from state legislatures, and the only practical way to get uniformity is through a Federal statute."[17]

Just before Roosevelt left the presidency, Pearson later recalled, there was a "rush" in National Association headquarters to "get as many executive orders for bird reservations as possible signed." On February 25, 1909, Roosevelt signed orders establishing seventeen bird reservations; two days later he signed five more. By his own count, he created fifty-one bird reservations during his nearly two terms as president, thus placing the United States in "the front rank in the world work of bird protection." In those eight years, he believed, "more was accomplished for the protection of wild life in the United States than during all the previous years, excepting only the creation of the Yellowstone National Park." By his reckoning, the record of the president and the Congress together included the creation of five national parks, four big-game refuges, and fifty-one bird reservations, as well as the adoption of laws protecting wildlife in Alaska, in the District of Columbia, and on the bird reservations.[18] These were notable achievements, but they could not be credited, at least as far as bird protection was concerned, to the "conservation movement."

# 18

# The South's First State Wildlife Commission Eviscerated

## *(1909)*

WHEN THE GENERAL ASSEMBLY opened in Raleigh in January 1909, Pearson had little reason to doubt that most legislators would be friendly to the Audubon cause. "I have just returned from Raleigh where our Legislature is in session," he wrote to Dutcher, "and yesterday I had the pleasure of naming the members of the Game Protection Committees of both Houses. I shall probably ask for some additional legislation." Two of his bills were adopted. One established in Guilford County a closed season for hunting ducks and squirrels and prohibited killing or capturing Wood Ducks at any time. The other, intended to offer birds statewide protection from dogs and cats during nesting seasons, was reduced to a prohibition against allowing hunting dogs to run at large during Northern Bobwhite breeding seasons in ten counties, including Guilford.[1]

The time seemed propitious for Pearson to persuade the legislature to adopt his bill prohibiting the sale of Northern Bobwhites and Ruffed Grouse anywhere in the state for two years. During the

192

previous summer, heavy rains had depleted the bobwhite population so greatly that the need for protection was easy to demon-
strate. In Virginia and South Carolina, such laws had already been
enacted. At Pearson's request, the game committees met in joint
session and listened to him discuss the problem. After the meeting
Pearson wrote to Dutcher, "A large number of Representatives
have pledged me their support to vote for this measure, and the
Chairman of each Committee is working hard on the proposition."
Brooke G. Empie, senate game committee chairman and Audubon
Society member, introduced the measure and two days later reported it favorably from his committee. It foundered in the house
among efforts to make exceptions to its provisions; thirty-two
representatives offered amendments on one day alone. Finally,
against the game committee's wishes, it was tabled.[2]

Apparently because Dutcher was not well, Pearson went to
New York to administer the National Association office for a few
days. After a week, he abruptly returned to Raleigh. "Word has
reached me," he explained in a letter to Dutcher, "that a very
damaging amendment to our license law will come up in the North
Carolina legislature by special order on Wednesday so I am forced
to go South this afternoon. Nothing of importance has come up in
the office this week other than what we were able to attend to."
Like the bill introduced in the special session of 1908, the new bill
would permit a wide range of nonresidents to hunt without buying
a license, thus sharply reducing the Audubon Society's revenues.
Pearson succeeded in having it modified before its adoption; the
only persons exempted from the license requirement were the
relatively small number of nonresident children and parents of
resident landowners.[3]

The suspicion that the bill may have been introduced as a
deliberate effort to weaken the Audubon Society made Pearson
hesitate over an invitation to address the Arkansas legislature about
a proposed state game protection system until he was assured by

friends that "the enemies of the Audubon Society were well in hand." He then decided to go to Texas as well. At Little Rock, he addressed a joint legislative session, conferred with members of the Arkansas Game Protective Association, and drafted a bill for the state game commission's establishment. At Austin, Texas, he met with State Fish and Game Commission officers; there and in San Antonio he delivered public lectures. In both cities he was told by Texans as well as by Mexican officials that hunters from the United States were "invading Mexico and slaughtering wild life at a frightful rate." They were said to enter Mexico by train, live in freight cars, and employ local men to kill ducks, turkeys, and deer, which they brought back to the United States and sold "at a good profit." Some hunters went to shallow lakes where wintering ducks flocked and set up batteries of guns that could be fired simultaneously by one person, sometimes as many as a hundred guns in a group. Men on horseback herded the floating birds into the line of fire.[4]

The time seemed right for Audubon work in Mexico. In Washington, Forbush visited the chairman of the Mexican delegation to the North American Conservation Conference, which was attended by delegates from Mexico, Canada, and the United States. The conversation encouraged him to believe that the Mexican government could be persuaded to take action in behalf of migratory birds. Pearson obtained letters of introduction from prominent Texas residents and went to Mexico City to visit President Porfirio Diaz. First he called on Porfirio Diaz, Jr., a wealthy businessman and sportsman. He "seemed to think well" of Pearson's proposals for preserving wildlife and took him to his father; they talked in "a great room in the Castle of Chapultepec." "I . . . laid before him a plan for organizing a national movement for game protection in Mexico, this to be followed up with restrictive measures on the killing of birds and game, the work to be supported by a hunters' license," Pearson wrote to Dutcher. President Diaz seemed much interested in Pearson's proposals, asked him many questions about wildlife protection elsewhere, and instructed his son to organize a protective society. Pearson would send him an outline for work to be done in Mexico, copies of constitutions and bylaws of wildlife organizations, and "all the available literature on the importance of birds to agriculture." Pearson believed action would soon be taken to protect Mexican wildlife and was pleased he had made the trip. "But I had not yet comprehended," he wrote later, "the full significance of the word manana." Moreover, he could not know that President Diaz and his son would two years later become powerless "political refuges."[5]

Only three weeks had passed since Pearson had left Raleigh. When he returned, trouble almost literally met him at the capitol door on Monday morning, March 1. As he later recalled events, a senator whom he identified merely as a friend of the Audubon cause told him that Senator Fred P. Latham, of Beaufort County, had introduced a measure oddly recorded as "a bill to be entitled an act for the better improvement of the game law for Beaufort and Currituck counties." At Latham's request the bill had been placed directly on the Senate calendar rather than referred to the game committee, read by title only, and, in deference to Latham, passed and ordered enrolled. Few senators were aware of what the apparently innocuous bill provided. It was sent to the house, where the word "improvement" in the title was changed to "enforcement" before the bill was referred to the game committee. Committee chairman M. B. Pitt had described the bill to Pearson's friendly senator, who like most of his colleagues had not known what it provided when it passed in the senate.[6]

The bill removed Beaufort and Currituck counties from the Audubon Society's jurisdiction. Existing laws protecting birds and game would remain in effect, but they would be enforced by the county commissioners, who would pay wardens by selling hunting licenses to nonresidents of the state. Licenses bought by nonresident hunters under the Audubon Act would not be acceptable

in Beaufort and Currituck; moreover, a license bought in Beaufort
would not be acceptable in Currituck, and vice versa. To hunt in
both counties, a nonresident would have to buy two licenses. Half
the money collected from license sales in each county could be
used for law enforcement; the other half would go into the school
fund.[7]

If the bill became law, most of the coast would still be within
Audubon jurisdiction, but the precedent could be dangerous.
Other counties might try to free themselves from Audubon regulation. Market hunters all along the coast wanted to be rid of
Audubon supervision. In Pearson's view, local supervision was
likely to mean no supervison, as had been the case before the
Audubon Act was passed. Pearson and the friendly senator considered ways of stopping the bill. "It was thought the best course
was for the Senate to recall the bill, to expose its contents and to kill
it," Pearson wrote later. "We repaired to the Senate where in a few
minutes the necessary action to recall the bill was taken. Then I
went across to the House to wait until the demand should be
presented and the bill ordered to be returned."[8]

For the first time in his six years of lobbying, Pearson was
outmaneuvered. Backers of Latham's bill had seen Pearson enter
the capitol. Quickly the news spread: the bill should be passed at
once, before he could organize opposition to it. Frank B. Hoover,
of Beaufort County, interrupted proceedings on the house floor
with a motion to take Latham's bill from the game committee and
place it on the calendar. The motion was adopted. Then A. S.
Roscoe, of Bertie County, moved the bill be "placed upon its
immediate passage." Again the motion was adopted. Few members
of the house understood the purpose of this sudden change in the
agenda, Pearson stated later. They voted for it primarily because
they were "impressed with the vigor of the proponents of the
motion" and because the bill applied to only two counties.[9]

Once they understood the bill, it had immediate appeal. Many

legislators were attracted to the possibility of selling county hunting licenses, keeping the money in the county, and dividing it
between the public schools and game protection. Local taxes were
the main support for the schools in each county, and Latham's bill
seemed to offer more revenue without raising them. More personal
economic motives increased the bill's attractiveness. Market hunters and shippers of game "smarted" (in Pearson's language) under
the Audubon Society's jurisdiction. Before the legislature met, one
legislator had warned Pearson he could no longer support the
society unless the Audubon Act was amended to permit him to
ship woodcock to northern markets. With a hundred wardens on
duty, in the Audubon year ending in March 1909 there had been
163 convictions in the courts for violations of the bird and game
laws. Half the convictions were for hunting on someone else's land
without permission; seventeen were for killing squirrels illegally,
sixteen for killing quails illegally, ten for hunting ducks and geese
illegally. There were individual convictions for killing woodpeckers, juncos, warblers, herons, jays, vultures, and nighthawks,
and one for selling mockingbirds.

Some legislators believed the Audubon Society's income from
hunting license sales to be much greater than it was, as much as
"thousands of dollars" from each county each year, but the state
treasurer's report for the fiscal year prior to the legislative session of
1909 showed $8,776 as the amount received from license sales in
the entire state. The slightly larger figure of $9,178.60 reported by
the Audubon Society as the amount of money received from the
state treasurer during the Audubon year March 1, 1908–February
28, 1909, included more of the hunting season of 1908–9 than the
state's fiscal year included. This was the year of the society's
highest revenue. The average income per county had been approximately $89.00 for the fiscal year, $93.00 for the Audubon year. In
some counties, including Beaufort and Currituck, many licenses
had been sold; in others, none.[10]

The strong influence that Pearson had often exerted through committees rankled some legislators. His unusual role as an official of both the National Association and the state society was at times misunderstood. The trips he made outside the state for the National Association and paid for by it were susceptible to being seen as pleasure trips financed by the state society. One legislator said that Pearson had "accumulated great wealth" as the society's secretary, all "at the expense of the tax-payers of North Carolina." In actuality, his salary as Audubon Society secretary for the current Audubon year was $1,599.97. He also received $744.30 as a commission on membership fees and contributions. From the National Association he received for the year ending October 20, 1908, a total of $2,303.77, much of which was for travel.[11]

Pearson later recalled that "Excitement ran high" when he entered the house chamber expecting the Latham bill to be recalled to the senate. Instead, he heard a "fiery speech" in the bill's behalf and watched helplessly as more speakers arose, exhibiting "something akin to mob-spirit in action in a legislative hall." A few representatives, including Speaker William A. Graham, defended the Audubon Society and argued against the bill. Many more not only spoke in the bill's favor; they also offered amendments adding their counties to the two counties covered by it. Forty such amendments were quickly adopted. The bill passed its second reading, the rules were suspended once more, and debate was resumed. Twelve more counties were added to the list. The bill passed its third reading and was sent to the senate.[12]

Pearson asked Governor William W. Kitchin for help in defeating the bill, but Kitchin declined to intervene. As governor-elect, he had not sent a representative to the joint conservation conference in Washington, though several other governors-elect had done so. In his inaugural address, he limited his remarks on natural resources to the need to drain swamp lands for farming. Nonetheless, he assured Pearson his former law partner, Senator E. L.

Travis of Halifax County, supported the Audubon Society. "That was true," Pearson wrote, "but the Governor's brother Paul, also in the Legislature, was one of our outspoken opponents." Audubon President Richard Lewis came to the capitol to help Pearson lobby, as did a few others, but "mostly it was a lone battle."[13] The Audubon system had been adopted chiefly because of Pearson's skillful advocacy and the legislators' acquiescence. Now that many legislators sought to establish a new system in their respective counties, Pearson had difficulty finding Audubon defenders. The legislators who supported him were primarily game committee members or representatives from counties where few hunting licenses were sold and where hunting would be unregulated without Audubon wardens.

The senate game committee finally succeeded in having the Latham bill referred to its custody but could hold it only until March 5, when it was taken from the committee and debated. Although enough Audubon support was mustered to withdraw twelve counties from the bill and return them to the society's jurisdiction, that achievement was temporary. A conference committee of two senators and three representatives compiled a list of fifty-two counties to be covered by the bill, leaving forty-six under the Audubon Society. Adopted by both houses on March 6, the bill became law two days later.[14]

"For stubbornness of contest, resourceful resistance on the one hand and determined aggressiveness on the other," wrote a reporter for the *News and Observer*, "no fight during the present session of the Legislature is comparable to that which has waged fierce on the bill designated as the anti-Audubon Society bill." Pearson concluded that the society had been the victim of action by excited men resentful of the centralized control of game, unjustifiably jealous and suspicious of him as well as the society, and deluded by thoughts of large sums of money for the public schools.[15] North Carolina, the first southern state to adopt a state system of bird and game protection, thus became one of the few southern states without such a system. By 1916, it was the only southern state other than Mississippi not to have such a system. It held that dubious distinction until 1927, when the North Carolina Game Commission was established.

Pearson went home on Sunday, March 7, feeling "disappointment and chagrin" over the "most bitter legislative defeat" of his career. Yet he was confident the Audubon Society had, as he put it in his annual report, "won for itself a place of appreciation in the hearts of the good people of North Carolina." "We know without doubt that to-day, as a result of its work, there are thousands of additional happy birds in the State which by their songs and usefulness are adding cheer and joy to people whose hearts are receptive to the messages of these beautiful creatures." Dutcher wrote a sympathetic letter, characterizing the Latham Act as having been "instigated by pure selfishness" and adding, "unfortunately, there are a great many people in this world who care little except for themselves, and provided they can get what they want, they give little thought for what is best for the rest of the people." Other letter writers offered assurances that the Latham Act would be repealed in 1911 and that the Audubon Society's full jurisdiction would be restored. Pearson was dubious.[16]

The defeat in North Carolina was not unique. In Arkansas, Florida, and Georgia, bills failed that Pearson had written providing for game commissions to be operated by the state rather than by an Audubon society. An important Audubon-sponsored plumage bill failed in New York. The law forbidding the sale of the plumage of birds killed in New York had been difficult to enforce because the plumage of birds killed in other states or countries could be legally sold; distinguishing one kind from the other after the feathers reached the market place was impossible. The National Association offered a bill, introduced in the legislature by James A. Francis in behalf of the Audubon Society of New York

State, to forbid traffic in the plumage of wild birds "irrespective of where the said plumage comes from." Thousands of copies of a circular explaining the bill were distributed; on four occasions, testimony was offered to the fish and game committee to which the bill was referred. But the "feather dealers" employed an attorney "who had great influence" in the legislature," Dutcher wrote, and the bill was blocked in committee. Chapman, unable to understand "why representatives from agricultural districts should side with feather-dealers," urged *Bird-Lore* readers to tell their legislators, "with emphasis," whether they preferred "birds as useless attachments to bonnets or as the protectors of our farms and orchards."[17]

Elsewhere in the nation the Audubon cause advanced. North Dakota and Oklahoma adopted the model law. Unlike New York, California adopted the state Audubon Society's bill forbidding the sale of wild bird feathers, "irrespective of whether said bird was captured or killed within or without the state." Missouri re-established a state warden system to protect birds and game, which had been established in 1905 and abolished in 1907. Missouri Governor Herbert S. Hadley, unlike Governor Kitchin in North Carolina, intervened in the legislation's behalf: "The value of birds to the agriculturist and the horticulturist is no longer a matter of speculation. Without the aid of birds, the production of harvests of grain and yields of fruit would, in a short time, become difficult, if not impossible." In Oregon, the illegal selling of plumage seemed to stop after ten prominent Portland milliners were convicted. In Illinois, the legislature adopted a law requiring school teachers to devote at least thirty minutes each week to teaching pupils "kindness and justice to, and humane treatment and protection of, birds and animals, and the important part they fulfil in the economy of nature." Any teacher who knowingly violated the law was to be penalized by a 5 percent reduction in pay for each month in which a violation occurred.[18]

Edward Forbush's lobbying in New England defeated what he reported was a "great mass of legislation adverse to bird protection." Moreover, Rhode Island, New Hampshire, and Vermont adopted laws requiring residents to buy hunting licenses, thus providing strong financial support for warden systems; attempts to repeal similar legislation in Massachusetts were defeated. Connecticut followed Massachusetts's example in establishing the office of state ornithologist.[19]

Pearson accepted re-election as secretary of the North Carolina society on condition he would give it "only such time as could be spared" from his National Association duties. He lowered his own salary sharply and notified Mary T. Moore her services as school secretary would end June 1. Moore stayed on until August, paid largely by the National Association as a substitute for Pearson after the board of directors, in a meeting Pearson did not attend, decided to put on a special campaign for memberships and contributions. "It is imperative that we have a larger membership and more money," Dutcher wrote to Pearson. For a few weeks, Dutcher in New York and Pennsylvania and Forbush in New England were to spend as much time as possible soliciting. Pearson was assigned to the "North Central" region, without instructions or pre-arrangements. "As far as I am able to do so," Dutcher wrote, "I am shifting responsibility, because the day will soon come when it will be shifted whether I want to have it so or not; and, therefore, I want you to work this proposition out yourself, as you will have to do on all occasions not very far in the future." Pearson visited cities in Ohio, Indiana, Illinois, and Wisconsin and corresponded with Audubon officials in other states. In Cincinnati, he visited the zoological garden, where he saw the last two known surviving Passenger Pigeons. He had never seen a live Passenger Pigeon before; he never saw one again. Five years later, both birds were dead, and the species was extinct. Though the special effort may have strengthened sentiment for the Audubon cause, it produced little additional income. The combined receipts for the year were only $326.70 more than those for the previous year.[20]

Pearson did not attend the First National Conservation Congress in Seattle in August 1909, but he followed its proceedings. William L. Finley, National Association Pacific Coast agent, relieved him of the burden of making the long trip. Finley was a member of the congress's committee on permanent organization, which defined the group's objective as being "to seek to overcome waste in natural, human, or moral forces." Extending far beyond natural resources, this broad definition opened the way for discussion of a wide variety of concerns by delegates from such groups as women's clubs, universities, and businesses. A North Carolina physician addressed the congress on the need for the "protection of our resources in our children." The "Grand Chief Templar of the United States" stressed the importance of conserving "manhood," the "greatest of all resources."[21]

Finley made a speech pleading for the protection of birds as one means of preserving the "balance of nature," perhaps influenced by George Abbey's *The Balance of Nature and Modern Conditions of Cultivation* (1909) or the writings of Greek philosophers who believed in a natural environmental harmony. Finley said, "In the struggle for existence every species is closely related to many other species, each acting as a force in itself to hold the equilibrium which is called the balance of nature." He blamed most illegal bird destruction on women and plume hunters, saying "as long as women demand these plumes men will be found to supply them."[22]

In New York, Dutcher continued to emphasize the primary importance of teaching children the economic value of birds. If children were well taught about economic value, he said at the National Association's meeting in October, the "esthetic value" would "make itself known." The teaching should take place at every level of education, "from the kindergarten to the university."

He proposed establishing "a great school or university devoted solely to the work of fitting teachers to be instructors about birds in their relation to man." Pearson appears to have ignored this proposal, probably viewing it as impractical. Although he believed the education of children to be a paramount need, he preferred to rely on a dispersion of knowledge through the National Association's publications and through field agents who could teach as he did, by writing for publication, lecturing, and corresponding. In addition to Pearson, Finley on the Pacific coast, Forbush in New England, and Moore in the Carolinas, the National Association was employing, part-time, M. B. Davis in Texas, Gretchen L. Libby in California, and Katherine Stuart in Virginia.[23]

More and more women were joining the Audubon movement. Although the National Association's officers and directors were all men, four women served as advisory directors and more than 40 percent of the association's nearly 1,250 individual members were women. Twenty of the thirty-three state society annual reports to the National Association for 1909 were written by women. Mrs. Kingsmill Marrs, chairman of the Florida Audubon Society's executive committee, believed women by themselves might save birds from feather hunters: "If women decided the aigrette was not to be worn, the aigrette would not be for sale." Katherine S. Wraight, Louisiana Audubon Society secretary, agreed with Dutcher that a strong effort should be made to reach farm children, but she favored nurturing an affection for birds rather than trying to teach them about birds and crops. She viewed the farmer as "a pretty skeptical old fellow, whom 'you can't fool with a cartload of statistics,' but who would be generous enough to make a free gift of a little fruit and grain to the birds his children have learned to love."[24]

The Audubon Society of North Carolina, surprisingly, grew during the year after its authority was curtailed. By March 1910, adult membership was 2,333; junior membership had risen more than 20 percent, from 900 to 1,100. Even with reduced receipts, the society supplied literature on birds in response to requests that came from "teachers and others in great numbers." Perhaps the legislative defeat had stirred interest and sympathy. So complicated were the game laws that the society could no longer afford to supply upon request copies of all the game laws in force. While reducing the society's jurisdiction, the legislature also enacted, by Pearson's count, eighty-three new local laws regulating game. Pearson compiled the laws applicable to the Audubon counties and distributed thousands of copies. The number of Audubon wardens declined to sixty-two during the year.[25]

For all practical purposes the experiment of using a private agency to enforce the state bird and game laws was almost over. Begun when the North Carolina legislature was unwilling to appropriate money to enforce the bird protection law, the effort had been well worthwhile. For six years, a strong educational program about the value of birds had reached every part of the state. Each warden had served as both field agent and law enforcement officer. Populations of birds had grown, especially of the seabirds that had been decimated. The model law was in place and could be enforced, on the coast at least, by National Association wardens. Moreover, the North Carolina Audubon Society had provided an impetus to the Audubon movement at a critical time and had given Pearson an opportunity to develop as the movement's one full-time executive, second only to Dutcher in status and rapidly becoming first in influence.

# 19

# New York

## (1909–1910)

NEW YORK WAS the center of the U.S. trade in wild bird feathers. Though state and national legislation, along with shifting sentiment among women, had greatly reduced use of feathers on hats, the business continued. Plumes, feathers, wings, and entire small bird bodies still came to market on the premise that the birds had been killed outside the state and could be legally sold. The agreement between milliners and Audubon societies had ended in 1906.

In December 1909, the National Association and the Audubon Society of the State of New York renewed efforts to persuade the legislature to prohibit sale of feathers of birds protected by law in the state, even if the birds were killed out of state. Dutcher arranged for Pearson to address the annual meeting of the New York Forest, Fish, and Game League at Syracuse, hoping his oratory could induce members to push the legislation. Pearson approached the subject obliquely, emphasizing game protection and the role of game wardens as teachers who could lecture on the "beauty of wild life and the importance of preserving it." The applause was so great that Dutcher announced that he would send Pearson to speak to sportsmen anywhere in the state. "At least twenty men," Pearson wrote later, immediately left their seats to ask for talks.[1]

206

From Syracuse, Dutcher and Pearson went to Albany to court State Game Commissioner James S. Whipple, who had opposed the Audubon feather bill at the last legislative session. Having criticized Whipple openly and intemperately, Dutcher now saw the need for diplomacy. He knew that Pearson and Whipple had in the past amicably delivered joint talks; so, in Albany, Pearson went alone to see Whipple. After raising objections, the commissioner finally conceded that the bill could be useful and agreed to support it—on the condition that Dutcher stay away from Albany. "The condition he imposes is very easy to comply with," Dutcher told Pearson with a smile.[2]

On the train back to New York, the two men decided that Dutcher would remain in the city, scheduling Pearson's lectures and mailing requests urging citizens to write their representatives, and Pearson would travel, speak, and lobby. Within the next few weeks, Pearson delivered fifteen lectures in fourteen cities and towns, including Ticonderoga, Henderson, Syracuse, and Newark. Local farmers and sportsmen assembled big audiences. Each meeting adopted resolutions favoring the feather bill. A lecture in Canton was arranged by Whipple, who shared the platform and spoke on forest preservation. "Our reception . . . was little short of an ovation," Pearson later recalled. In Watertown, he talked in the afternoon to children assembled by the school superintendent, who was also vice-president of the Jefferson County Sportsmen's Association, and again in the evening to adults. He showed slides, described ways in which humans destroyed birds, told stories from his personal experiences, and defended all species except House Sparrows as useful and worthy of preservation. "Mr. Pearson delivered his lecture in a most entertaining manner, making it impossible for the listener to lose any of it," wrote one news reporter.[3]

The prospect of lobbying New York legislators held "something terrifying," Pearson recalled. He feared they would be "particularly formidable," more "shrewd" and "resourceful" than legislators elsewhere. In the secretary of state's office, he uneasily registered as a lobbyist; no southern state had such a formality. He spent evenings with lobbyists and legislators in the Kenmore and Ten Eyck hotels, where he said nothing about the feather bill until he had developed friendships. When anecdotes were exchanged, he talked about human life in the South, rather than bird life, and found tales "in the dialect of Negro plantation hands" well received. He pretended to like beer, an "abomination." [4]

The feather bill was introduced in the senate on January 24, 1910; two days later it was introduced in the assembly by James Shea, whose name Pearson often applied to it thereafter. The bill prohibited killing most bird species in New York, as provided in the existing law, and forbade selling protected birds' feathers or feathers of any birds belonging to the same family as the protected species no matter where the birds were killed. Game bird feathers were exempted, as were feathers of other birds that could be legally killed: crows, "crow blackbirds" (grackles), hawks, kingfishers, House Sparrows, Snowy Owls (*Nyctea scandiaca*), and Great Horned Owls (*Bubo virginianus*). [5]

Advised to let the bill "rest for a time," Pearson attended to other business. In Richmond, he talked with the Virginia legislator's game committees about the state Audubon society's bills to protect robins and doves. Then he went to New Orleans to chair the fifth convention of the National Association of Game and Fish Wardens and Commissioners. In an address described as "very eloquent," he advocated increased protection for nongame birds and laws forbidding the sale of game birds. The convention elected him president, endorsed the National Association's work, and adopted a resolution favoring national laws to protect migratory birds and fish. "I spoke . . . yesterday and the Convention received my speech about like they did at Syracuse," Pearson wrote proudly to Dutcher. "From the enclosed clipping you will notice that they elected your lieutenant president for the coming year."

He would hold the presidency for two years. From New Orleans, Pearson went to Jackson, Mississippi, where the legislature was in session. Although the state Audubon society was small and weak, a comprehensive bill for bird and game protection had been introduced that included establishing a state game commission. Several changes suggested by Pearson were made in the bill, and Governor Edmund F. Noel assured him he would support it. Nonetheless, the bill failed.[6]

After attending to Audubon Society business in Greensboro for a week, Pearson resumed lobbying in Albany. Legislators were receiving citizen letters solicited by Dutcher, and twice Pearson wrote to all members of both houses. Early in March, he sent them each a bound set of National Association leaflets. In a notebook he recorded the views of legislators and of other persons of influence: among those who approved of the feather bill were Assembly Speaker James W. Wadsworth, Jr., and Franklin D. Roosevelt, who studied birds and who later in the year was elected to the senate, where he was appointed chairman of the forest, fish, and game committee. Governor Charles Evans Hughes declined to comment on the bill, maintaining he should not pass judgment until the legislature had made a decision.[7]

Attorneys for the Eastern Millinery Association and the Feather Importers' Association, along with several independent milliners, lobbied against the feather bill. At a forest, fish, and game committee hearing on March 9, they offered what seemed to Pearson to be strong though fallacious arguments: egrets and other herons were harmful birds undeserving of protection, John James Audubon had shown no disapproval of egret killing, and the trade in egret plumes was important to the economy. Even if egrets ought to be protected, the milliners said, the feather bill was unnecessary: the birds were not killed in the plume gathering because the plumes were picked up from the ground only after the birds had shed them. Pearson, Dutcher, a National Association attorney, another attorney representing two independently interested women, and a Camp Fire Club of America representative testified in the bill's behalf. In the three-hour hearing, Dutcher wrote to a friend, the "temperature was very hot."[8] Apparently neither Pearson nor Dutcher had expected to hear again the falsehood that egret plumes were gathered from the ground. Plumes shed by the birds were too old to be marketable except at very low prices; only the freshly grown plumes were pretty enough to command the high prices making the plume business profitable.

During the two weeks that Pearson and Dutcher waited for the forest, fish, and game committee to act, the legislative committee of the Republican League of Clubs of New York State endorsed the feather bill and asked all Republicans in the legislature to support it. On March 23, the assembly committee reported the bill favorably to the floor. Three days later, an oddly critical editorial entitled "Piffling Legislation" appeared in the *New York Times*, written by someone who was apparently familiar with only part of the bill. "It is not proposed to stop the killing of wild game birds for the markets. But the feathers of those birds must not be sold. The law prohibits the sale, but neglects to indicate any other way to dispose of the feathers." Except for the author's ignorance of the bill's provision exempting game bird feathers, the editorial was a strong statement in the milliners' behalf. Copies were sent by the Feather Importers' Association to all the legislators, some of whom may have reacted negatively to the editorial's distortions. The bill passed the assembly by a vote of 108 to 15. At hearings held by the senate committee on forest, fish, and game laws, Pearson rebutted the assertion that feather hunters picked up egret plumes from the ground by exhibiting plumes still attached to skin stripped from egret backs. The feather bill was reported favorably to the senate and approved there by a large vote on April 21, 1910.[9]

On the assumption that Governor Hughes would soon sign the bill, Dutcher suggested Pearson return to North Carolina for a "little rest" before he would be needed in New York again. Dutcher had made plans to attend an ornithological congress in Berlin and would be away from New York for several weeks. During his absence, Pearson would administer the National Association from the New York office. Pearson had been in Greensboro long enough to prepare for a field trip to the coast with H. H. Brimley when a telegram came from Dutcher. Governor Hughes had granted the milliners a hearing on the feather bill, and Pearson's services were needed. In Albany, more witnesses volunteered to testify in the bill's behalf than could be accepted. During the hearing on May 3, Pearson "searched the face of Governor Hughes," trying without success to determine how he was responding to the testimony. The governor "neither smiled nor frowned, nor did he show that he was pleased or displeased at anything that was said." [10]

Four days later, Hughes signed the feather bill and it became law, to take effect on July 1, 1911. Many advocates of the law, Pearson later wrote, regarded it as having "sounded the death-knell of the wild-bird feather business throughout the civilized world." He credited Dutcher with responsibility for "all that took place in winning the struggle" and characterized his own role as that of Dutcher's "field marshal." In a report in *Bird-Lore*, he acknowledged the importance of help from Game Commissioner Whipple, the "Audubon Society of New York State, the Camp Fire Club of America, representatives of many game protective clubs, and hundreds of individuals working privately." [11]

A similar bill, much less significant in potential influence, was introduced in the New Jersey legislature. "Before its enemies realized its character," wrote the New Jersey Audubon Society secretary, the assembly approved it. When it reached committee in the senate, milliners expressed their opposition and the bill was held there. Dutcher and National Association chief clerk Beecher S. Bowdish went to Trenton to try to find a way "to force the bill on to the floor." Just before dawn on April 7, 1910, in the senate's closing hours, the bill was called out, voted upon, and rejected. The rejection was attributed by the Audubon Society secretary to "a total misunderstanding on the part of the Senators regarding its real character" and "a lack of organized public sentiment." Embarrassed by having been of slight help to the National Association in lobbying for the bill, the Audubon Society's officers made plans to reorganize and become a "banner organization." [12]

At last Pearson escaped to the North Carolina coast for a five-day outing with Brimley. They camped on "an almost uninhabited peninsula, the northern tip of which forms the right bank of the inlet at the mouth of the Cape Fear River." Pearson made notes; Brimley carried a gun in order to hunt or collect specimens for the state museum but seldom used it. At dusk, the two men sat on the crest of the dunes, looking toward the sea and watching birds. They rarely talked. "Human speech seemed a sort of desecration in these surroundings." They broke camp reluctantly, Brimley to return to Raleigh, Pearson to Greensboro and then to New York to substitute for Dutcher, who sailed for Europe on May 17. [13]

In New York Pearson asked Mrs. Russell Sage to help finance an educational campaign for laws prohibiting the hunting of American Robins, which were still being legally killed by the thousands in several southern states, including North Carolina. Mrs. Sage had inherited about seventy million dollars from her financier husband, who had died in 1906. Author of "Opportunities and Responsibilities of Leisured Women" in the *North American Review,* she had by 1910 spent millions on philanthropic causes and established the Russell Sage Foundation to improve American social and living conditions. Seemingly sympathetic toward all neglected or mistreated beings, she had been a life member of the National Association since its first year of existence. [14]

Toward the end of May, Mrs. Sage sent Pearson a check for five hundred dollars to help open a campaign. He wrote an educational leaflet and engaged an artist to paint a picture of an American Robin singing among apple blossoms. "It is good to watch the Robins when a touch of autumn is in the air and the *Wander-Lust* is strong upon them. On rapidly beating wings they drive swiftly across the fields, or pause on the topmost spray of a roadside tree and look eagerly away to the southward. Their calls are sharp and inquisitive. Clearly the unsuppressed excitement of starting on a long journey pervades their nature." The pamphlet was immensely popular. More than five million copies were eventually distributed.[15]

After the robin campaign was under way, Pearson asked Mrs. Sage to help with an enlarged program of education in the South, particularly among children. Robert W. de Forest, Russell Sage Foundation president, questioned him about the National Association. Afterward, Pearson recorded the essence of de Forest's comments: "You have made the impression upon me that I hoped you would and I am authorized by Mrs. Russell Sage to say that she will give to the Audubon Association $5,000 a year for three years to be used for your educational work in the South." Pearson wrote at once to Palmer, who was "delighted" and who favored immediately making specific plans for using the money so that Mrs. Sage and de Forest could be reassured as to the gift's importance.[16]

The decision was made to use much of the money to encourage public school teachers in the South to form junior Audubon societies. Participating teachers would organize classes of ten or more students, each of whom would pay an annual fee of ten cents. The teachers would report to Pearson in Greensboro, who would send them, for each pupil, leaflets, colored pictures of birds, outline drawings for coloring, and an Audubon button bearing the picture of a mockingbird. Every participating teacher would receive a free subscription to *Bird-Lore* and give at least one lesson a month on birds. Pearson later characterized Mrs. Sage's gift as a "momentous event" that supported the "beginning of a phase of the Association's work which in time was to enrich the thought of many millions of children throughout the United States and Canada, and greatly hasten the development of the public mind in favor of wild-life preservation."[17] Nonetheless, it was not a new phase of work. He had for several years solicited junior memberships in the National Association, and junior programs had long been common among the state societies, including the one in North Carolina.

Late in June at the Summer School of the South, Pearson urged the teachers and local residents who came to his classes, bird walks, and public lectures to form junior Audubon societies and lobby for laws protecting robins. The Tennessee Audubon Society founded in 1899 had died, but during the four months following Pearson's summer visit, residents of Knoxville established the East Tennessee Audubon Society and, with the aid of Sage Fund money, organized junior societies. The West Tennessee Audubon Society was founded in Memphis; during the next year, eighteen hundred school pupils enrolled in junior societies, the city park commission established a bird refuge in Overton Park with bird feeders and shrubbery for nesting, and the Goodwyn Institute sponsored lectures.[18]

Pearson went from Knoxville to Atlanta. He understood the vulnerability of a private organization functioning as a public regulatory agency but apparently believed no other way was open in Georgia, and he had again arranged for his bill making the Georgia Audubon Society the state game commission to be introduced in the legislature. The need seemed particularly great. "Here Robins are probably shot as extensively as in any other single section of the South; it is here that the famous 'Dove shoots' take place, sometimes resulting in the slaughter of thousands of Doves in a day in a single field. It is in Georgia that the trappers of live birds for market have their last strongholds." Again the bill was defeated. "The milliners of the State had joined with the market-hunters."[19]

Dutcher returned from the Fifth International Ornithological Congress in Berlin, the only American delegate to attend. Representing the National Association, AOU, Smithsonian Institution, and U.S. State Department, he had delivered a paper on the Audubon movement's history and another on the necessity for international cooperation in bird protection. "America cannot protect her own birds if the countries of the Old World offer a market for the plumage of American birds, as they are doing now." There was also trade in the other direction. Every year thousands of songbirds were shipped from Europe to America to be kept in cages; equally large numbers of European game birds were annually eaten in fashionable American hotels and restaurants. At the congress, an international committee for bird protection was appointed and resolutions were adopted calling upon the nations represented to prohibit traffic in bird feathers except for scientific purposes. Dutcher warned that the committee must "not sleep," but it never functioned, perhaps because he became too ill to stimulate it.[20]

Dutcher's declining health generated solicitude among the National Association's leaders. While he was in Europe, William W. Grant, who was soon thereafter placed on the board of directors, suggested that a small fund be raised to help defray Dutcher's expenses and allow him "entertainment." Pearson welcomed the suggestion but said he believed Dutcher would prefer that the money be set aside for bird protection rather than for his own pleasure. The decision was made to create a bird protection fund as a memorial to Dutcher's daughter, Mary, who had often helped her father without compensation in the National Association's work and who had died of tuberculosis in January 1909. Solicitations quickly brought in almost seven thousand dollars. At a special luncheon in New York, the Mary Dutcher Memorial Fund was presented to Dutcher as an endowment for the National Association.[21]

Pearson did not appear on the program at the Second National

Conservation Congress, which met in St. Paul, Minnesota, in September 1910, and no one who did appear showed any interest in wild creatures. Although Pearson represented the National Association, he was registered under the congress's rules as a delegate from North Carolina. The state's only delegate, he was appointed to the resolutions committee, which at his instigation included in its report the simple but important statement: "We recommend that the Federal Government conserve migratory birds and wild game animals." Evening lectures on natural history by Frank Chapman and artist Radclyffe Dugmore, not part of the formal program, were omitted in the published proceedings. Anyone who depended upon the proceedings for information about the congress would not have readily discerned that the National Association had participated in any way. The League of American Sportsmen fared a little better by getting into the proceedings a report recommending objectives it shared with the association: protection of migratory birds by the national government, additional national wildlife refuges, and uniform state laws enforced by state wardens.[22]

Reporting on the congress in *Bird-Lore*, Pearson wrote with goodwill and reassurance that the participants "gave due consideration to the question of wild-bird and animal protection." Years later, however, after attending several congresses of the National Conservation Association, he was more candid: "We were disappointed in the lack of interest exhibited in birds and mammals at these Congresses. . . . Contending with us for recognition . . . were many who had pet theories of government, and others who were representatives of large business interests. They were always on hand and exhibited amazing ability in securing assignments for the best places on the programs." The "fortunes of wild birds and wild mammals" were considered by most persons at the congresses to be "of slight importance." Even in North Carolina, despite Pearson's efforts to convince people of birds' value to agriculture,

State Geologist Joseph Hyde Pratt excluded all wildlife other than fish from his definition of "natural resources."[23]

From St. Paul, Pearson went to Canada to stimulate interest in international cooperation for migratory bird protection. In Manitoba and Ontario he talked with public officials and other persons known to be concerned about birds. Because of the high commercial value of ducks and geese, he emphasized those species, pointing out that some of them nested in Canada but wintered in the United States, Central America, and South America. The governments of the countries over which the birds ranged should "legislate cooperatively," he maintained.[24]

He returned to Greensboro in time to be with Elsie for the birth of their third and last child, who followed Elizabeth and Thomas Gilbert, Jr. "Early last night the stork visited our home and left us with a fine boy of 9½ pounds," Pearson wrote to Palmer on October 15, 1910. "We are very fond of him already, and having high hopes for his usefulness in life we have named him William Theodore Pearson—have named him for the two men whose kindness and inspiration have meant so much to his father,— William Dutcher and Theodore S. Palmer." A similar letter went to Dutcher. Palmer replied he hoped the boy would inherit "his mother's grace of manner" and "his father's happy disposition."[25]

A "beautiful letter" of acknowledgement, Pearson later recalled, came from Dutcher. It was the last letter Pearson received from him. On October 19, Dutcher had a stroke from which he never recovered. He was sixty-four. Although he lived ten more years, he did not regain the power to speak or to write anything other than his name. Prior to the stroke, the strains and tensions of his life had steadily mounted. After his daughter's death, a sister died. The trip to Europe may have added stress. In September, he wrote to Pearson that he was "broken up with a bad cold" and that his wife had "broken down nervously" and had "gone away for a rest." He still struggled to carry on his insurance business by day and administer the National Association by night. There was rarely time for field studies that might have helped to keep his body strong. His problems were compounded by occasional sharp scoldings from other National Association board members who resented his autocratic and sometimes erratic manner of administration. At the time of his stroke, Pearson wrote later, Dutcher "felt much hurt by criticism of his management."[26]

# 20

# When Wildlife
# Protectors Quarrel

## *(1910–1911)*

PEARSON WENT TO New York on October 20, not knowing until he arrived that Dutcher had suffered a stroke the day before. "Thus ended the work of one who deeply loved his fellow-men as well as the birds; whose smile came from a heart overflowing with kindness and whose honesty of purpose, tolerance and unselfishness made of his life at once an inspiration and a benediction," he wrote later. Pearson immediately took charge of the National Association office; on January 4, 1911, the board of directors formally gave him executive officer status.[1]

The National Association was, in his words, "the one sizable organization" in the United States "devoting its entire energies to the field of wild-life preservation." Its staff was growing, its activities expanding. Whereas Dutcher had worked at the office largely at night, Pearson was there all day, sharing a small area with clerks, files, and stacks of publications. He found two rooms on the corner of Broadway and 67th Street, near subway and elevated railway stops, that offered more space at no additional cost. In April, the association moved from 141 Broadway to 1974 Broadway.[2]

Outside the office, Pearson felt estranged in New York. "How lonely a stranger can be in a great city, I was to learn in full measure." He lived in a hotel for fourteen months, during which, as best he could remember later, he was a guest in only two homes. "Most of the people I met entertained on a scale that I could not afford to repay in kind, so I sought to avoid rather than to welcome their hospitality, and buried myself in work." He went to the office early and stayed late. In his room at night, he read, wrote newspaper articles, and composed letters. Sometimes for exercise he "wandered down Broadway to 42nd street or on to 33rd." Generally the people he saw "seemed to be pleasure bent." They "poured in and out" of theaters and gathered in cafes and cabarets. When on rare occasions he went into one of "these places of amusement," he experienced a "feeling of depression and loneliness." He was never able to adjust to that part of New York life. Even after he had lived in the city for more than twenty-five years, he still shunned "The Great White Way." [3]

At intervals, he returned to Elsie and the Audubon Society of North Carolina. There seemed to be little likelihood the society could ever regain statewide jurisdiction. The system that was succeeding in other states, which in several instances Pearson had helped establish, consisted of a totally public agency financed by the sale of licenses to all hunters. Instead of asking the legislature of 1911 to restore full jurisdiction to the Audubon Society, he wrote a bill creating a game commission administered by the state and supported by the sale of licenses to all hunters and fishermen. He engaged the services of Aycock and Winston, the Raleigh law firm of Audubon Society Vice-President Charles B. Aycock. For day-to-day lobbying, Pearson employed Milford W. Haynes, a former warden, who worked in Raleigh for three-and-a-half months. [4]

Representative John H. Dillard of Cherokee County introduced the bill. Although Governor Kitchin "spoke very favorably" of it privately to Haynes, in his biennial message he merely com-

mended it to the legislators' "careful consideration." Haynes and
Aycock compiled a list of men they wanted on the house game
committee. After Aycock submitted the list to the speaker and the
committee membership was announced, Haynes reported to Pearson that he was "quite sure" the committee would approve the
Audubon bill. It did, but by the time the bill was called up for a
floor vote, several game committee members had decided to vote
against it, having heard from constituents who objected to buying
licenses to hunt and fish. It was rejected 60 to 28. North Carolina
continued to have more local variations in hunting regulations than
any other state. "It is practically impossible for any man to become
thoroughly familiar with the Game Laws of North Carolina,"
Pearson had written before the 1911 legislature met.[5] By session's
end, the laws were more complex than ever.

In South Carolina, the unsolved Audubon warden's murder in
1908 apparently convinced the society that it was inadequate for
the task it had undertaken, even though in an unrelated case,
Arthur Lambert, notorious poacher and plume hunter, was caught
and convicted. A bill similar to laws already adopted in Alabama
and in several states outside the South was drafted to establish a
state warden system separate from the society and supported by
license sales to all hunters. In 1910 the legislature created the
position of chief game warden and imposed a nonresident hunting
license requirement. Audubon Secretary James H. Rice was appointed chief warden. With no money to employ a staff, Rice could
do little to enforce laws protecting birds. Egret rookeries on the
coast were plundered by plume hunters, he reported, and no one
was arrested. In 1911, Pearson employed National Association
wardens on the South Carolina coast. Only four egrets were
known to have been killed during that summer. "All the Egret
colonies did well, and there will be a noticeable increase next
season of our slender stock of these fine birds," Rice reported.[6]

In Oregon and California as well as in South Carolina, Audubon leaders moved into government service as game protection was accepted as a state responsibility. William L. Finley, the National Association's West Coast representative, became Oregon's game warden. Gretchen L. Libby, California Audubon Society school secretary, was added to the State Board of Fish and Game Commissioners' staff.[7]

Pearson abandoned his plan for an Audubon warden system in Georgia and drafted a bill providing for a state system financed by license sales to all hunters. When the bill was adopted in 1911, he was elated. "This is the end of a five years campaign on our part and this splendid news has given me a glow which will last for many days," he wrote to Richard H. Lewis.[8]

Before the Shea plumage act could take effect in New York, the millinery industry sponsored a bill to repeal it. Introduced in the assembly by A. J. Levy of New York City, the bill seemed to Pearson to go beyond simple repeal of the Shea Act; it could possibly "open the way for the sale of the plumage of all birds." A "long and spirited" hearing was held on April 26, 1911, by the assembly committee on forest, fish, and game, chaired by Franklin D. Roosevelt. Once again the milliners claimed that egret and heron feathers were gathered from the ground; again the National Association and cooperating organizations maintained that most feathers on the market came from slaughtered birds. When the milliners offered testimony from a Frenchman who had employed Venezuelan natives to collect feathers from the ground, Pearson countered with testimony from a New York resident who for five years had bought feathers from Venezuelans whose custom it was "to shoot the birds while the young are in the nest." Roosevelt's committee reserved judgment and passed the bill to the rules committee, which in turn surrendered it to the assembly floor, where it was rejected.[9]

A continuing concern had been that the New York millinery industry, if it failed to have the Shea Act repealed, would move across the river to New Jersey, where the Audubon plumage bill had been rejected by the legislature in 1910. Such a move was blocked when the reorganized New Jersey Audubon Society sponsored the bill again, this time successfully. It became law on April 18, 1911.[10]

Another part of the bird market was closed in New York by Senator Howard R. Bayne's bill prohibiting the sale of game, including game birds. Pearson had failed to persuade the North Carolina legislators to adopt such a bill, but by 1911, according to his count, nineteen legislatures had done so. He later credited George Bird Grinnell with having appealed generally for no-sale-of-game laws and William T. Hornaday, director of the New York Zoological Society's Zoological Park, as "largely responsible" for the Bayne bill's introduction.[11] "At first the no-sale-of-game bill looked like sheer madness," Hornaday wrote, "but no sooner was it fairly launched than supporters came flocking from every side. All the organizations of sportsmen and friends of wild life combined in one mighty army, the strength of which was irresistible." With amendments permitting the sale of game raised in captivity, the Bayne bill was passed. Pearson stated in *Bird-Lore* that its enactment should mean "the immense shipments of Quail and Wild Duck which have hitherto been made from the southern states to New York City must now be discontinued."[12]

While wildlife protectors were harmoniously lobbying legislators, one of Pearson's money-raising efforts led to a divisive quarrel. Upon request, he met in May with Winchester Repeating Arms Company representatives led by Second Vice-president Harry S. Leonard to hear their proposal for organizing a strong national game-protection association. Sales of guns and ammunition to hunters accounted for much of the company's business, they explained; a continuous supply of game species was important. Pearson was asked how much money would be required to found a new organization. On the basis of his National Association experience, he offered an estimate of $25,000 a year for at least five years and suggested participation by several companies. Invited to head the new association, he countered by recommending the money be given to the National Association. Later on the same day, Leonard wrote to Pearson, saying the $25,000 Pearson had recommended could be raised, again inviting him to head the new organization, and expressing the sponsors' willingness, if Pearson declined the invitation, to donate the money to the National Association for a game protection program, on condition that Pearson administer it. "As we told you, we have looked the situation over very thoroughly and decided, for ourselves at least, that you were the one who could best handle an organization of this kind and make it productive of results." The National Association would be expected to provide Pearson with an "adequate salary, this to be not less than $6,000 a year."[13]

Pearson appears not to have anticipated hostile reactions to the proposal. He was following what seemed to him a logical and desirable course. His Audubon career had been spent associating with hunters to protect game almost as much as working with bird lovers to save nongame species. Dutcher, a hunter, had praised and encouraged him; the North Carolina Audubon Society, a game commission, had been regarded a model. The National Association had accepted Willcox's large gift with the requirement it would protect "wild birds and animals," including game. All the association's agents worked closely with hunters for state laws regulating, not prohibiting, the taking of game. Money was solicited wherever it could be obtained. When the U.S. Cartridge Company helped Pearson raise money for the National Association in Boston, no protest erupted in the organization. Although large corporate donations to philanthropic causes were not yet common, gifts from wealthy businessmen and corporate executives were.

The points to which Pearson perhaps should have been sensitive were the gun manufacturers' stipulations that he administer the funds and that his salary be increased to $6,000. Such stipulations seemed reasonable to him, showing the manufacturers' faith in his ability and their willingness to pay him fairly. The proposed salary was roughly equal to what he already made working part-time for the National Association and part-time for the North Carolina Audubon Society. For the year ending October 1910, he had received almost $4,500 in salary and expenses from the National Association. Although the Audubon Society treasurer's report for the year ending March 1911 has not been located, the report for the previous year—the first year of reduced jurisdiction—shows that he received approximately $2,100 in compensation, including expenses. On that basis, his total annual income amounted to more than $6,000.[14] If he resigned from the Audubon Society to devote full time to the National Association, he hoped to do so without making a financial sacrifice.

Yet what seemed appropriate to him stirred resentment and jealousy in some quarters. Just as some North Carolinians in 1909 had not understood his role in the National Association, in 1911 some wildlife protection leaders, including two National Association board members, seemed unaware of his continuing work in North Carolina. Board members might also have resisted the stipulation that they must keep Pearson as their executive officer. In addition, jealousies might have arisen outside the association.

Pearson reported the offer to the advisory committee of the National Association's board of directors, saying that he would stay with the organization and recommending that the gun manufacturers' offer of money be accepted. The committee in turn recommended acceptance to the full board of directors. In a second letter to Pearson, Leonard assured him that the manufacturers would impose no further conditions. "The Association . . . will be absolutely free at all times to administer the work of game protection in such manner as the Association may deem most advisable and in the best interests of the conservation of the wild life of the country."[15]

No decision was reached at a board meeting on May 20; on June 2, a majority voted to accept the offer. By that time six men— William W. Grant, Jonathan Dwight, Gifford Pinchot, Andrew D. Meloy, George O. Shields, and William T. Hornaday—had united to try to prevent the gift from being accepted. They were an unlikely group to oppose a majority of the board of directors, most of whom were founding members. Only two of the six, Grant and Dwight, were board members. Pinchot was an advisory director but not a dues-paying member of the association. Meloy, an association life member since 1910, owed his primary allegiance to another organization, the New York State Fish, Game and Forest League, of which he was president. Neither Hornaday nor Shields had ever belonged to the National Association and each headed a competing effort: Hornaday had established his own wildlife protection fund and Shields presided over the League of American Sportsmen, which was dying for lack of money.

Grant believed the gun manufacturers to be "sincere and solicitous" but feared that the National Association's image would be tarnished by the gift; he favored establishing a "commission" to accept the gift and convey it to the National Association. Dwight, suspicious of the gun manufacturers' motives, apparently without knowing exactly why, was concerned about the "row these subscribers could kick up if they did not get what they would expect"; moreover, as the National Association's treasurer, he considered Pearson and the rest of the staff "overpaid" already and preferred to "see them all go rather than raise salaries." Pinchot warned Pearson that the National Association could become dependent on the annual gift and be tempted to modify its policies to persuade the donors to continue contributing. "It is not the active dictation of the contributor which is to be feared, but the quiet shaping of actions and policies which follows from the fears that the contribution may perhaps be discontinued."[16]

At the June 2 meeting, the National Association board decided to keep its favorable vote confidential until a written statement had been submitted to all board members and approved. Apparently alerted by Grant and Dwight, Meloy and Shields broke the story to a *New York Times* reporter. They ignored the gun manufacturers' principal objective, to obtain Pearson's services as administrator of a game protection effort. They ignored the group's willingness to give the money for game protection to the National Association only because Pearson, declining to abandon the association, assured them it could carry out an effective game protection program. As Meloy and Shields told the story, the manufacturers had offered the National Association a bribe, and the board had agreed to accept it. The manufacturers' purpose, according to Meloy and Shields, was to buy the National Association's silence on the issue of whether automatic guns, or pump guns, should be permitted in hunting. Meloy went still further. Pearson, he charged, had persuaded the National Association board to accept the manufacturers' money in order to get a pay raise.[17] Nothing has been located in the records to support any of those assertions.

On the evening of June 2, Pearson, Grinnell, Allen, Brewster, and National Association attorney Samuel T. Carter learned that the board's confidentiality had been violated and that interviews with Meloy and Shields would appear in the *New York Times* the following morning. As second vice-president and acting president, Allen signed a statement summarizing the board's position: the gun manufacturers had an understandable interest in protecting game; in offering the contribution they asked only that it be spent for game protection and that Pearson direct the spending; the "policy of the association" would be "unchanged" and its "field of influence" would be "greatly extended." The National Association had never opposed the use of automatic guns in hunting and the gun manufacturers would not be buying any service, the *New York Times* reporter covering the story was told. Furthermore, Pearson's salary was going to be raised anyhow, gift or not, because of his increased duties.[18]

The *New York Herald* as well as the *Times* carried articles about the controversy. Pearson clipped them and sent them to Palmer, explaining, insofar as he could, what had happened. "I understand that our friends, the opposition, made an effort to get the story in all the eight morning dailys. These are the only two that carried them." Brewster and Carter, "very much exercised" because some board members had apparently told Meloy and Shields about the board's actions, suggested that Pearson seek Palmer's advice. "Both of these gentlemen asked me to lay the matter before you and to ask whether it was not in your opinion wise to determine who, if any one, was guilty of the breach of faith."[19]

Without waiting for Palmer's answer, Pearson went by train to see him. They agreed that Pearson, for his own part, should reject the gun manufacturers' offer. Apparently they also decided not to attempt to expose the board member or members who had collaborated with Meloy and Shields. Pearson wrote to Leonard the following day, having concluded that he must reject the offer to administer the funds, not because the plan was in itself undesirable but because "the matter could be construed and very likely would be construed by the public in a way to be of very great detriment to the work of the Association."[20]

Pearson's decision did not commit the board as a whole; another meeting was scheduled for June 16. In the interim, Pinchot telegraphed Pearson, Allen, and Grinnell that he would resign as advisory director and publicize his resignation if the gun manufacturers' gift were accepted. Meloy wrote to Mrs. Dutcher. Apparently neither Pearson nor any other board member had attempted to ascertain what Dutcher's view of the proposal might be. Still paralyzed, Dutcher was unable to speak or write. Although Mrs. Dutcher believed his mind was "clear," the board members had not regarded him as sufficiently competent to understand the issue or to have an opinion meriting consideration. Meloy apparently wrote to Mrs. Dutcher along the same lines that he followed in his press statement, accusing Pearson of persuading the board to accept a bribe to get a pay raise. When Mrs. Dutcher read Meloy's letter to her husband, he exhibited a "strong feeling against anything savoring of bribery," she reported to Meloy, and "was most emphatic in his evidence of his disapproval." She also accused Pearson, on her husband's behalf, of taking "advantage of his helplessness." "I am greatly disappointed in your friendship for Mr. Dutcher," she added, "and now look upon you as one of his greatest enemies, inasmuch as you have taken the opportunity of doing him the greatest injury."

Concerned that her letter might be intemperate and unfair, she sent it not to Pearson but with her letter to Meloy, whose motives and veracity she apparently did not question. "If you think me too severe, return the letter and I will destroy it." She did not know how her husband felt about her letter to Pearson. "I tried to read this to Mr. Dutcher," she wrote to Meloy, "to know if it meets his approval, but I had to give it up, as it is too much for me and only grieves Mr. Dutcher to see me troubled. . . . I wonder more of Mr. Dutcher's friends do not come to see him? It means a very bright spot in his very monotonous life."[21]

Copies of Mrs. Dutcher's letters were circulated among the disputants. "If the action of the Board is satisfactory to Mr. Dutcher's friends, and the real friends of the organization," Hornaday wrote to Pinchot, "these letters will not be published; but if the action is open to suspicion, they will be published." Grinnell, the strongest advocate of accepting the proposal, remained unchanged in his views. He politely acknowledged Pinchot's telegram threatening to resign as advisory director and did not attempt to dissuade him. Characterizing newspaper criticisms of the National Association as the "vaporings of young reporters who are anxious to make a sensational story," he quoted an "old and conservative newspaper," the Philadelphia *Evening Bulletin*: "The members of the Audubon Society should restrain their indignation, hold their peace, and proceed to make good use of the money which is tendered to them."[22]

Although advisory directors did not ordinarily attend board meetings, Meloy and Hornaday urged Pinchot to go to the June 16 meeting. When the board met at 1:30 P.M. at the American Museum of Natural History, Pinchot was there. It was clear to regular board members that he, Meloy, and Hornaday were determined to cause further embarrassment if the gun manufacturers' offer were accepted. Frank Chapman, an original board member, had returned to New York on the previous day from a South American expedition and was also present. "Welcome home again!" Pearson had written. "I regret to trouble you with an unpleasant matter the instant you land." Pearson described the problem briefly, said he would show Chapman "the correspondence in the matter," and told him about the scheduled meeting. "Some members who voted to accept the gift" at the June 2 meeting had decided it should be rejected, "to save the good name and usefulness of the Association," Pearson added. "The situation is somewhat tense and I hope you will withhold judgment until the full facts can be placed before you." After talking with Pearson, Chapman agreed that the gun manufacturers' offer should be declined. The National Association had been organized primarily for the protection of song and insectivorous birds, he argued at the meeting; accepting the gift might cause it to give priority to the protection of game birds. "Clubs for the protection of the birds ranked as game abound, but the Audubon Society is practically the only organization effectively engaged in the protection of non-game birds," he explained a month later to readers of *Bird-Lore*.[23]

When the vote was taken, Pinchot noted cryptically in his diary, "George B. Grinnell and Mrs. _____ [apparently he could not remember Wright's name at the moment and never went back to fill in the blank space] voted to keep it [the proposed gift], all the others against. I spoke against." Like the men on the board, Wright was comfortable with hunting, hunters, and businesses providing guns and ammunition. To James S. Whipple's statement that the National Association was "against all killing of birds and animals," she had replied, "This is all tommy-rot, we believe in the proper taking of food birds, commonly called game birds, at the proper season & under proper circumstances." Grinnell was annoyed by the board's action. "Of course Hornaday and his friends have won a triumph." After the meeting, Pearson issued a statement to the press announcing that the gun manufacturers' proposed gift had been rejected. On the following morning he sent Palmer clippings from four New York newspapers. "It may be possible you have not seen all of these," he wrote. "The World seems very calm this morning!"[24]

Had the National Association accepted the gun manufacturers' money without disruptive dissension, Pearson could have put the money to good use. The first year's gift of $25,000 would have increased the organization's income in 1911 by two-thirds and financed more field agents, more publications, and more lobbying for protective state laws. In terms of immediate publicity, there were advantages in rejecting the offer. "The idea that any board of directors should fail to accept a gift of $125,000," Pearson wrote later, "was such an unusual news-item that the story of our declining the offer must have been printed in virtually every paper in the United States and Canada, and the commendations we received were numerous."[25]

Although Meloy believed that the controversy had inflicted wounds that might take a "long time to heal," the matter was apparently set quickly aside, at least for the time being. Only Meloy himself seems to have become sufficiently excited to anticipate bearing resentments into the future. Only he had publicly shown personal animosity, attributing the controversy to Pearson's "ambitions." Hornaday's opinion of Pearson's behavior was almost diametrically opposed to Meloy's. In a letter to Pinchot, Hornaday characterized Pearson as "weak," "lacking in initiative," and submissive to the will of other persons on the board of directors, although during the course of the controversy Pearson and Hornaday cooperated in persuading the New York legislature to reject the Levy bill and pass the Bayne bill. (Fifteen years later, Hornaday would supply information about the 1911 controversy to new Pearson adversaries.) Pearson remained friends with Shields, of whom he later wrote, "To him, more than to any other man, is due the credit of arousing public sentiment against the excessive killing of game. . . . " Pinchot continued as a National Association advisory director, accepting Pearson's invitation to hold office for another term "with great pleasure." By September, and possibly before, Mrs. Dutcher had renewed her friendship with Pearson. "Mrs. Dutcher has just written, asking me to come out to visit them," Pearson wrote to Palmer. "She seems to think it will cheer Mr. Dutcher, and I shall probably go in a few days."[26]

Once more the gun manufacturers invited Pearson to leave the National Association to found a new game protection organization. Again he declined. The offer was then extended to John B. Burnham, deputy commissioner of fish and game of the state of New York. The American Game Protective and Propagation Association (later the American Game Protective Association and now the Wildlife Management Institute) was organized in September 1911, with Burnham as president. Several Audubon founders and leaders, including Grinnell, Merriam, Brewster, and John Thayer (but not Pearson), along with nature writer and poet John Burroughs, a hunter, were listed as "Honorary and Associate Members" of the board of directors. The new organization adopted many National Association objectives, including protection of insectivorous birds, more wildlife refuges, bag limits, uniform game laws, and prohibition of the sale of wild native game.[27]

# 21

# In New York to Stay

## *(1911)*

ON JUNE 22, 1911, six days after the National Association board meeting in New York, Pearson resigned as North Carolina Audubon Society secretary. P. D. Gold, Jr., of Raleigh, chairman of the society's board of directors, accepted the secretary's position after Pearson assured him that the work could be done "without any great annoyance or labor." Headquarters were moved to Raleigh and ceased to function as the National Association southern office. Gold referred questions about bird life to Pearson and sent him Warden Jennett's reports on the seabird colonies for interpretation, saying the reports were "all dutch" to him. Pearson wrote the society's brief annual report for *Bird-Lore* at year's end in Gold's name.[1]

Although the society was slowly dying, it employed thirty-five wardens and won more than sixty convictions in the courts during 1911. Pearson provided $200 from the National Association treasury to help pay the costs of employing Jennett and operating the launch *Dovekie*. The seabird colonies "thrived" during the spring and summer and almost eleven thousand young terns, gulls, and skimmers were raised in the colonies Jennett guarded. The Least Terns raised 1,592 young, nearly one hundred times the sixteen raised in 1903, the first year of the Audubon Society's work, to become "by far the largest nesting group of these birds on the Atlantic Coast of the United States." The seven Sandwich Terns raised in 1911 were the only young of that species raised during that season on the entire U.S. east coast, insofar as Pearson could determine.[2]

Pearson intended to keep his family in Greensboro, probably for his children's sake. "I expect to continue to live in North Carolina and will hope to have the pleasure of seeing you from time to time," he wrote to Governor Kitchin. He and the Brimleys worked on the North Carolina bird book, for which the North Carolina Audubon Society board of directors appropriated $1,200 for paintings and drawings by Rex Brasher and Bruce Horsfall. From New York in September, Pearson reported to H. H. Brimley that Horsfall had spent a half day with him and another half day in the American Museum of Natural History "working on our pictures." Horsfall's painting of a Fox Sparrow (*Passerella iliaca*) and a White-throated Sparrow together were "particularly pleasing," and the disappointing Wood Duck portrait was not surprising. "I have never yet seen an artist who could make a picture of the Wood Duck that will convey to your mind half the beauty which one sees 'gazing on the matchless beauty of a male Wood Duck.'"[3]

Early in July, Pearson escaped on a field trip to Maine to examine the seabird colonies guarded by fifteen of the National Association's thirty-nine wardens. He was especially interested in the Herring Gull colonies, which were not known to occur on the Atlantic coast south of Maine. At Portland, he was met by the Maine Audubon secretary, Arthur H. Norton, who "knew more about the wild life of the Maine coast than any other man." On the island of No-Man's-Land, they counted an estimated twenty thousand birds. Pearson was amused by the young birds. "Although hard to catch they at once become docile when picked up." He tested their willingness to remain still when being handled by placing them on their backs in a row. They lay motionless until he had perhaps as many as six together. Then they grew bold, rolled over, and scuttled away.[4]

On Machias Seal Island, a Canadian possession at the mouth of the Bay of Fundy, terns and Atlantic Puffins (*Fratercula arctica*) nested among the rocks; Leach's Storm-Petrels (*Oceanodrama leucorhoa*) had burrows in the island's four acres of soil. A dog owned by the lighthouse keeper's son entertained itself by digging the storm-petrels out and killing them. Pearson counted 147 storm-petrels that the dog had killed. "I spoke to the lighthouse-keeper about the law protecting them. He said he doubted if the laws of New Brunswick covered such birds." Pearson went to Fredericton, found a copy of the game law, and learned the lighthouse keeper's opinion was correct. Then he returned to the island and gave the lighthouse keeper twenty-five dollars to send the dog to the mainland for the rest of the summer. Back in New York, Pearson wrote to the Canadian Department of Marine and Fisheries, pointing out the importance of the coastal bird colonies and asking that they be protected. In response to his request, instructions were sent to all Canadian lighthouse keepers to protect the birds nesting in their neighborhoods.[5]

Possibly too great an emphasis was being placed on defending birds by stressing their usefulness to agriculture. In *Bird-Lore* Mabel Wright reported a conversation with an articulate farmer in which she noted the value of birds in raising crops. "Of course there's truth in what you say," the farmer commented. "All the same, if I just stood by and waited for them to do my chores of potato-bug picking, and hunting cut worms and spraying for currant and canker worms, and tree blight, I should be standing barefoot instead of in a good pair of boots." He told Wright she should talk to farmers about saving birds because of their "pretty ways and friendliness." They were "surely good company" and made "chore time seem shorter." Wright reported the conversation along with the conclusion to which it had led her: "Our standards,

as a whole, are becoming pitifully, if necessarily, intensely material. Let us, therefore, dwell first upon the undeniable beauty and
cheer of the birds of the air, and less upon their economic value."[6]

Sympathy and affection for birds were far more widespread
than they had been when Pearson had begun to write and speak in
their behalf almost twenty years earlier. He could see evidence of
the change as he read the National Association's mail. Many
protests against the "needless killing" of birds were received when
a man was employed in Montclair, New Jersey, to shoot into trees
where birds flocked at summer's end. A similar flocking was
handled differently in Greensboro, where in August Pearson saw
the flock of approximately one hundred thousand Purple Martins
that had been roosting in trees near the courthouse for several
weeks. In response to complaints that the birds were a "nuisance
and a menace to health," a fire hose was "brought to bear on the
trees and the birds were drenched and frightened away." The next
evening, few of the birds returned. A children's essay contest on
bird protection, sponsored by the Michigan Audubon Society, was
won by a girl who persuaded a group of boys to stop shooting at a
bird. "Do you think it is right to shoot at such a little bird, who can
only protect himself by flying. It has as much right to the world as
you have, so why don't you let the poor little creature alone." Near
Detroit, Henry Ford had five hundred nesting boxes put up on his
estate and arranged with the Michigan Audubon Society to make
an "ornithological survey" of his grounds, so he might do other
things to nurture bird life. Pearson believed that the changing
popular views toward birds were "evidence of the rapidly increasing refinement of sentiment that comes with advancing civilization." Many Americans had reached the point, a historian later
wrote, at which "in the sight of a chickadee or the song of a
sparrow, even in the mention on a printed page," they found
"much that was sincerely moving."[7]

In Pearson's first year of being fully in charge of the National

Association, he displayed his skills in fund-raising and management. "I asked help from nearly every person with whom I became
acquainted, if that person impressed me as an encouraging prospect." The income from all sources rose to slightly more than
$44,600, an increase of $6,000 over the previous year. By cutting
costs, Pearson paid off a deficit in the general fund and built up a
surplus of $7,812.95.[8]

The increasing number of southern junior Audubon classes
pleased him greatly. By June 1911, the end of the first year of the
Sage Fund project, 533 classes had a total membership of 10,595 in
twelve states. "No one can estimate the good accomplished by the
systematic instruction in bird study and bird protection given to
these . . . children," he wrote. Late in the year, a National Association member demanding anonymity contributed five thousand
dollars to extend the Audubon junior project outside the South.[9]

In spite of all the protective measures, Snowy and Great Egrets
were still highly vulnerable. The feather markets had been closed
in New York, New Jersey, Louisiana, Missouri, Massachusetts,
Oregon, and California, but in other states "outstretched hands"
were "beckoning to the inhabitants of the southern swamps to send
on the snowy product." Egret plumes, worth "more than twice
their weight in gold," sold for eight pounds sterling per ounce in
London. With the help of an anonymous "Friend of the Birds"
who contributed $500, Pearson solicited special funds for egret
protection. Agents sent out to locate egret colonies reported a total
of ten in South Carolina, North Carolina, Georgia, and Florida,
containing about 1,400 Great Egrets and 250 Snowy Egrets. On
Avery Island, Louisiana, Edward A. McIlheny built a large
"artificial colony." For $250.20, the National Association bought
Bird Island, thirty-five acres in size, in Orange Lake, Alachua
County, Florida, where sixty-six pairs of Great Egrets and fifty-
seven pairs of Snowy Egrets nested.[10] Wardens were assigned to all
the known colonies except McIlheny's private preserve.

The Audubon movement had taken hold across the nation. Counting the two societies in Tennessee, there were thirty-eight state and territorial societies. Excepting Arizona and Kansas, every state or territory having an Audubon society also had adopted the model law. Even in Kansas, as a consequence of the Audubon Society's efforts, the game laws were modified to protect most nongame birds.[11]

In New York in October 1911, Pearson greeted the delegates to the National Association meeting in a buoyant, optimistic, and grateful spirit. "It is no small privilege to live at this time in history, among the beginnings of so many things which make for material and spiritual uplift." He pointed out how far the association had come since 1902, when a "little band of bird lovers, headed by Mr. William Dutcher," formed the National Committee of Audubon Societies. The growth did not "simply happen"; it was the result of the work of "many human beings, reaching forward for better things." Although he did not mention God, as he had so often, he emphasized the inherent goodness in what was being accomplished, the spiritual value of laboring "joyeously [sic] and without stint" to "form a line of defence as best we may between the wild creatures and the greed of thoughtless men." Rather than citing the value of birds to agriculture, he spoke of the importance of all "wild animal life" to the "joy of human existence." The appreciation of wild beings would now spread quickly, he predicted, and the Audubon movement would "grow to large proportions."[12]

Confident about his own future as well, Pearson decided to move with his wife and children to New York. Elsie came to Philadelphia to be with him at the AOU meeting in November; one participant was William Beebe, New York Zoological Society curator of ornithology, who lived at University Heights in New York City. After the meeting, the Pearsons went to New York, where, Pearson wrote in his autobiography, the Beebes "took us to see a house in Loring Place, which seemed to meet our needs, and there we have ever since resided."[13] They moved in January 1912 and were still living there on September 3, 1943, when T. Gilbert Pearson died.

# Notes

*Abbreviations Used in the Notes*

| | |
|---|---|
| *Adventures* | T. Gilbert Pearson. *Adventures in Bird Protection, an Autobiography*. New York: Appleton-Century, 1937. |
| ASNC | Audubon Society of North Carolina. |
| ASP | National Association of Audubon Societies Papers. |
| *Birds* (1919) | T. Gilbert Pearson, Clement S. Brimley, and Herbert H. Brimley. *Birds of North Carolina*. Raleigh: Edwards & Broughton, 1919. |
| *Birds* | T. Gilbert Pearson, Clement S. Brimley, and Herbert H. Brimley. *Birds of North Carolina*. Rev. ed. Raleigh: Bynum Printing Company, 1942. |
| *GC* | *Guilford Collegian*. |
| GCR | Guilford College Records, Greensboro, North Carolina. |
| NCGS | North Carolina Geological Survey Papers, University of North Carolina at Chapel Hill. |
| Pearson folder, AMNH | T. Gilbert Pearson folder, Department of Ornithology Historical Correspondence, American Museum of Natural History. |
| SNIC | State Normal and Industrial College, Greensboro, North Carolina. |
| UNC | University of North Carolina. |

## Chapter 1

1. T. Gilbert Pearson, *Adventures in Bird Protection*, 15 (hereinafter, *Adventures*).

2. Ibid., 1–3; United States, Tenth Census, 1880, Indiana, Wayne County, Microfilm Census Schedules, vol. 38, sheet 1, Enumerating District 62, microfilm reel 322.

3. *Adventures*, 3–5; Carl Webber, *The First Eden of the South . . . Alachua County, Florida*, 73, 96–97, and 127.

4. United States, Tenth Census, reel 322.

5. *Adventures*, 9, 10.

6. Ibid., 12.

7. Ibid., 9–10.

8. Pearson, "A Day with the Herons in Florida," 8–9.

9. Frank H. Lattin, *The Oologists' Hand-book, 1885. Adventures*, 18.

10. Ibid., 17–18.

11. Pearson, "Collecting Experience," 25–26.

12. *Adventures*, 12–15.

13. Florida Superintendent of Public Instruction, *Biennial Report, 1883–84*, 5, and *Annual Report, 1888*, 33–35; *Adventures*, 13 and 19.

14. Ibid., 16–22; F. W. Buchholz, *History of Alachua County*, 406–7.

15. Pearson, "The Ibises of Ledworth Lake," 99–100. Pearson, "Notes on the Herons of Central Florida," 133.

16. Pearson, "Nesting of the Pied-billed Grebe," 152–53, "The American Anhinga," "The Wood Duck," and "The Herons of Alachua County, Florida." On the grebe's nesting habits, Pearson, "Pelicans, Cormorants, Loons, and Grebes," in National Geographic Society, *The Book of Birds* 1:14–15, and "Nesting of the Pied-billed Grebe," 152–53.

17. Pearson, *Stories of Bird Life*, 153–60.

18. Ibid., 71–80.

19. Pearson, "The Arredondo Sparrow Hawk," 2–6; Pearson, "Notes from Alachua Co., Florida," 150; *Adventures*, 17–18.

## Chapter 2

1. On Coues's book, *Adventures*, 22. Witmer Stone, "American Ornithological Literature," in American Ornithologists' Union, *Fifty Years' Progress*, 29–49; John K. Terres, *The Audubon Society Encyclopedia of North*

*American Birds*, 109. On Coues, see Palmer et al., *Biographies of Members of the American Ornithologists' Union*, 148–49; *Who Was Who in America, 1897–1942*, 265. Also Paul R. Cutright and Michael J. Brodhead, *Elliott Coues*. Elliott Coues, *Key to North American Birds*, xi and 60.

2. Coues, *Key to North American Birds*, xxx. On mounting, *Adventures*, 22.

3. Webber, *First Eden of the South*, 5; Buchholz, *History of Alachua County*, 284–85; Frank M. Chapman, *Frank Chapman in Florida*, 27–28, 76, and 86.

4. Frank M. Chapman, *Autobiography of a Bird-Lover*, 20, 23, 29, 32–34, and 36–37; Chapman, *Frank Chapman in Florida*, 1–4 and 27; Chapman, "A List of Birds Observed at Gainesville, Florida," 267–77; *Dictionary of American Biography, Supplement Three*, 161–62.

5. *Adventures*, 10–11; Robert Cushman Murphy, interview with the author, September 4, 1967.

6. Pearson to Chapman, April 8, 1891, Pearson folder, AMNH.

7. Ibid., July 17, 1891.

8. Ibid., July 17 and August 8, 1891.

9. *Auk* 9 (January 1892): xx; Pearson to Chapman, August 8, 1891, Pearson folder, AMNH; Coues, *Key to North American Birds*, xxi; Joel A. Allen, *The American Ornithologists' Union*, 1; Terres, *Audubon Society Encyclopedia*, 640.

10. Nuttall Ornithological Club, *Bulletin* 8 (October 1883): 221–26; Cutright and Brodhead, *Elliott Coues*, 261–73.

11. *Who Was Who in America, 1897–1942*, 18; Daniel J. Preston, "The AOU's Fledgling Years"; Robin W. Doughty, *Feather Fashions and Bird Preservation*, 53 and 58.

12. On Brewster, *Auk* 1 (October 1884): 376. Doughty's *Feather Fashions and Bird Preservation* has extensive statistics on the international feather trade. On legislative action, Charles L. Flynn, Jr., *White Land, Black Labor*, 125–28. On committee members, *Who Was Who in America, 1943–1950*, 369; Henry E. Clepper, ed., *Leaders of American Conservation*, 145–46; *Dictionary of American Biography, Supplement II*, 264–65; Palmer, *Biographies*, 55–56.

13. On the *Code*, Allen, *American Ornithologists' Union*, 2–8. On Merriam, *Auk* 1 (October 1884): 376–78; 2 (April 1885): 223; 3 (January 1886): 117–20 and (July 1886): 416; 4 (January 1887): 59; 7 (October 1890): 414; and 8 (January 1891): 81; Keir B. Sterling, *Last of the Naturalists*, 56–90.

14. *Auk* 3 (January 1886): 120 and 143; *Audubon Magazine* 1 (April

1887): 55; Palmer, *Biographies*, 213, 277–78, and 514–15; American Ornithologists' Union Committee on the Protection of North American Birds, Minutes (hereinafter cited as AOU Committee Minutes), 3–5.

15. AOU Committee Minutes, 3–21.

16. Ibid., 25–26; *Forest and Stream*, March 11, 1886.

17. Quotations in the preceding paragraphs are from the supplement to *Science*, February 26, 1886. See also John F. Reiger, *American Sportsmen and the Origins of Conservation*, 45–49, and James B. Trefethan, *An American Crusade for Wildlife*, 106–14.

18. *Science*, August 6, 1886, 118–19; AOU Committee Minutes, 27–30.

19. On endorsements, *Bird-Lore* 7 (January–February 1905): 51–52; *Audubon Magazine* 1 (February 1887): 16; John G. Mitchell, "A Man Called Bird," 95–96. On pledges, AOU Committee Minutes, 43. On incorporation, *Bird-Lore* 7 (January–February 1905): 52; Mitchell, "A Man Called Bird," 96. For Allen's report, see *Science*, August 6, 1886, 118–19. On the second bulletin, *Auk* 4 (January 1887): 59. On Audubon membership, *Audubon Magazine* 1 (February 1887): 19. On Sennett's report, *Auk* 4 (January 1887): 59. On the magazine's goals, *Audubon Magazine* 1 (February 1887): 5.

20. Ibid., 2 (January 1889): 262; *Bird-Lore* 7 (January–February 1905): 52–55; *Adventures*, 127–28

21. On Pearson's plume hunting, ibid., 15–16. On other plume hunters, Pearson, "Notes on the Herons," 134.

22. Ibid., 132–34.

23. *Adventures*, 10, 20.

24. Ibid., 17 and 19; see also Altus L. Quaintance, "The Pileated Woodpecker in Florida," 86–87.

25. *Adventures*, 19, 22. Earlham College does not have complete registration records for the years prior to 1900. The college catalogs for 1875–76 and 1876–77 list Pearson's brother, Charles E. Pearson, as a student in the preparatory department.

26. *Adventures*, 22–24; *GC* 6 (December 1893): 116; Dorothy L. Gilbert, "T. Gilbert Pearson and Guilford College," 1–8.

*Chapter 3*

1. Guilford College, *Catalogue, 1890–91*, 22–23 and 34.

2. *Adventures*, 24–25.

3. *GC* 4 (September 1891), unpaged advertisement, and 6 (December 1893): 116; Guilford College, *Catalogue, 1890–91*, 30.

4. *GC* 4 (October 1891): 53 and (January 1892): 128; Guilford College, *Catalogue, 1891–92*, 44. On the collection's growth, *GC* 4 (January 1892): 128 and 6 (December 1893): 116.

5. Guilford College, *Catalogue, 1890–91*, 22–23, 34.

6. *Adventures*, 28, 24. *GC* 4 (January 1892):126.

7. *Auk* (January 1892): 57; *Bird-Lore* 7 (January–February 1905): 55.

8. *Adventures*, 28, 29. *Ornithologist and Oologist* 17 (January 1892): 13.

9. Pearson, "Some Notes on the Wild Turkey," 293–94.

10. Pearson, "Some Spring Notes from Guildford [*sic.*] County," 76.

11. *Adventures*, 27–29.

12. Pearson, "The Wild Turkey," 168–69. Mike Seamster, "Big Bird is Back!"

13. On his first debate, *Adventures*, 31 and 34. Pearson, "The Destruction of Our American Birds."

14. *Adventures*, 34. *GC* 4 (June 1892):251.

15. *Adventures*, 35.

16. Pearson, "In the Great Dismal Swamp," 26–28.

17. *Birds* (1919), 264; Pearson, "Collecting on Cobb's Island, Va.," 191–93.

18. Pearson, *Stories of Bird Life*, 64–66.

19. *Adventures*, 35.

20. On cabinet additions, *GC* 5 (March 1893): 173–74; 5 (September 1892): 26; 5 (December 1892): 110; 5 (February 1893): 143 and 5 (April 1893): 207. On the exposition display, *Oologist* 10 (March 1893): 90 and 11 (January 1894): 14–20.

21. *Adventures*, 26–27. Dorothy L. Gilbert, *Guilford*, 206; *Adventures*, 53.

22. *GC* 5 (February 1893): 149 and 5 (March 1893): 174.

23. SNIC, *Catalogue, 1892–93*, 6–7, and *Catalogue, 1893–94*, 4–5 and 55; *GC* 7 (April 1895): 207; photograph dated May 1893 in archives of UNC at Greensboro.

24. *Adventures*, 38; Elsie Weatherly to Charles D. McIver, July 25, 1892, McIver Papers; Gilbert, *Guilford*, 209–10; *GC* 5 (June 1893): 266–67.

25. *Adventures*, 38. Guilford College, "Minutes of the Board of Trustees, 1873–1918," GCR, 196.

26. Guilford College, *Catalogue, 1892–93*, 43–44.

27. On the YMCA, Gilbert, *Guilford*, 197–98; *GC* 6 (December 1893): 114. On the conference, *Adventures*, 37. Also *GC* 5 (June 1893): 263; 6 (December 1893): 115; and 6 (April 1894): 253.

28. *Adventures*, 38; *GC* 6 (March 1894): 225.

29. On Moore, Gilbert, *Guilford*, 153–56; Joseph Moore, "The Greatest Factor in Human Evolution," 240–44. *Adventures*, 38.

30. *GC* 6 (September 1893): 18.

*Chapter 4*

1. *Auk* 10 (October 1893): 386–87; 11 (January 1894): 89–90; and 14 (January 1897): 108.

2. Elliott Coues, "The Presidential Address," in E. Irene Rood, ed., *Papers Presented to the World's Congress on Ornithology*, 15.

3. Pearson, "Notes on the Herons," 132–35.

4. Doughty, *Feather Fashions and Bird Preservation*, 64–65.

5. *GC* 6 (November 1893), unpaged advertisement; Guilford College, "Minutes of the Board of Trustees, 1873–1918," December 11, 1893, GCR. On his holidays, *GC* 6 (January 1894): 176.

6. *Our Animal Friends* 21 (February 1894): 121–23.

7. Pearson, "Hunting the Brown Pelican," 83–86; *GC* 7 (September 1894): 16 and (November 1894): 73.

8. *GC* 6 (November 1893): 80–81 and 88–90 and (December 1893): 144; and 7 (May 1895): 227–31 and 249.

9. *GC* 6 (December 1893): 115.

10. Pearson to Chapman, July 13, 1895, Pearson folder, AMNH.

11. On "Bird Day," *Auk* 11 (October 1894): 341. On Chapman, 12 (July 1895): 282–84.

12. *Harper's Bazaar* and New York *Evening Post*, quoted in *Auk* 11 (October 1894): 342. Dutcher wrote in *Bird-Lore* 7 (January–February 1905): 55.

13. *Adventures*, 43–44. On the clubs, see also *GC* 8 (October 1895): 49, (January 1896): picture facing p. 107, and (February 1896): 151; and 8 (May 1896): 253.

14. Pearson, "Evolution in Its Relation to Man," 107–11. *GC* 8 (April 1896): 214.

15. *Adventures*, 39. Pearson, *Stories of Bird Life*, 82–89.

16. Pearson, "How We Got Our Man-o-War Bird," 76–78, and *Ad-*

*ventures*, 40. On the Tampa Bay specimens, *GC* 9 (September 1896): 16; *Adventures*, 39. On decline of waders, Pearson, "Passer Domesticus at Archer, Fla., and Other Florida Notes," 99.

17. *GC* 9 (November 1896): 80–81.

18. Peter J. Schmitt, *Back to Nature*. On natural history's spreading popularity, *Auk* 14 (January 1897): 23–28 and (April 1897): 297. Rood, ed., *Papers Presented to the World's Congress on Ornithology*; Doughty, *Feather Fashions and Bird Preservation*, 65.

19. Massachusetts Audubon Society, *This Statement Was Made by Mrs. Augustus Hemenway and Miss Minna B. Hall*. Pearson, "Notes on the Herons," 135. Robert H. Welker, *Birds and Men*, 207. Massachusetts Audubon Society, "Profile on Massachusetts Audubon Society" and *First Report*. Also Stephen Fox, *John Muir and His Legacy*, 152–53; Carl W. Buchheister and Frank Graham, "From the Swamps and Back," 7–10.

20. *Auk* 14 (January 1897): 116; *Bird-Lore* 1 (December 1899): 203 and 7 (January–February 1905): 47.

21. *Auk* 14 (January 1897): 116.

22. On the survey, *Auk* 13 (July 1896): 268. Theodore S. Palmer, "A Review of Economic Ornithology in the United States," 259. On Dutcher, *Auk* 14 (January 1897): 32. Massachusetts Audubon Society, *First Report*, 11.

23. On the murre, *Auk* 14 (April 1897): 202; *Birds*, 185–86. On museum conditions, *GC* 7 (November 1894): 73 and 8 (December 1895): 97. On the Duke donation, *GC* 9 (April 1897): 238–41.

24. On Holmes's lecture, *GC* 8 (April 1896): 210. *Adventures*, 44–45.

25. Pearson to Joseph Austin Holmes, January 20 and February 2, 1897, and Dixie Lee Bryant to Holmes, January 9, 1897, NCGS.

26. *Adventures*, 46–47.

27. Pearson to Holmes, February 2, 1897, and Holmes to Pearson, March 22, 1897, NCGS.

28. *GC* 9 (May 1897): 284 and 290–91.

29. Ibid., (April 1897): 249. Pearson to Holmes, May 2 and 26 and July 9, 1897, NCGS.

*Chapter 5*

1. *Hellenian, 1898*, 36; *Hellenian, 1899*, 43; Dialectic Society Records, S-93: 132, 138, and 140–41.

2. Pearson, "The Story of a Snow-Bird's Nest," 13. Also *State Normal Magazine* 1 (February 1898): 218–19; Pearson, "The Flamingo Feather."

3. *Birds*, xxi–xxvi, 381, 386, and 388; Marcus B. Simpson, "The Letters of John S. Cairns to William Brewster, 1887–1895."

4. George F. Atkinson, "Preliminary Catalogue of the Birds of North Carolina"; *Dictionary of American Biography*, 1: 407–8. John W. P. Smithwick, "Ornithology of North Carolina."

5. *Dictionary of North Carolina Biography* 1:227–28; *Birds*, 381–85; Herbert H. Brimley, *A North Carolina Naturalist*, xi–xvi.

6. Pearson, "Preliminary Catalogue of the Birds of Chapel Hill, N.C."

7. Pearson to Chapman, March 15, 1898, Pearson folder, AMNH; Pearson, "An Addition and a Correction to the List of North Carolina Birds." *North Carolina University Magazine*, 15 (April 1898): 166.

8. Pearson to Chapman, March 15, 1898, Pearson folder AMNH; *Adventures*, 48. Herbert H. Brimley, "Thomas Gilbert Pearson."

9. *Adventures*, 48–49.

10. *Birds* (1919), 32, and *Birds*, 170–71.

11. *Adventures*, 49.

12. *Birds*, 33, 234. On the New River swallows, Eloise F. Potter, James F. Parnell, and Robert P. Teulings, *Birds of the Carolinas*, 238. On the eagles, *Birds* (1919), 171.

13. *Birds*, 126; Pearson, "Notes on Some of the Birds of Eastern North Carolina," 246.

14. *Birds*, 114.

15. Pearson, "The Quest for the Cormorant's Nest," 81–84.

16. Pearson, ed., *Birds of America*, I, 97. Pearson, "Nesting Habits of Some Southern Forms of Birds in Eastern North Carolina," 19–21.

17. *Birds*, 19; Potter, Parnell, and Teulings, *Birds of the Carolinas*, 55–56; Terres, *Audubon Society Encyclopedia*, 106; Alexander Sprunt, Jr., *Florida Bird Life*, 18–19.

18. Pearson, "The City of the Longlegs," 208–11; *Birds* (1919), 102.

19. *Birds*, 20; Frank M. Chapman, *Handbook of Birds of Eastern North America*, 93. Pearson, "Notes on Some of the Birds of Eastern North Carolina," 248. National Geographic Society, *The Book of Birds*, 1:20.

20. *Adventures*, 50–52; *Birds*, 164; Pearson, "Notes on Some of the Birds of Eastern North Carolina," 249.

21. On time with Wilson, Pearson, "Preliminary Catalogue," 34; H.

H. Brimley to Holmes, May 26, 1898, and N.C. State Geologist, *Biennial Report, 1899–1900*, 17, Pearson to Holmes, July 27, 1898, and H. H. Brimley to Holmes, August 29, 1898, NCGS; "List of Marine Material Collected in Vicinity of Beaufort, N.C. by T. Gilbert Pearson—Summer of 1898," T. Gilbert Pearson file, N.C. State Museum of Natural Sciences. Pearson, "The Fish Scrap and Fish Oil Industry in North Carolina"; Pearson to Holmes, August 14, 1898, NCGS.

22. Pearson to Holmes, July 27 and August 14, 1898, and Holmes to Pearson, July 30, 1898, NCGS.

*Chapter 6*

1. *Adventures*, 52; N.C. State Geologist, *Biennial Report, 1899–1900*, 18; *Hellenian, 1899*, 43; inscribed photographs, in Lewis Lyndon Hobbs and Mary Mendenhall Hobbs Papers; *GC* 16 (January 1904): 80. Theodore S. Palmer to Pearson, September 21, 1898, NCGS. On Pearson's paper, *Hellenian, 1899*, 43; *North Carolina University Magazine*, 16 (October 1898): 48; Pearson, "Nesting Habits."

2. *North Carolina University Magazine* 16 (October 1898): 48; UNC, *Catalogue, 1898–99*, 120; *Dictionary of North Carolina Biography* 1:114–15; Pearson, "Preliminary Catalogue," 34–36.

3. Charles L. Lewis, *Philander Priestley Claxton*, 98.

4. *Auk* 16 (January 1899): 58. Pearson, "The Economic Value of Bird Study," 5.

5. *Auk* 16 (January 1899): 66–69. George T. Angell, *Autobiographical Sketches and Personal Recollections*.

6. *Auk* 14 (January 1897): 32, 14 (April 1897): 257, 14 (July 1897): 344, 15 (January 1898): 82–100, and 21 (January 1904): 167; *Audubon Naturalist News* 13 (February 1987): 9; Frank Graham, Jr., *Audubon Ark*, 18; *Bird-Lore* 7 (January–February 1905): 47.

7. *Auk* 15 (January 1898): 83–89, 90–92, 111 (Merriam quote); 82, 110, 14 (Dutcher quotes).

8. Ibid., 80.

9. *Auk* 16 (January 1899): 60 and 70; *Bird-Lore* 1 (June 1899): 100, 2 (December 1900): 201, 7 (January–February 1905): 47 and 75, and 8 (November–December 1906): 272–73; Graham, *Audubon Ark*, 18; Pearson, *Adventures*, 209.

10. *Bird-Lore* 1 (February 1899): 30–32 and (June 1899):101–2.

11. Ibid., 1 (August 1899), 125–27; *Auk* 16 (January 1899): 59 and 61.

12. Welker, *Birds and Men*, 194.

13. *Adventures*, 336–45; Theodore W. Cart, "The Lacey Act," 4–13.

14. *Bird-Lore* 2 (April 1900): 60. Also, *Auk* 16 (January 1899): 56–57; *Adventures*, 259–60; Welker, *Birds and Men*, 207.

15. On Deane, *Auk* 16 (January 1899): 56. On Beal, Waldo L. McAtee, "Economic Ornithology," in American Ornithologists' Union, *Fifty Years' Progress*, 113 and 120; *Bird-Lore* 1 (February 1899): 30–31; *Auk* 14 (October 1897): 421–22.

16. Pearson, "Life on the Holiday Campus," 153.

17. Ibid.

18. *Adventures*, 54; Pearson, "Preliminary Catalogue," 34.

19. Stone's recommendation, *Auk* 16 (January 1899): 74. *Bird-Lore* 1 (February 1899): 28 (book sales) and 29–32 (Wright's plea).

20. Chapman, *Autobiography*, 181. Edmund Morris, *The Rise of Theodore Roosevelt*, 90. Theodore Roosevelt, *Theodore Roosevelt, an Autobiography*, 23–30.

21. Morris, *The Rise of Theodore Roosevelt*, 383–84; Reiger, *American Sportsmen*, 114–41.

22. *Bird-Lore* 1 (April 1899): 65.

23. Pearson, "Woodland Carpenters."

24. Pearson, *Stories of Bird Life*, 127–29.

25. Ruthven Deane to Pearson, March 3, 1899, NCGS.

26. N.C. State Geologist, *Biennial Report, 1899–1900*, 20, Holmes to Pearson, July 30, 1898, and Pearson to Holmes, August 1, 1899, and March 18, 1900, NCGS; *North Carolina University Magazine*, 16 (June 1899): 363.

27. *Adventures*, 55.

28. UNC, *Catalogue, 1898–99*, 51–52; *North Carolina University Magazine*, 16 (June 1899): 367.

29. Henry V. Wilson, "The Laboratory of the U.S. Fish Commission at Beaufort, N.C." *Adventures*, 56; Pearson to Holmes, June 17 and 28, 1899, NCGS. On the frigatebird, *Birds*, 22–23.

30. On Elsie's job, *State Normal Magazine* 1 (December 1897): 164 and 6 (October 1901): 84. *Adventures*, 57.

31. Pearson to Holmes, August 1, 1899, NCGS. *Adventures*, 57.

32. Pearson to Holmes, August 1, 1899, NCGS.

*Chapter 7*

1. *Adventures*, 58; *GC* 12 (October 1899): 25; Guilford College, *Catalogue, 1899–1900*, 32–33.

2. On the biology class, Gilbert, *Guilford*, 206–8. On the zoology course, Guilford College, *Catalogue, 1899–1900*, 33. The article was "The Study of Birds in the Public Schools," 11.

3. Pearson, "Preliminary Catalogue." *Auk* 17 (January 1900): 82; *Adventures*, 55–56.

4. Pearson, "The Spring Migration of Birds."

5. *North Carolina Journal of Education* 3 (November 1899): 6; *GC* 12 (February 1900): 180–81.

6. *Bird-Lore* 1 (December 1899): 192, 2 (February 1900): 12–13, and 3 (January–February 1901): 20.

7. *Adventures*, 59.

8. On Pearson as manager, *GC* 12 (October 1899): 19. On Claxton and the journal, *North Carolina Journal of Education* 3 (June 1900): 1 and 4 (February 1901): 1; manuscript tipped into Library of Congress copy, *Atlantic Educational Journal* 4 (August 1901): 1; Lewis, *Philander Priestley Claxton*, 98–111.

9. *Auk* 18 (April 1900): 199 and (January 1901): 76–103. Also *Bird-Lore* 2 (February 1900): 33 and 2 (June 1900): 90.

10. Cart, "The Lacey Act." *Bird-Lore* 2 (June 1900): 93, 3 (January–February 1901): 41, and 2 (June 1900): 98.

11. On merchants' offer, *Bird-Lore* 2 (June 1900): 93–98. Wright quotes, ibid., (August 1900): 129-30, and 1 (December 1899): 203. On Seton, ibid., 2 (October 1900): 166. On Stone, *Auk* 18 (January 1901): 71. On status by 1900, *Bird-Lore* 7 (January–February 1905): 47; *Auk* 19 (January 1902): 36.

12. On society numbers, *Bird-Lore* 7 (January–February 1905): 47; 2 (June 1900): 94, (October 1900): 164, and (December 1900): 202.

13. *GC* 13 (December 1900): 56–57.

14. *Adventures*, 61.

15. Ibid., 61–63; *State Normal Magazine* 9 (October 1904): 30–31.

16. *Adventures*, 63; UNC, *Catalogue, 1900–1901*, 104 and *Catalogue, 1901–1902*, 117 and 121; *GC* 13 (Commencement 1901): 213.

17. *Adventures*, 63; Pearson to Charles McIver, June 1 and 11, 1901, McIver Papers.

18. *Adventures*, 63; UNC, *Catalogue, 1900–1901*, 104, and *Catalogue*,

*1901–1902*, 117 and 121; Harvard University, *Catalogue, 1900–01*, 423, and *Catalogue, 1901–02*, 196 and 413.

## *Chapter 8*

1. SNIC, *Catalogue, 1901–1902*, 38, 48, and 79.

2. *Adventures*, 65. SNIC, *Catalogue, 1901–1902*, 25–27 and 54.

3. Virginia Brown Douglas, "Mindpower Past," 17-19, and "T. Gilbert Pearson," 7–10.

4. SNIC, *Catalogue, 1906–1907*, 27.

5. On the reviews, *Bird-Lore* 4 (March–April 1902): 68; *Auk* 19 (January 1902): 105; *State Normal Magazine* 6 (February 1902): 275–77. On school reactions, *Atlantic Educational Journal* 5 (November 1902): 45; *State Normal Magazine* 6 (December 1901): 172.

6. On Dutcher's appeal to Pearson, *Adventures*, 66. On state efforts, *Auk* 19 (January 1902): 34–63. On Henderson, N.C. *Senate Journal, 1901*, 406; *Bird-Lore* 3 (March–April 1901): 78.

7. On the leaflets, *Adventures*, 66–67. Pearson, "The Economic Value of Bird Study." Pearson, "Suggestions for Private Bird Study."

8. SNIC, "Minutes of Meetings of Faculty Council, October 1895–June 1905," 148–49.

9. Pearson to H. H. Brimley, March 10, 1902, and Brimley to W. L. Poteat, March 8, 1902, Brimley Papers (A&H).

10. Audubon Society of North Carolina, *First Annual Report*, 1; *Bird-Lore* 5 (January–February 1903): 38–39; *Adventures*, 67. Oliver H. Orr, *Charles Brantley Aycock*, 315. The society is hereinafter cited as ASNC.

11. ASNC, *Constitution of the Audubon Society of North Carolina*.

12. Pearson to R. H. Sykes, March 27, 1903, NCGS.

13. Pearson to H. H. Brimley, April 18, 1902, Brimley Papers. Also Pearson to Brimley, March 10, 1902, Brimley Papers; Francis Sharman to "Dear Sir," undated circular, NCGS; *Adventures*, 67.

14. On the branch societies, ASNC, *First Annual Report*, 1; on the articles, *Adventures*, 67; ASNC, *The Audubon Bird Identification Blank*.

15. ASNC, *Purposes and Plans*. Pearson to "Dear Sir," May 12, 1902, National Audubon Society files.

16. On the Thayer fund, *Auk* 20 (January 1903): 155. On the Biltmore activity, Harold T. Pinkett, *Gifford Pinchot*, 26–27; Davis, ed., *Encyclopedia of American Forest and Conservation History*, 2: 593–94; Carl A. Schenck,

*The Biltmore Story,* 152; *Auk* 20 (January 1903): 152; Terres, *Audubon Society Encyclopedia,* 641.

17. Pearson, "The Song Sparrow" and "March Birds."

18. On the cuckoo, *Birds* (1919), 187; *Birds,* 194. On the collection, *Birds* (1919), 179; *Birds,* 5 and 203–4.

19. SNIC, *Catalogue, 1901–1902,* 39–42. Pearson to McIver, May 23, 1902, McIver Papers. On Brown's writing, Douglas, "Mindpower Past" and "T. Gilbert Pearson"; *Greensboro News and Record,* November 26, 1983.

20. ASNC, *First Annual Report,* 1–2. On Blair, *Dictionary of North Carolina Biography* 1:171–72. On the park association, Davis, *Encyclopedia* 2:496.

21. *Atlantic Educational Journal* 5 (May 1902): 44 and 5 (August 1902): 35; Lewis, *Philander Priestley Claxton,* 126–40.

22. *Adventures,* 68. On the wedding, Douglas, "T. Gilbert Pearson"; *State Normal Magazine* 6 (June 1902): 472; *GC* 16 (February 1904): unnumbered page of advertisements.

23. *Adventures,* 68.

24. On attendance, *Atlantic Educational Journal* 5 (August 1902): 35. Also Lewis, *Philander Priestley Claxton,* 32–36; *State Normal Magazine* 6 (February 1902): 244–45. *Adventures,* 68. Also Pearson to H. H. Brimley, undated letter, Brimley Papers; Pearson to Chapman, July 15, 1902, Pearson folder, AMNH; University of Tennessee, Summer School of the South, *Announcement, 1902,* 23.

25. On the faculty, *Atlantic Educational Journal* 5 (August 1902): 35–37. Pearson to H. H. Brimley, undated letter, Brimley Papers.


*Chapter 9*

1. Potter, Parnell, and Teulings, *Birds of the Carolinas,* 334; *Birds,* 327; (1919), 248–49.

2. Pearson, "A Pair of Brown Thrashers"; *Adventures,* 68–69.

3. Pearson to H. H. Brimley, undated letter, and H. H. Brimley to Pearson, August 16, 1902, Brimley Papers.

4. Pearson to McIver, August 11, 1902, McIver Papers. *Adventures,* 69–70.

5. *Adventures,* 71.

6. ASNC, *Certificate of Incorporation of the Audubon Society of North Carolina Company.* Orr, *Charles Brantley Aycock,* 266–67; letterhead, Pear-

son to McIver, November 7, 1902, McIver Papers. Pearson to "Dear Sir," October 30, 1902, Brimley Papers.

7. Pearson, "The Audubon Societies."

8. Theodore S. Palmer, *Legislation for the Protection of Birds Other Than Game Birds*, 107–8; Palmer and H. W. Olds, *Game Laws for 1902*, 18–19, and *Laws Regulating the Transportation and Sale of Game*, 71–72; Donald B. Hayman, *Resource Management in North Carolina*, 18–19.

9. Pearson to H. H. Brimley, November 10 and December 6, 1902, Brimley Papers; *Bird-Lore* 4 (May–June 1902): 104.

10. *Auk* 20 (January 1903): 102–3, 108, 110, and 158–59.

11. On attendees, *Adventures*, 73; *Bird-Lore* 4 (November–December 1902): 207–8. On Pearson's paper, Washington *Evening Star*, November 18, 1902; *Auk* 20 (January 1903): 61.

12. *Adventures*, 72. *Bird-Lore* 4 (November–December 1902): 208.

13. *Auk* 20 (January 1903): 102, 112–13.

14. On committee actions, *Bird-Lore* 4 (November–December 1902): 208. On discussions with Dutcher, Pearson to H. H. Brimley, December 6, 1902, Brimley Papers; Pearson, *The Passing of Our Sea Birds*, 3.

15. *Auk* 20 (January 1903): 59–63 and 157; *Bird-Lore* 4 (November–December 1902): 207–8.

*Chapter 10*

1. Pearson to C. S. Vann, December 5, 1902, Pearson to H. H. Brimley, December 6, 1902, and Brimley to Pearson, December 11, 1902, Brimley Papers.

2. ASNC, *Report of the State Audubon Society. January 1, 1911*, 4. On precedents, Robert W. Williams, *Game Commissions and Wardens*, 105 and 152–55.

3. Pearson to H. H. Brimley, December 11, 1902, Brimley Papers. *State* v. *Gallop*, 126 NC 635; Bean, *The Evolution of National Wildlife Law*, 16.

4. Pearson to H. H. Brimley, December 11, 1902, and Brimley to Pearson, December 12, 1902, Brimley Papers.

5. On the trip, *Adventures*, 77; *Auk* 20 (January 1903): 155. On the stereopticon, Pearson to McIver, May 8, 1902, and September 10, 1903, McIver Papers. On the *Dovekie*, *Birds* (1919), 25.

6. *Auk* 19 (January 1902): 59–70; *Science*, February 26, 1886, 204;

*Adventures*, 84–85; N.C. House of Representatives, *H.B. 304, Session 1903*, sec. 4.

7. Chapman, *Handbook*, 282–83. Also Terres, *Audubon Society Encyclopedia*, 1007–9; Edgar M. Reilly, *The Audubon Illustrated Handbook of American Birds*, 433–34; Michael J. Brodhead, "Elliott Coues and the Sparrow War."

8. On starlings, Terres, *Audubon Society Encyclopedia*, 837–38; Chapman, *Handbook*, 259–60; *Birds*, 285–86. On the pigeon, Terres, *Audubon Society Encyclopedia*, 731; *Birds*, 188.

9. *Birds*, 329–31; Terres, *Audubon Society Encyclopedia*, 939.

10. N.C. House of Representatives, *H.B. 304, Session 1903*, sec. 4; *Birds*, 88–106, 195–205, 241–43, 333, and 336–40; *Adventures*, 84.

11. N.C. House of Representativess, *H.B. 304, Session 1903*, secs. 4 and 5.

12. Ibid., secs. 10 and 14.

13. Charles B. Aycock, "Biennial Message," 45. Pearson to H. H. Brimley, January 12, 1903, Brimley Papers. On the bill in the legislature, *Adventures*, 79. Also Pearson to H. H. Brimley, December 8, 1902, and Pearson to J. F. Jordan, January 8, 1902[3], Brimley Papers.

14. ASNC, *Main Provisions of the Audubon Bill*.

15. On house dates, N.C. *House Journal, 1903*, 277. *Adventures*, 82; *Auk* 21 (January 1904): 192–93; N.C. *House Journal, 1903*, 310–28.

16. *Auk* 21 (January 1904): 204.

17. Pearson, "Birds of Tennessee."

18. *Nashville American*, quoted in *Auk* 21 (January 1904): 192–93. Also *Tennessee Public Laws, 1903*, chap. 118.

19. N.C. *House Journal, 1903*, 402 and 426. *Adventures*, 80–81.

20. *Adventures*, 85; N.C. *House Journal, 1903*, 426; N.C. General Assembly, *An Act To Incorporate the Audubon Society of North Carolina*, sec. 4.

21. N.C. General Assembly, *An Act to Incorporate*, secs. 7 and 11.

22. *Adventures*, 87. On other states, *Auk* 18 (January 1901): 77–82; *Bird-Lore* 7 (January–February 1905): 47; Palmer, *Chronology and Index of the More Important Events in American Game Protection, 1776–1911*, 38–39.

23. Pearson to H. H. Brimley, March 17, 1903, Brimley Papers. Pearson, "The Mocking Bird," 266.

24. Pearson to H. H. Brimley, March 23, 1903, Brimley Papers. Also ibid., April 13, 1903, Brimley Papers.

*Chapter 11*

1. ASNC, *First Annual Report*, 4; photograph of sign, National Audubon Society files; Pearson to H. H. Brimley, April 13, 1903, Brimley Papers.

2. Pearson to H. H. Brimley, April 13, and May 6 and 14, 1903, Brimley papers.

3. ASNC, *Second Annual Report*, 15.

4. Pearson to H. H. Brimley, June 13, 1903, Brimley Papers.

5. Pearson, "Bird Life in July"; University of Tennessee, Summer School of the South, *Announcement, 1903*. *Atlantic Educational Journal* 6 (July–August 1903): 24. Lewis, *Philander Priestley Claxton*, 111.

6. On MacIver, Douglas, "T. Gilbert Pearson." Douglas, "Mindpower Past"; SNIC, *Catalogue, 1902–1903*, 27–29 and 68, and *Catalogue, 1903–1904*, 7; *Greensboro News & Record*, November 26, 1983.

7. ASNC, *Second Annual Report*, 12–13.

8. Ibid., 13–16.

9. On the arrest, ibid., 7–8; *Adventures*, 92. *Bird-Lore* 5 (September–October 1903): 174. Wright to Chapman, October 13, 1903, Historical Correspondence, AMNH.

10. *Adventures*, 92–94.

11. Pearson, *Protect the Insect-Eating Birds* (1903), 1–3.

12. ASNC, *Second Annual Report*; Pearson, ed., *Portraits and Habits of Our Birds*.

13. ASNC, *Second Annual Report*, 5–6 and 16–17. On the Library Act, Orr, *Charles Brantley Aycock*, 207–8.

14. *Bird-Lore* 5 (January–February 1903): 40 and (March–April 1903): 70–72; ASNC, *Report of the Treasurer*.

15. *Adventures*, 92–94. Also ASNC, *Second Annual Report*, 8.

16. On the myth-making shipment, *Adventures*, 101–2. On later smuggling, ASNC, *Second Annual Report*, 10–11.

17. ASNC, *Second Annual Report*, 8–10.

18. Ibid., 19–30.

19. Ibid., 1 and 20–29.

20. On Fuertes, Wright to Chapman, June 3, 1904, Historical Correspondence, AMNH. On *Bird-Lore*, ibid., October 13, 1903. On Dutcher, ibid., undated latter, ca. 1903–4.

21. Elisha Mitchell Scientific Society, *Journal* 20 (no date): 15–16 and (December 1904): 122–23.

22. *Auk* 21 (January 1904): 97–99.

23. On the thirty-three wardens, ibid., 201–4.

24. Ibid., 122; Chapman, *Autobiography of a Bird-Lover*, 181–82; *Adventures*, 236–37; *Bird-Lore* 13 (May–June 1911): 175–77.

25. *Bird-Lore* 5 (May–June 1903): 104–5 and 5 (September–October 1903): 171–72; *Auk* 21 (January 1904): 102.

26. On urging the government, ibid., 106–9. For Wright's quote, *Bird-Lore* 5 (January–February 1903): 37.

27. On finances, ASNC, *Report of the Treasurer.* Pearson's praise, ASNC, *Second Annual Report*, 11. Letter to Dutcher, *Auk* 21 (January 1904): 185.

28. *State Normal Magazine* 8 (February 1904): 114–17 and 124; Rose Howell Holder, *McIver of North Carolina*, 232–34.

## Chapter 12

1. Pearson to H. H. Brimley, January 28, 1904, Brimley Papers.

2. *Adventures*, 341; *Recreation* 20 (April 1904): 307–12 and 319–20; Dian Olson Belanger, *Managing American Wildlife*, 10–11 and 17–18.

3. On Winston, Orr, *Charles Brantley Aycock*, 205; ASNC, *Second Annual Report*, 24. ASNC, *Some Possibilities of Game Protection in North Carolina*, 12–19.

4. ASNC, *Some Possibilities*, 1–12.

5. ASNC, *Second Annual Report*, 2, and *Third Annual Report*, 2. Also Pearson to Theodore S. Palmer, March 16, 1904, Palmer Papers.

6. Ibid. On the 5,000 copies, ASNC, *Third Annual Report*, 4.

7. Pearson, "The Botanist" and "The Gander of Roanoke." For Chapman's views, *Bird-Lore* 6 (January–February 1904): 32; Schmitt, *Back to Nature*, 45–55.

8. *State Normal Magazine* 9 (October 1904): 37; ASNC, *Financial Statement*; SNIC, *Catalogue, 1902–1903*, 5.

9. Pearson, "The Cormorants of Great Lake."

10. On Pearson's observations and the fishermen, Pearson, "With the Carolina Sea Birds," 8–12. On the warden's reports, ASNC, *Third Annual Report*, 9.

11. *Bird-Lore* 7 (January–February 1905): 81 and 118; *Auk* 21 (January 1904): 133–34; *State Normal Magazine* 9 (October 1904): 37.

12. On Pearson's job, SNIC, *Catalogue, 1901–1902*, 79, and *Cata-*

*logue, 1904–1905*, 80; *State Normal Magazine* 9 (October 1904): 30–31. On the lessees, Palmer, Diary, November 9–12, 1904, Palmer Papers; ASNC, *Third Annual Report*, 14–23.

13. Ibid., 14–15; *Birds* (1919), 57.

14. ASNC, *Third Annual Report*, 15–16.

15. Ibid., 4; *Bird-Lore* 7 (January–February 1905): 100–101.

16. ASNC, *Third Annual Report*, 9. Also ASNC, *Financial Statement*, 2; ASNC, *Fourth Annual Report*, 39.

### Chapter 13

1. *Adventures*, 130; *Bird-Lore* 6 (January–February 1904): 35, (May–June 1904): 105, (July–August 1904): 140, and (September–October 1904): 174.

2. *Appletons' Cyclopedia of American Biography* 6:516; *Who Was Who in America, 1897–1942*, 1349; *New York Times*, August 19, 1906.

3. *Adventures*, 130.

4. Ibid., 130–31; *Auk* 22 (January 1905): 71–76; *Bird-Lore* 7 (November–December 1905): 349–50.

5. ASNC, *Financial Statement*, 3. On McIver's reaction, *Adventures*, 131. On Bryant, SNIC, *Catalogue, 1903–1904*, 5, and *Catalogue, 1904–1905*, 7; Pearson to Laura Coit, December 26, 1904, McIver Papers.

6. Pearson to Chapman, February 15, 1905, and Chapman to Pearson, February 28, 1905, Pearson folder, AMNH. On the letters, *Bird-Lore* 6 (November–December 1904): 215–16 and 7 (January–February 1905): 41–42 and (March–April 1905): 141–42.

7. On incorporation, ibid., 7 (January–February 1905): 39–40. *Auk* 22 (January 1905): 110.

8. *Adventures*, 439–40; *Auk* 22 (April 1905): 232.

9. *Adventures*, 130. On the residents' actions, ASNC, *Third Annual Report*, 12–13. *Adventures*, 132.

10. *Dictionary of American Biography* 9:409–10; *Adventures*, 132–33. Also ASNC, *Third Annual Report*, 17; *Bird-Lore* 7 (January–February 1905): 120 and (November–December 1905): 348.

11. *Auk* 22 (April 1905): 232.

12. Pearson to H. H. Brimley, October 26, 1905, Brimley Papers. ASNC, *Fourth Annual Report*, 40.

13. *Adventures*, 133–35; ASNC, *Fifth Annual Report*, 5–6 and 20–22.

14. On the statistics, ASNC, *Fourth Annual Report*, 11. On the tern colony, Pearson, "The Least Tern"; *Bird-Lore* 8 (November–December 1906): 244. On the herons, ASNC, *Fourth Annual Report*, 8.

15. *Adventures*, 135–36.

16. *Boston Directory, 1900*, 470; *Who Was Who in America, 1897–1942*, 547; *Dictionary of American Biography* 4:518–19; *Bird-Lore* 7 (January–February 1905): 117 and (November–December 1905): 346.

17. *Bird-Lore* 7 (January–February 1905): 100 and (November–December 1905): 317. On Wayne, Palmer, et al., *Biographies*, 592–93. On the reorganization, *Adventures*, 137; *Bird-Lore* 7 (November–December 1905): 343.

18. *Bird-Lore* 7 (July–August 1905): 218 and (September–October 1905): 251 and 8 (January–February 1906): 34–35; *Auk* 22 (October 1905): 443.

19. *Adventures*, 137–38. For the quote on martins, Pearson, ed., *Birds of America* 3:83.

20. H. H. Brimley to Pearson, August 19, 1905, Brimley Papers.

21. Ibid., June 30, 1905, and August 12, 1905.

22. Pearson to Brimley, February 23, 1906; see also Brimley to "My Dear Albert," April 29, 1908, Brimley Papers.

23. Pearson to Brimley, March 14, 1906, Brimley Papers.

*Chapter 14*

1. On the North Carolina move, *State Normal Magazine* 10 (November 1905): 26; *Greensboro, N.C. Directory, 1905–06*, 258. *Bird-Lore* 7 (November–December 1905): 296 and 345–50.

2. *Bird-Lore* 7 (November–December 1905): 296–300; ASNC, *Fourth Annual Report*, 23.

3. *Bird-Lore* 7 (November–December 1905): 303–6.

4. On South Carolina, *Adventures*, 138; *Bird-Lore* 8 (November–December 1906): 232. On Georgia, *Adventures*, 141–42. Also *Bird-Lore* 8 (July–August 1906): 144–45.

5. Pearson, "Florida Bird Notes," 8.

6. Ibid., 10. Pearson, "The White Egrets," 64.

7. *Adventures*, 139–40.

8. *Bird-Lore* 8 (November–December 1906): 228–29.

9. Ibid., 7 (November–December 1905): 298–300 and 8 (July–August 1906): 145.

10. *Adventures*, 142.

11. *State Normal Magazine* 11 (June 1907): 255–56; ASNC, *Fourth Annual Report*, 28 and 38–40.

12. Raleigh *News and Observer*, June 20, 1906, clipping, National Audubon Society files. Also ASNC, *Fourth Annual Report*, 4.

13. ASNC, *Fourth Annual Report*, 4. *Charlotte Chronicle* (quoted in *Greensboro Record*, March 8, 1906), *Wilmington Star*, November 25, 1906, and *Greensboro Record*, March 8, 1906, clippings, National Audubon Society files.

14. ASNC, *Fourth Annual Report*, 11–12.

15. Pearson to H. H. Brimley, March 14, 1906, Brimley Papers. *Wilmington Star*, August 4, 1906, clipping, National Audubon Society files; *Bird-Lore* 8 (November–December 1906): 219.

16. On Dutcher's and Bond's appeals, *Congressional Record*, January 26, 1906, 1626, and February 23, 1906, 2900; *Bird-Lore* 8 (July–August 1906): 145.

17. Pearson to Palmer, June 12, 1906, Palmer Papers. *Congressional Record*, June 11, 1906, 8238, June 23, 1906, 9032, and June 29, 1906, 9722. Also "An Act to Protect Birds and Their Eggs in Game and Bird Preserves" (34 Stat. 536).

18. *Adventures*, 143. *New York Times*, August 19, 1906. On details of the bequest, *Bird-Lore* 8 (November–December 1906): 225 and 9 (November–December 1907): 368; *Adventures*, 143; *Auk* 24 (January 1907): 120.


*Chapter 15*


1. *Bird-Lore* 9 (January–February 1907): 55. *Adventures*, 147; *Bird-Lore* 9 (November–December 1907): 345.

2. Robert B. Glenn, "The Governor's Message," 23. Pearson to Dutcher, January 12, 1907, Audubon Societies Papers. N.C. *Senate Journal, 1907*, 28; N.C. *House Journal, 1907*, 50.

3. Pearson to Dutcher, January 19, 1907, and February 2, 1907, Audubon Societies Papers (hereinafter ASP).

4. Pearson to Dutcher, February 15, 1907, Raleigh *News and Observer*, February 15, 1907, clipping, Busbee and Busbee to Dutcher, February 7, 1907, and Dutcher to Busbee and Busbee, February 9, 1907, ASP.

5. *Adventures*, 148. Pearson to Dutcher, January 19, 1907, ASP. On the bills, Pearson to Dutcher, January 12, 1907, ASP; *Bird-Lore* 9 (May–June 1907): 142; N.C. *Public Laws, 1907*, chaps. 358 and 422. On abandoning the game-bird bill, ASNC, *Fifth Annual Report*, 20.

6. Pearson to Dutcher, January 19, 1907, ASP. Also John L. Cheney, *North Carolina Government, 1585–1974*, 480 and 484–85.

7. On the increase, *Adventures*, 119. Pearson to Dutcher, February 16, 1907, ASP. On the arrests, ASNC, *Fifth Annual Report*, 16–17. Pearson to Dutcher, February 23, 1907, ASP. N.C. *House Journal, 1907*, 469.

8. *Bird-Lore* 9 (November–December 1907): 303–7 (quote), 290, and 352–53.

9. ASNC, *Sixth Annual Report*, 25–26; Pearson to Dutcher, July 8, 1907, ASP.

10. ASNC, *Sixth Annual Report*, 26–27.

11. William W. Cocks to Allen, January 26, 1907, ASP. See especially Sterling, *Last of the Naturalists*, 258–73. Dutcher to Pearson, January 28, 1907, ASP.

12. *Adventures*, 149.

13. On the original bill, Dutcher to Pearson, Febuary 2, 1907, and Pearson to Dutcher, January 30, 1907, ASP. For the quote, *Adventures*, 150.

14. Pearson to Dutcher, January 30, 1907, ASP; *Adventures*, 150.

15. On lobbying efforts, *Adventures*, 151. On the results, Pearson to Dutcher, February 26 and March 1, 1907, ASP; Sterling, *Last of the Naturalists*, 272.

16. Williams to Dutcher, March 20, 1907, ASP.

17. *Bird-Lore* 9 (November–December 1907): 300–303.

18. Ibid., 301, and *Adventures*, 152–55.

19. *Auk* 25 (April 1908): 246–47.


## Chapter 16

1. Pearson to Dutcher, January 22, 1907, ASP. On organizing, Pearson to Dutcher, April 11, 1907, ASP; *Bird-Lore* 9 (January–February 1907): 56, (March–April 1907): 102, and (November–December 1907): 355.

2. On activities in the cities, Pearson to Dutcher, April 11, 1907, ASP. For the quote, *Bird-Lore* 9 (March–April 1907): 102.

3. *Birds*, 347.

4. *Bird-Lore* 13 (September–October 1911): 273–74.

5. ASNC, *Fifth Annual Report*, 18–19.

6. Pearson to Dutcher, June 29, 1907, ASP. Also *Bird-Lore* 9 (May–June 1907): 142; *Birds*, 179–80; ASNC, *Sixth Annual Report*, 14. On the warden's estimates, Pearson, "Mortality among Birds."

7. On the description of the tern, *Birds*, 179–181; Pearson to Dutcher, June 29, 1907, ASP; Pearson, "Cabot's Tern."

8. ASNC, *Sixth Annual Report*, 10 and 18–21, and *Fifth Annual Report*, 10.

9. Pearson to Dutcher, January 10, 1908, ASP; ASNC, *Sixth Annual Report*, 29; *Bird-Lore* 9 (November –December 1907): 355–56; *Adventures*, 155.

10. Pearson to Dutcher, January 28, 1908, ASP. On restaurants and hotels, Pearson to Dutcher, January 22, 1908, ASP. On Charleston and arrests, *Bird-Lore* 11 (January–February 1909): 49.

11. Pearson, "Ornithological Work in North Carolina."

12. On his travel, Pearson to Dutcher, January 22, 1908, and June 17, 1908, ASP. On writing Georgians, Pearson to Dutcher, June 20, 1908, ASP. On Wallace and the bill, Pearson to Dutcher, June 17, 1908, and August 5, 1908, ASP; *Bird-Lore* 10 (July–August 1908): 185; *Adventures*, 159.

13. On Elsie, Pearson to Dutcher, August 8, 1908, ASP. On summer school, Pearson to Dutcher, August 5, 1908, ASP. On the Indiana meeting, *Bird-Lore* 20 (November–December 1908): 301–2. On Porter, *Adventures*, 160. Also Deborah Dahlke-Scott and Michael Prewitt, "A Writer's Crusade To Portray Spirit of the Limberlost."

14. Pearson to Dutcher, August 5 and 8, 1908, ASP; *Adventures*, 159.

15. *Bird-Lore* 11 (January–February 1909): 50–51. Pearson to Dutcher, January 14, 1908, ASP.

16. On Aycock, Pearson to Dutcher, September 9, 1908, ASP; ASNC, *Sixth Annual Report*, 3–4. On the bill, Pearson to Bowdish, January 30, 1908, ASP; N.C. *House Journal, 1908*, 35. On the junior secretary's request, ASNC, *Seventh Annual Report*, 25–29. Dutcher to Pearson, June 9, 1908, ASP.

17. On Dutcher's actions, Chapman to Wright, November 29, 1907, Palmer to Chapman, undated, and Chapman to Palmer, January 3, 1908, Historical Files, AMNH.

18. Pearson to Dutcher, February 1, 1908, and Dutcher to Pearson, February 3, 1908, ASP. Pearson, "Warden of Our Bird Life."

*Chapter 17*

1. Davis, ed., *Encyclopedia* 1:246, and 2:528–29.
2. Pinkett, *Gifford Pinchot*, 102–11; M. Nelson McGeary, *Gifford Pinchot*, 86–87; National Conservation Commission, *Report* 1:123; Conference on Conservation of Natural Resources, *Proceedings of a Conference of Governors*, v–xii. Also Samuel P. Hays, *Conservation and the Gospel of Efficiency*, 127–30.
3. On the request, Dutcher to Pearson, September 28, 1908, ASP. On Roosevelt, National Conservation Commission, *Report* 1:3–4 and 123.
4. Conference on Conservation of Natural Resources, *Proceedings*, 412.
5. For the quote, ibid., 192–94. National Conservation Commission, *Report* 1:115–19.
6. Fourth International Fishery Congress, *Proceedings*, pt. 1, 3–13. On Dutcher and the delegates, *Bird-Lore* 11 (January–February 1909): 53–54. Jean Delacour, interview with the author. Pearson to Palmer, September 29, 1908, Palmer Papers.
7. Pearson to Dutcher, September 28, 1908, ASP.
8. On the committee, *Bird-Lore* 10 (November–December 1908): 275; Dutcher to Pearson, November 5, 1908, ASP. On the address, *Bird-Lore* 10 (November–December 1908): 277–84.
9. *Bird-Lore* 10 (November–December 1908): 274–75 and 284–87 and 11 (November–December 1909): 278 and 348.
10. Dutcher to Pearson, December 4, 1908, and Pearson to Dutcher, telegram, December 3, 1908, ASP. Conference on Conservation of Natural Resources, *Proceedings*, 123; National Conservation Commission, *Report* 1:28–35 and 117.
11. Pinchot, *Breaking New Ground*, 375. On Taft's remarks, National Conservation Commission, *Report* 1:124.
12. Pearson to Dutcher, December 9, 1908, and December 15, 1908, ASP; National Conservation Commission, *Report* 1:249–63 and (for Merriam's report) 3:316–40.
13. *Bird-Lore* 11 (November–December 1909): 295; Pearson to Dutcher, December 15, 1908, and January 7, 1909, and Dutcher to Pearson, December 16, 1908, ASP.

14. Pearson, "Suggested Outline Plan for Investigative Work by the Audubon Society Committee of the National Conservation Commission," December 15, 1908, and Pearson to Dutcher, December 15, 1908, ASP.

15. *Bird-Lore* 11 (January–February 1909): 48. On the commission's fate, McGeary, *Gifford Pinchot*, 99–100.

16. Chapman, *Autobiography*, 200 ff.; Palmer et al., *Biographies*, 521–22; *Bird-Lore* 7 (November–December 1905): 348; Trefethan, *An American Crusade for Wildlife*, 148-50; Pearson, *Adventures*, 275.

17. Trefethan, *An American Crusade for Wildlife*, 150; *Bird-Lore* 11 (January–February 1909): 54–56 and (March–April 1909): 98.

18. *Adventures*, 254. Roosevelt, *Theodore Roosevelt*, 460–61; also *Bird-Lore* 11 (November–December 1909): 291–93.


*Chapter 18*

1. Pearson to Dutcher, January 7, 1909, ASP. On the committees, N.C. *Senate Journal, 1909*, 12; N.C. *House Journal, 1909*, 31. N.C. *Public Laws, 1909*, chaps. 338 and 775. ASNC, *Seventh Annual Report*, 20.

2. Pearson to Dutcher, January 16, 1909, ASP. N.C. *Senate Journal, 1909*, 59, 68, 89–90, 103–4, and 140–1. N.C. *House Journal, 1909*, 575.

3. Pearson to Dutcher, January 23, 1909, ASP. N.C. *Senate Journal, 1909*, 52, 68, 72, and 93; N.C. *Public Laws, 1909*, chap. 185.

4. On the invitation, *Adventures*, 162; Pearson to Beecher S. Bowdish, February 5, 1909, ASP. On activities in Arkansas and Texas *Bird-Lore* 11 (March–April 1909): 99 and 11 (July–August 1909): 189; *Adventures*, 162–63.

5. On the delegation, *Bird-Lore* 11 (November–December 1909): 299; McGeary, *Gifford Pinchot*, 107–8; Pinchot, *Breaking New Ground*, 361–66. On Pearson and Diaz, *Adventures*, 167–68; *Bird-Lore* 11 (March–April 1909): 99.

6. *Adventures*, 168–69; N.C. *House Journal, 1909*, 673; N.C. *Senate Journal, 1909*, 403 and 417.

7. *Adventures*, 170; N.C. *Public Laws, 1909*, chap. 840.

8. *Adventures*, 169.

9. Ibid.; N.C. *House Journal, 1909*, 748.

10. ASNC, *Seventh Annual Report*, 30–31; *Adventures*, 170.

11. *Adventures*, 169; ASNC, *Seventh Annual Report*, 30–31; *Bird-Lore* 10 (November–December 1908): 327.

12. *Adventures*, 170–71; N.C. *House Journal, 1909,* 748.

13. William W. Kitchin, "Inaugural Address"; *Adventures,* 171–72.

14. N.C. *Senate Journal, 1909,* 504, 539, 543, 602–4, and 655–56; N.C. *Public Laws, 1909,* chap. 840.

15. *Adventures,* 170–73 (Raleigh *News and Observer,* March 6, 1909, quoted on 172).

16. ASNC, *Seventh Annual Report,* 24. *Adventures,* 173.

17. On the southern bills, *Adventures,* 173; Palmer, *Chronology and Index,* 13. On Francis's bill, *Bird-Lore* 11 (March–April 1909): 98, and on Chapman, 11 (May–June 1909): 141–44. *Bird-Lore* 11 (May–June 1909): 134.

18. On other states, ibid., 146–48, and on Oregon, ibid., (November–December 1909):301–2 and 285.

19. Ibid., (November–December 1909): 297–99.

20. On Pearson's and Moore's jobs, ASNC, *Eighth Annual Report,* 5–6; *Bird-Lore* 11 (November–December 1909): 346; Dutcher to Pearson, April 29, 1909, and Mary T. Moore to Board of Directors, April 22, 1909, and to Dutcher, May 26, 1909, ASP. On Pearson's assignments and travels, *Adventures,* 177–78; see also *Bird-Lore* 11 (November–December 1909): 295. On receipts, *Bird-Lore* 10 (November-December 1908): 326 and 11 (November-December 1909): 345.

21. *Adventures,* 346. First National Conservation Congress, *Addresses and Proceedings,* 64 and 181–82.

22. First National Conservation Congress, *Addresses and Proceedings,* 108–14. For information about balance of nature theories, see Ernst Mayr, *The Growth of Biological Thought,* 482–83.

23. *Bird-Lore* 11 (November–December 1909): 286–87 (for the quotes) and 289–96.

24. Ibid., 305–44.

25. ASNC, *Seventh Annual Report,* 24 and 29, and *Eighth Annual Report,* 3–5.

*Chapter 19*

1. *Adventures,* 178–81.

2. Ibid., 179–80. Also *Bird-Lore* 12 (November–December 1910): 265.

3. *Adventures,* 180–83. On the Canton lecture, *Bird-Lore* 12 (Novem-

ber–December 1910): 269. On Watertown, *Watertown Standard*, January 11, 1910, and *Watertown Times* (?), January 11, 1910, clippings, ASP.

4. *Adventures*, 181–82.

5. Ibid., 183–84; *Bird-Lore* 12 (January–February 1910): 50; Chapman, *Handbook*, 269–71.

6. On "rest," *Adventures*, 184. On Richmond, *Bird-Lore* 12 (November–December 1910): 305. On his New Orleans address, *Picayune*, February 8, 1910, clipping, ASP. Pearson to Dutcher, February 8, 1910, ASP; Belanger, *Managing American Wildlife*, 184–86. On the Jackson activities, *Adventures*, 185; Pearson to Dutcher, February 16, 1910, ASP; *Bird-Lore* 11 (November–December 1909): 318.

7. Edgar B. Nixon, ed., *Franklin D. Roosevelt and Conservation* 1:3–4 and 11; *Adventures*, 186-88.

8. *Adventures*, 190.

9. Ibid., 186–90; *New York Times*, March 24, 1910, and (for the quote) March 26, 1910. On the assembly vote, ibid., April 13 and 18, 1910; *Adventures*, 192–93, and on the senate vote, 195; *New York Times*, April 22, 1910.

10. On Dutcher's plans, *Auk* 27 (July 1910): 365. On the hearing, *Adventures*, 195–96.

11. *Adventures*, 196–97. *Bird-Lore* 12 (May–June 1910): 128–29.

12. *Bird-Lore* 12 (November–December 1910): 295–96.

13. *Adventures*, 198–200. Also *Birds* (1919), 144.

14. *Dictionary of American Biography* 8:291–93; *Bird-Lore* 13 (November–December 1911): 387; *Adventures*, 201.

15. *Adventures*, 201; *Bird-Lore* 12 (September–October 1910): 206–9.

16. *Adventures*, 203. Palmer to Pearson, June 13, 1910, ASP.

17. On the junior societies, *Bird-Lore* 12 (November–December 1910): 268. The quote is from *Adventures*, 203–4.

18. *Adventures*, 204; *Bird-Lore* 12 (November–December 1910): 269, 303–4, and 260, and 13 (November–December 1911): 383–84.

19. *Bird-Lore* 13 (September–October 1911): 274. *Adventures*, 205.

20. *Bird-Lore* 12 (July–August 1910): 169–72.

21. *Bird-Lore* 12 (July–August 1910): 172 and 12 (November–December 1910): 267; *Auk* 38 (October 1921): 508–9; *Adventures*, 204.

22. National Conservation Congress, *Proceedings*, iv, ix, 145, (on the recommendation) 311, and (on the league report) 415–16; *Bird-Lore* 12 (September–October 1910): 218 and 12 (November–December 1910): 270.

23. *Bird-Lore* 12 (September–October 1910): 218. *Adventures*, 347; Joseph Hyde Pratt, "The Conservation and Utilization of Our Natural Resources."

24. *Bird-Lore* 12 (November–December 1910): 270.

25. Pearson to Palmer, October 15, 1910, Palmer Papers. Also *Adventures*, 206. Palmer to Pearson, October 21, 1910, Palmer Papers.

26. Dutcher to Pearson, September 16, 1910, ASP. Also E. H. Howard to Palmer, January 18, 1909, Palmer Papers. *Adventures*, 206, for Pearson's quotes.

*Chapter 20*

1. *Adventures*, 206. On Pearson's move, *Bird-Lore* 13 (January–February 1911): 59.

2. *Adventures*, 219, and on the staff and move, 229; *Bird-Lore* 13 (March–April 1911): 119 and (November–December): 399.

3. *Adventures*, 211–12.

4. Ibid., 174 and 214; ASNC, *Ninth Annual Report*, 7–8; Pearson to J. Swan Frick, January 20, 1911, Milford W. Haynes to Pearson, January 7, 11, 12, and 13 and February 16, 1911, Aycock and Winston to Pearson, January 7, 1911 (telegram), and Pearson to Aycock and Winston, January 14, 1911 (telegram), ASP.

5. On Kitchin, Haynes to Pearson, January 7, 1911, ASP; William W. Kitchin, "Biennial Message," 30. Also Pearson to P. D. Gold, July 1, 1911, ASP. On the committee, N.C. *House Journal, 1911*, 58, 133, and 331; Haynes to Pearson, January 7 and 10, 1911, ASP. On the vote, Pearson to J. H. Dillard, February 17, 1911; N.C. *House Journal, 1911*, 988–89. On state game laws, ASNC, *Ninth Annual Report*, 5. Also *Adventures*, 175.

6. *Bird-Lore* 13 (November–December 1911): 381–82. Also ibid., 11 (January–February 1909): 48–50 and (November–December 1909): 305 and 331–32, and 12 (November–December 1910): 302–3; Palmer, *Chronology and Index*, 41.

7. *Bird-Lore* 13 (July–August 1911): 227–28 and (November–December 1911): 379–80.

8. Pearson to Richard H. Lewis, August 23, 1911, ASP. Also *Bird-Lore* 12 (November–December 1910): 266, 13 (September–October

1911): 273–74 and (November–December 1911): 335; Palmer, *Chronology and Index*, 45.

9. On the bill and hearing *Bird-Lore* 13 (March–April 1911): 119–20 and 171–72; *Adventures*, 220–23. On feather collecting and the committee, *Adventures*, 220–24; *Bird-Lore* 13 (May–June 1911): 171–74; Nixon, ed., *Franklin D. Roosevelt and Conservation*, 1:7.

10. *Bird-Lore* 13 (May–June 1911): 178; *Adventures*, 220.

11. *Adventures*, 225–26. Also *Bird-Lore* 13 (March–April 1911): 120.

12. William T. Hornaday, *Our Vanishing Wild Life*, 308. Also William Bridges, *Gathering of Animals*, 279. *Bird-Lore* 13 (July–August 1911): 225.

13. *Adventures*, 231–33. H. S. Leonard to Pearson, May 5, 1911, Gifford Pinchot Papers.

14. *Bird-Lore* 12 (November–December 1910): 317–18; ASNC, *Eighth Annual Report*, 4.

15. Leonard to Pearson, May 11, 1911, Pinchot Papers.

16. William W. Grant to Palmer, May 26, 1911, and Jonathan Dwight to Palmer, May 31, 1911, Palmer Papers. Pinchot to Pearson, May 27, 1911, Pinchot Papers.

17. On confidentiality, Pearson to Palmer, June 3, 1911, Palmer Papers. *New York Times*, June 3, 1911.

18. *New York Times*, June 3, 1911.

19. Pearson to Palmer, June 3, 1911, Palmer Papers.

20. On the train trip, Pearson to Palmer, June 3, 1911 (telegram), Palmer Papers. On Pearson's decision, Pearson to Pinchot, June 16, 1911, and Hornaday to Pinchot, June 14, 1911, Pinchot Papers.

21. Pinchot to Grinnell, Allen, and Pearson, June 10, 1911 (telegram), and Hornaday to Pinchot, June 10, 1911 (telegram), Pinchot Papers. Catherine O. Dutcher to Meloy, June 12, 1911, and to Pearson, June 12, 1911, Palmer Papers.

22. Hornaday to Pinchot, June 14, 1911, and Grinnell to Pinchot, June 14, 1911, Pinchot Papers.

23. Pearson to Chapman, June 15, 1911, Historical Correspondence, AMNH. On Chapman at the meeting, *New York Times*, June 17, 1911. *Bird-Lore* 13 (July–August 1911): 212.

24. Pinchot, diary, June 16, 1911, Pinchot Papers. Wright to Grant, May 25, 1911, Palmer Papers. On Grinnell, Fox, *John Muir and His Legacy*, 156. Pearson to Palmer, June 17, 1911, Palmer Papers.

25. *Adventures*, 234.

26. Meloy to Pinchot, June 17, 1911, and Hornaday to Pinchot, June

14, 1911, Pinchot Papers. On Hornaday later, Irving Brant, *Adventures in Conservation with Franklin D. Roosevelt*, 4. For Pearson's quote, *Adventures*, 345. Pinchot to Pearson, November 10, 1911, Pinchot Papers. Pearson to Palmer, September 8, 1911, Palmer Papers.

27. *Adventures*, 233–34 and 354–55; *Bird-Lore* 14 (January–February 1912): 76–77; Clepper, ed., *Leaders of American Conservation*, 51–52.

*Chapter 21*

1. *Adventures*, 223. Pearson to Gold, July 1, 1911, Gold to Pearson, July 27, 1911, and, on the annual report, Gold to Pearson, October 30, 1911 (with Pearson's draft), ASP.

2. On the $200, Pearson to Gold, July 20, 1911, ASP. On the 11,000 birds, *Bird-Lore* 13 (November–December 1911): 378 and, on the terns, 338.

3. Pearson to Kitchin, July 1, 1911, ASP. On the art appropriation, Gold to Pearson, September 12, 1911, and enclosures and C. S. Brimley to Pearson, January 11, 1911, ASP; *Birds*, xviii. On Horsfall, Pearson to H. H. Brimley, September 1, 1911, ASP.

4. On Maine and Norton, *Adventures*, 230. Also *Bird-Lore* 13 (November–December 1911): 338 and 372. On the birds, Pearson, *Birds of America* 1:42–45.

5. *Adventures*, 231. Also *Bird-Lore* 13 (September–October 1911): 277, 273.

6. *Bird-Lore* 12 (November–December 1910): 253–54.

7. On Montclair, ibid., 13 (September–October 1911): 274–75, on martins, 276, on the essay contest and Ford, 278, Pearson on the changing view, 275. Schmitt, *Back to Nature*, 44.

8. *Adventures*, 234. On finances, *Bird-Lore* 12 (November–December 1910): 316–18, 13 (November–December 1911): 397–99, and 14 (November–December 1912): 391; *Adventures*, 234.

9. *Bird-Lore* 13 (July–August 1911): 226 and, on the $5000, (November–December 1911): 388, and *Adventures*, 425.

10. On feather markets, *Bird-Lore* 13 (May–June 1911): 173. On egret plumes, *Adventures*, 229. On the $500, *Bird-Lore* 13 (May–June 1911): 174 and, on colonies and McIlheny, (November–December 1911): 339, and *Who Was Who in America, 1943–1950*, 361. On Bird Island, *Bird-Lore* 13 (November–December 1911): 338.

11. *Bird-Lore* 13 (November–December 1911): 326 and 370; maps on letterhead, Pearson to Palmer, April 29, 1911, Palmer Papers.

12. *Bird-Lore* 13 (November–December 1911): 333–34.

13. *Auk* 29 (January 1912): 97. On Beebe, *Who Was Who in America, 1961–1968*, 72. *Adventures*, 235.

# Selected Bibliography

*Manuscript Sources*

American Ornithologists' Union, Committee on the Protection of North American Birds Minutes, December 12, 1885–February 17, 1887. National Audubon Society, New York.

Brant, Irving. Papers. Library of Congress, Washington, D.C.

Brimley, Herbert H. Papers. North Carolina Division of Archives and History, Raleigh. (Cited in notes as Brimley Papers [A&H].

Brimley, Herbert H. Papers. North Carolina State Museum of Natural Sciences, Raleigh. (Cited in notes as Brimley Papers.)

Department of Ornithology Historical Correspondence. American Museum of Natural History, New York.

Dialectic Society Records. University of North Carolina at Chapel Hill.

Guilford College Records. Guilford College, Greensboro, North Carolina.

Historical Correspondence. See Department of Ornithology Historical Correspondence.

Hobbs, Lewis Lyndon, and Mary Mendenhall Hobbs Papers. Guilford College, Greensboro, North Carolina.

McIver, Charles D. Papers. University of North Carolina at Greensboro.

National Association of Audubon Societies Papers. Astor, Lenox and Tilden Foundations. Rare Books and Manuscripts Division, New York Public Library. (Cited in notes as "Audubon Societies Papers" [ASP], the collection's former title.)

National Audubon Society files. National Audubon Society, New York.

North Carolina Geological Survey Papers. University of North Carolina at Chapel Hill.

Palmer, Theodore S. Papers. Library of Congress, Washington, D.C.

Pearson, T. Gilbert. File. North Carolina State Museum of Natural Sciences, Raleigh.

Pinchot, Gifford. Papers. Library of Congress, Washington, D.C.

State Normal and Industrial College Records. University of North Carolina at Greensboro.


*Works by T. Gilbert Pearson*

"An Addition and a Correction to the List of North Carolina Birds." *Auk* 15 (July 1898): 275.
*Adventures in Bird Protection, an Autobiography*. New York: Appleton-Century, 1937.
"After Fifty Years." *Guilford Collegian* 9 (December 1894): 108–10.
"The American Anhinga." *Ornithologist and Oologist* 16 (April 1891): 49–50.
"The Arredondo Sparrow Hawk." *Guilford Collegian* 13 (October 1900): 2–6.
"The Audubon Societies." *Atlantic Educational Journal* 5 (October 1902): 24.
"Bird Life in July." *Atlantic Educational Journal* 6 (July–August 1903): 12–13.
*The Bird Study Book*. Garden City, N.Y.: Doubleday, Page, 1917.
"Bird Study in Elementary Schools." *North Carolina Journal of Education* 4 (February 1901): 30–32.
"Birds in May." *Atlantic Educational Journal* 5 (May 1902): 22–23.
*Birds of America*. Editor and contributor. 3 vols. New York: The University Society, Inc., 1917.
*Birds of North Carolina*. With Clement S. Brimley and Herbert H. Brimley. Raleigh: Edwards & Broughton, 1919. Rev. ed. Raleigh: Bynum Printing Company, 1942.
"Birds of Tennessee." *State Normal Magazine* 8 (April 1903): 197–202.
"A Bob-White Family." *Guilford Collegian* 13 (March 1901): 138–48.
"Bob-White; Quail; Partridge (Colinus virginianus)." *Atlantic Educational Journal* 5 (May 1902): 23–24.
"The Botanist." *State Normal Magazine* 8 (February 1904): 110–12.
"Brunnich's Murre (*Uria lomvia*) at Newberne, N.C." *Auk* 14 (April 1897): 202.
"Cabot's Tern (Sterna sandvicensis acuflavida) Breeding in North Carolina." *Auk* 25 (July 1908): 312.
"The Childhood of Ring-Neck." *North Carolina Journal of Education* 3 (March 1900): 26–28.

"The City of the Longlegs." *Guilford Collegian* 12 (March 1900): 208–11.

"Collecting Experience." *Oologist* 7 (February 1890): 25–26.

"Collecting on Cobb's Island, Va." *Oologist* 9 (August 1892): 191–93.

"The Cormorants of Great Lake." *Bird-Lore* 7 (March–April 1905): 121–26.

"Cuckoo, the Rain Prophet." *North Carolina Journal of Education* 3 (December 1899): 23–24.

"A Day with the Herons in Florida." *Oologist* 5 (January 1888): 8–9.

"The Destruction of Our American Birds." *Guilford Collegian* 4 (June 1892): 240–42.

"The Development of Modern Science." *Guilford Collegian* 7 (May 1895): 227–31.

"The Dialectic Literary Society." *North Carolina University Magazine* 16 (December 1898): 84–89.

"The Eastern Snowbird: Junco hymelis." *Atlantic Educational Journal* 5 (February 1902): 21.

*Echoes from Bird Land. An Appeal to Women.* With message from Eula L. Dixon, "State Supt. Dept. of Mercy, W.C.T.U., Snow Camp, N.C.," July 1895. Unpaged circular.

"The Economic Value of Bird Study." *Atlantic Educational Journal* 4 (July 1901): 4–5.

"Evolution in Its Relation to Man." *Guilford Collegian* 8 (January 1896): 107–11.

"The Fall Migration of Birds in the Southern States." *Atlantic Educational Journal* 4 (November 1901): 17–18.

"February Birds." *Atlantic Educational Journal* 5 (February 1902): 20–21.

"Fifty Years of Bird Protection in the United States." In American Ornithologists' Union, *Fifty Years' Progress of American Ornithology, 1883–1933.* Rev. ed. Lancaster, Pa.: 1933.

"The Fish Scrap and Fish Oil Industry in North Carolina." *Guilford Collegian* 13 (February 1901): 81–87.

"The Flamingo Feather." *North Carolina University Magazine* 15 (April 1898): 152–56.

"Florida Bird Notes." *Bird-Lore* 9 (January–February 1907): 6–10.

"The Gander of Roanoke." *State Normal Magazine* 7 (October 1900): 13–35.

"George Bird Grinnell." *Bird-Lore* 14 (January–February 1912): 77–80.

"The Herons of Alachua County, Florida." *Ornithologist and Oologist* 17 (March 1892): 36–37, and (May 1892): 71–72.

"How We Got Our Man-o-War Bird." *Guilford Collegian* 9 (November 1896): 76–78.

"Hunting the Brown Pelican." *Guilford Collegian* 7 (December 1894): 83–86.

"The Ibises of Ledworth Lake." *Oologist* 9 (April 1892): 99–100.

"In the Great Dismal Swamp." *Ornithologist and Oologist* 18 (February 1893): 26–28.

"John James Audubon, the Ornithologist." *North Carolina Journal of Education* 3 (October 1899): 13–15.

"The Least Tern." *Bird-Lore* 20 (September–October 1918): 380–83.

"A Legend of Braiden Castle." *Guilford Collegian* 9 (February 1897): 169–73.

"A Lesson on Woodland Carpenters." *North Carolina Journal of Education* 2 (January 1899): 15–16.

Letter to readers. *North Carolina Journal of Education* 3 (June 1900): 1.

"Life on the Holiday Campus." *North Carolina University Magazine* 16 (February 1899): 150–55.

"March Birds." *Atlantic Educational Journal* 5 (March 1902): 18–19.

"The Mocking Bird." *Guilford Collegian* 12 (June 1900): 266–69.

"Mortality Among Birds." *Bird-Lore* 10 (May–June 1908): 124–26.

"Neighbors of Mine." *North Carolina University Magazine* 15 (February 1898): 72–77.

"Nesting Habits of Some Southern Forms of Birds in Eastern North Carolina." Elisha Mitchell Scientific Society, *Journal* 15 (January–June 1898), pt. 1:17–22.

"Nesting of the Pied-billed Grebe." *Ornithologist and Oologist* 15 (October 1890): 152–53. Reprinted in the December issue.

"The New Georgia Law." *Bird-Lore* 13 (September–October 1911): 273–74.

"North Carolina." *Bird-Lore* 9 (May–June 1907): 142.

"Notes from Alachua Co., Florida." *Oologist* 5 (October–November 1888): 150.

"Notes from North Carolina." *Bird-Lore* 10 (September–October 1908): 228–29.

"Notes on Some of the Birds of Eastern North Carolina." *Auk* 16 (July 1899): 246–50.

"Notes on the Herons of Central Florida." In *Papers Presented to the World's Congress on Ornithology*, edited by E. Irene Rood, 132–35. Chicago: Charles E. Sergel, 1896.

*Objects and Plans.* No. 5. Greensboro: Audubon Society of North Carolina, 1903.

"An Old Barred Owl." *North Carolina Journal of Education* 3 (June 1900): 20–22.

"Ornithological Work in North Carolina." Elisha Mitchell Scientific Society, *Journal* 24 (June 1908): 33–43.

"Our Chimney Dwellers." *Guilford Collegian* 12 (October 1899): 11–13.

"Our Summer Birds." *Guilford Collegian* 5 (May 1893): 231–32.

*Our Wild Birds in Agriculture.* No. 2 (rev.). Greensboro: Audubon Society of North Carolina, November 1902.

"A Pair of Brown Thrashers (*Harporhynchus rufus*)." *Atlantic Educational Journal* 5 (October 1902): 23–24.

"Passer domesticus at Archer, Fla., and Other Florida Notes." *Auk* 14 (January 1897): 99.

*The Passing of Our Sea Birds.* No. 3. Greensboro: Audubon Society of North Carolina, 1902.

"A Peep in the Autumn Woods." *Guilford Collegian* 8 (November 1895): 64–66.

*Portraits and Habits of Our Birds.* Editor. 2 vols. New York: National Association of Audubon Societies, 1920–21.

"Preliminary Catalogue of the Birds of Chapel Hill, N.C., with Brief Notes on Some of the Species." Elisha Mitchell Scientific Society, *Journal* 16 (January–June 1899), part 1, 33–51.

"Prof. John Tyndall." *Guilford Collegian* 6 (February 1894): 193–94.

*Protect the Insect-Eating Birds.* No. 6 and rev. ed. Greensboro: Audubon Society of North Carolina, 1903(?) and 1907(?).

"The Quest for the Cormorant's Nest." *Guilford Collegian* 12 (December 1899): 81–84.

"The Robin." *Bird-Lore* 12 (September–October 1910): 206–9.

"Ruffle Breast, the Shrike." *North Carolina Journal of Education* 3 (January 1900): 30–32.

"A Second Lesson on Woodland Carpenters." *North Carolina Journal of Education* 2 (February 1899): 19–20.

*Some Common Birds on the Farm.* Supplement to September Bulletin, 1909, North Carolina Department of Agriculture. Raleigh: E. M. Uzzell.

"Some Notes on the Wild Turkey." *Oologist* 10 (November 1893): 293–94.

"Some Spring Notes from Guildford [sic.] County, N.C." *Ornithologist and Oologist* 17 (May 1892): 76.

"The Song Sparrow." *Atlantic Educational Journal* 5 (March 1902): 19.

"South Carolina." *Bird-Lore* 9 (May–June 1907): 143.

"The Spring Migration of Birds." *North Carolina Journal of Education* 3 (February 1900): 12–13.

*Stories of Bird Life.* Richmond: B. F. Johnson Publishing Company, 1901.

"The Story of a Snow-Bird's Nest." *North Carolina University Magazine* 15 (December 1897): 9–14.

"The Study of Birds in the Public Schools." *North Carolina Journal of Education* 2 (September 1898): 11–12.

"Suggestions for Private Bird Study." *Atlantic Educational Journal* 4 (August 1901): 13.

*Tales from Birdland.* Garden City, N.Y.: Doubleday, Page, 1918.

"To the Editor." *Ornithologist and Oologist* 17 (January 1892): 13.

"Trying to Hatch Rotten Eggs." *Oologist* 6 (December 1889): 235.

"An Untimely End of a Set of Brown-headed Nuthatch Eggs." *Oologist* 6 (August 1889): 152–53.

"The Value of Southern Birds." *Atlantic Educational Journal* 5 (November 1902): 21–22.

"The Warden of Our Bird-Life." *World's Work* 16 (May 1908): 10244–47.

"Water and Land Birds Every Boy Should Know." In *Nature's Secrets*, edited by George Clyde Fisher, vol. 1, 34–134. New York: University Society, 1933.

"The White Egrets." *Bird-Lore* 14 (January–February 1912): 62–69.

"The Wild Turkey." *Guilford Collegian* 4 (March 1892): 168–69.

"With the Carolina Sea Birds." *State Normal Magazine* 9 (October 1904): 8–12.

"The Wood Duck." *Ornithologist and Oologist* 16 (September 1891): 134–35.

"Woodland Carpenters." *North Carolina Journal of Education* 2 (January 1899): 15–16; (February 1899): 19–20; (March 1899): 24–25; and (April 1899): 13–14.

"Work of the Audubon Society." *Guilford Collegian* 12 (February 1900): 176–77. An unsigned article apparently written by Pearson.


*Other Published Works*


Abbey, George. *The Balance of Nature and Modern Conditions of Cultivation.* New York: E. P. Dutton, 1909.

Allen, Joel A. *The American Ornithologists' Union, a Seven Years' Retrospect.* New York: American Ornithologists' Union, 1891.

———. "Bird-Destruction," *Science*, August 6, 1886, 118-19.

American Ornithologists' Union. *Fifty Years' Progress of American Ornithology, 1883–1933*. Rev. ed. Lancaster, Pa.: American Ornithologists' Union, 1933.

Angell, George T. *Autobiographical Sketches and Personal Recollections*. Boston: Franklin Press, Rand, Avery, 1884.

Atkinson, George F. "Preliminary Catalogue of the Birds of North Carolina." Elisha Mitchell Scientific Society, *Journal* 4 (1887) pt. 2: 44–87.

Audubon Society of North Carolina. Annual Reports, 1903–11.

———. *The Audubon Bird Identification Blank*. Richmond: B. F. Johnson, 1902.

———. *The Audubon Society of North Carolina for the Study and Protection of Birds and the Preservation of Game*. Greensboro, 1910(?).

———. *Constitution and By-Laws of the Audubon Society of North Carolina*. Greensboro, 1905.

———. *Constitution of the Audubon Society of North Carolina*. Greensboro, 1902(?).

———. *Financial Statement of the North Carolina Audubon Society for the Year Ending March 10, 1905*. Greensboro, 1905.

———. *The First One Hundred Sustaining Members of the Audubon Society of North Carolina, November 15th, 1902*. Greensboro, 1902.

———. *Main Provisions of the Audubon Bill*. Greensboro, 1903.

———. *Purposes and Plans*. No. 1. Greensboro, April 1902.

———. *Report of the Treasurer of the Audubon Society of North Carolina . . . 1904*. Greensboro, 1904.

———. *Some Possibilities of Game Protection in North Carolina, by Dr. T. S. Palmer, Washington, D.C. History of Game Protection in North Carolina, by Judge Francis D. Winston, Windsor, N.C. Addresses Delivered at the Annual Meeting of the Audubon Society of North Carolina . . . 1904*. Greensboro, 1904(?).

———. *The Value of North Carolina Birds*. No. 2. Greensboro, April 1902.

Aycock, Charles B. "Biennial Message of Charles B. Aycock, Governor of North Carolina, to the General Assembly, Session 1903." North Carolina *Public Documents, 1903*, doc. 1.

Bates, J. Leonard. "Fulfilling American Democracy: The Conservation Movement, 1907 to 1921." *Mississippi Valley Historical Review* 44 (June 1957): 29–57.

Beal, F. E. L. *Some Common Birds in Their Relation to Agriculture*. Farmers'

Bulletin No. 54. Washington, D.C.: Government Printing Office, 1898.

Bean, Michael J. *The Evolution of National Wildlife Law.* Rev. and expanded ed. New York: Praeger Publishers, 1983.

Belanger, Dian Olson. *Managing American Wildlife: A History of the International Association of Fish and Wildlife Agencies.* Amherst: University of Massachusetts Press, 1988.

Brant, Irving. *Adventures in Conservation with Franklin D. Roosevelt.* Flagstaff, Ariz.: Northland Publishing, 1988.

Brewster, William. *October Farm.* Cambridge: Harvard University Press, 1936.

Brewster, William, and Frank M. Chapman. "Notes on the Birds of the Lower Suwannee River." *Auk* 8 (April 1891): 125–38.

Bridges, William. *Gathering of Animals, an Unconventional History of the New York Zoological Society.* New York: Harper & Row, 1974.

Brimley, Herbert H. *A North Carolina Naturalist.* Edited by Eugene P. Odum. Chapel Hill: University of North Carolina Press, 1949.

———. "Thomas Gilbert Pearson." *Chat* 7 (1943): 50–52.

Brodhead, Michael J. "Elliott Coues and the Sparrow War." *New England Quarterly* 44 (September 1971): 420–23.

Buchheister, Carl W., and Frank Graham. "From the Swamps and Back: A Concise and Candid History of the Audubon Movement." *Audubon* 75 (January 1973): 4–45.

Buchholz, F. W. *History of Alachua County, Florida, Narrative and Biographical.* Saint Augustine: Record Company Printers, 1929.

Burroughs, John. "In Warbler Time." *Bird-Lore* 1 (February 1899): 3–5.

Cart, Theodore W. "The Lacey Act: America's First Nationwide Wildlife Statute." *Forest History* 17 (October 1973): 4–13.

Chapman, Frank M. *Autobiography of a Bird-Lover.* New York: Appleton-Century, 1933.

———. *Bird-Life, a Guide to the Study of Our Common Birds.* New York: D. Appleton, 1897.

———. *Frank Chapman in Florida: His Journals and Letters.* Compiled and edited by Elizabeth S. Austin. Gainesville: University of Florida Press, 1967.

———. *Handbook of Birds of Eastern North America.* New York: D. Appleton, 1895.

———. "A List of Birds Observed at Gainesville, Florida." *Auk* 5 (July 1888): 267–77.

Cheney, John L. *North Carolina Government, 1585–1974*. Raleigh: North Carolina Department of the Secretary of State, 1975.

Clepper, Henry E., ed. *Leaders of American Conservation*. New York: Ronald Press Co., 1971.

Conference on Conservation of Natural Resources, Washington, 1908. *Proceedings of a Conference of Governors in the White House, Washington, D.C. May 13–15, 1908*. Washington, D.C.: Government Printing Office, 1909.

Connor, Robert D. W. *North Carolina: Rebuilding an Ancient Commonwealth, 1584–1925*. 4 vols. Chicago and New York: American Historical Society, Inc., 1928–29

Coues, Elliott. *Key to North American Birds*. 4th ed. Boston: Estes and Lauriat, 1890.

Cutright, Paul R., and Michael J. Brodhead. *Elliott Coues, Naturalist and Frontier Historian*. Urbana: University of Illinois Press, 1981.

Dahlke-Scott, Deborah, and Michael Prewitt. "A Writer's Crusade to Portray Spirit of the Limberlost." *Smithsonian* 7 (April 1976): 64–69.

Davis, Richard C., ed. *Encyclopedia of American Forest and Conservation History*. 2 vols. New York: Macmillan, 1983.

Doughty, Robin W. *Feather Fashions and Bird Preservation, a Study in Nature Protection*. Berkeley: University of California Press, 1975.

Douglas, Virginia L. Brown. "Interdependence in Wood Life." *State Normal Magazine* 8 (April 1904): 133–40.

———. "Mindpower Past: Turn-of-the-Century Faculty Launched Global Attack on Bird-Killers." *Alumni News* (Fall 1981): 17–19.

———. "T. Gilbert Pearson, Some Recollections." *Biophile Bulletin* 5 (1968): 7–10.

Drummond, Henry. *Natural Law in the Spiritual World*. New York: J. Pott, 1884.

Dunlap, Thomas R. *Saving America's Wildlife*. Princeton, N.J.: Princeton University Press, 1988.

Ehrlich, Paul R. *The Machinery of Nature*. New York: Simon and Schuster, 1986.

Ehrlich, Paul R., and Anne Ehrlich. *Extinction: The Causes and Consequences of the Disappearance of Species*. New York: Random House, 1981.

Field, George W. "The Heath Hen." *Bird-Lore* 9 (November–December 1907): 249–55.

Flynn, Charles L. *White Land, Black Labor; Caste and Class in Late Nine-*

*teenth-Century Georgia.* Baton Rouge: Louisiana State University Press, 1983.

Fourth International Fishery Congress. *Proceedings of the Fourth International Fishery Congress . . . Held at Washington, U.S.A., September 22 to 26, 1908.* Washington, D.C.: Government Printing Office, 1910.

Fox, Stephen. *John Muir and His Legacy, the American Conservation Movement.* Boston: Little, Brown, 1981.

Frome, Michael. *The Forest Service.* 2d ed., rev. Boulder, Colo.: Westview Press, 1984.

Gilbert, Dorothy Lloyd. *Guilford, a Quaker College.* Greensboro, N.C.: Trustees of Guilford College, 1937.

_____. "T. Gilbert Pearson and Guilford College." *Guilford College Bulletin* 37 (January 1944): 1–8.

Glenn, Robert B. "The Governor's Message to the General Assembly of North Carolina of 1907." *North Carolina Public Documents, 1907*, doc. 1.

Graham, Frank, Jr. *The Audubon Ark: A History of the National Audubon Society.* New York: Alfred A. Knopf, 1990.

Grantham, Dewey W. *Southern Progressivism: The Reconciliation of Progress and Tradition.* Knoxville: University of Tennessee Press, 1983.

*Greensboro, N.C. Directory, 1905–06.* Greensboro: Hill Directory Co., 1905.

Hahn, Steven. *The Roots of Southern Populism: Yeomen Farmers and the Transformation of the Georgia Upcountry, 1850–1890.* New York: Oxford University Press, 1983.

Hayman, Donald B. *Resource Management in North Carolina.* Chapel Hill: Institute for Research in Social Science, University of North Carolina, 1947.

Hays, Samuel P. *Conservation and the Gospel of Efficiency.* Cambridge: Harvard University Press, 1959.

Holder, Rose Howell. *McIver of North Carolina.* Chapel Hill: University of North Carolina Press, 1957.

Hornaday, William T. *Our Vanishing Wild Life.* New York: C. Scribner's Sons, 1913.

_____. *Thirty Years War for Wild Life.* New York: Arno, 1931.

Howell, Arthur H. *Florida Bird Life.* New York: Coward-McCann, 1932.

Jordan, J. F. *To the Sportsmen of North Carolina.* No. 4. Greensboro: Audubon Society of North Carolina, 1902.

Joyner, J. Y. *Purposes and Plans.* No. 1. Rev. ed. Greensboro: Audubon Society of North Carolina, November 1902.

Kastner, Joseph. *A World of Watchers*. New York: Alfred A. Knopf, 1986.

Kitchin, William W. "Biennial Message." North Carolina *Public Documents, 1911*, doc. 1.

————. "Inaugural Address . . . 1909." North Carolina *Public Documents, 1909*.

Lattin, Frank H. *The Oologists' Hand-book, 1885*. Rochester, N.Y.: J. P. Smith, 1884.

————. *The Standard Catalogue of North American Birds Eggs*. 3d ed. Albion, N.Y.: F. H. Lattin, 1892.

Leopold, Aldo. *A Sand County Almanac*. New York: Oxford University Press, 1949.

Lewis, Charles Lee. *Philander Priestley Claxton, Crusader for Public Education*. Knoxville: University of Tennessee Press, 1948.

Lund, Thomas A. *American Wildlife Law*. Berkeley: University of California Press, 1980.

McGeary, M. Nelson. *Gifford Pinchot, Forester-Politician*. Princeton, N.J.: Princeton University Press, 1960.

Massachusetts Audubon Society. *First Report of the Massahusetts Audubon Society for the Protection of Birds. October, 1897*.

————. "Profile on Massachusetts Audubon Society." June 1986. Typescript.

————. *This Statement Was Made by Mrs. Augustus Hemenway and Miss Minna B. Hall*. Massachusetts Audubon Society. Leaflet.

Mayr, Ernst. *The Growth of Biological Thought*. Cambridge: Belknap Press of Harvard University Press, 1982.

Mitchell, John G. "A Man Called Bird." *Audubon* 89 (March 1987): 81–104.

Moore, Joseph. "The Greatest Factor in Human Evolution." *Guilford Collegian* 6 (April 1894): 240–44.

Moore, Mary Taylor. *To the School Teachers of North Carolina*. Greensboro: Audubon Society of North Carolina, 1907(?).

Morris, Edmund. *The Rise of Theodore Roosevelt*. New York: Coward, McCann & Geoghegan, 1979.

National Audubon Society. *Audubon Wildlife Report, 1985*. New York: National Audubon Society, 1985.

National Conservation Commission, Washington, D.C. *Report . . . February 1909*. 3 vols. Washington, D.C.: Government Printing Office, 1909.

National Conservation Congress. *Addresses and Proceedings*. Seattle, Washington, August 26–28, 1909. Washington, D.C.: The Congress, 1910.

―――. *Proceedings of the Second National Conservation Congress at Saint Paul, September 5–8, 1910.* Washington, D.C.: The Congress, 1910.

National Geographic Society. *The Book of Birds.* Edited by Gilbert Grosvenor and Alexander Wetmore. 2 vols. Washington, D.C.: National Geographic Society, 1939.

Nixon, Edgar B., ed. *Franklin D. Roosevelt and Conservation, 1911–1945.* 2 vols. Washington, D.C.: Government Printing Office, 1957.

North Carolina Academy of Science. "Proceedings of the Eighth Annual Meeting . . . 1909." Elisha Mitchell Scientific Society, *Journal* 25 (June 1909): 39–53.

North Carolina General Assembly. *An Act to Incorporate the Audubon Society of North Carolina and to Provide for the Preservation of the Song and Game Birds of the State.* Greensboro: Audubon Society of North Carolina, 1903.

North Carolina House of Representatives. *H. B. 304, Session 1903. Introduced by Mr. Roberson of Guilford. A Bill to Be Entitled an Act to Incorporate the Audubon Society of North Carolina and to Provide for the Preservation of the Song and Game Birds of the State.* Raleigh: E. M. Uzell, 1903.

*Notable Names in American History, a Tabulated Register.* Clifton, N.J.: James T. White, 1973.

Orr, Oliver H. *Charles Brantley Aycock.* Chapel Hill: University of North Carolina Press, 1961.

Palmer, Theodore S. *Chronology and Index of the More Important Events in American Game Protection, 1776–1911.* Washington: Government Printing Office, 1912. Biological Survey Bulletin No. 41.

―――. "In Memoriam: William Dutcher." *Auk* 38 (October 1921): 501–13.

―――. *Legislation for the Protection of Birds Other Than Game Birds.* Washington, D.C.: Government Printing Office, 1902. Biological Survey Bulletin No. 12. Rev. ed.

―――. "The Life Work of William Dutcher." *Bird-Lore* 22 (September–October 1920): 317–21.

―――. "A Review of Economic Ornithology in the United States." U.S. Department of Agriculture, *Yearbook, 1899,* 259–92. Washington, D.C.: Government Printing Office, 1900.

Palmer, Theodore S., and H. W. Olds. *Game Laws for 1902. A Summary of the Provisions Relating to Seasons, Shipment, Sale and Licenses.* Washington: Government Printing Office, 1902. Farmers' Bulletin No. 160.

————. *Laws Regulating the Transportation and Sale of Game.* Washington: Government Printing Office, 1900. Biological Survey Bulletin No. 14.

Palmer, Theodore, et al. *Biographies of Members of the American Ornithologists' Union.* Edited by Paul H. Oehser. Reprinted from *The Auk*, 1884–1954. Washington, D.C.: *The Auk*, 1954.

Pinchot, Gifford. *Breaking New Ground.* Seattle: University of Washington Press, (1947) 1972.

Pinkett, Harold T. *Gifford Pinchot, Private and Public Forester.* Urbana: University of Illinois Press, 1970.

Potter, Eloise F., James F. Parnell, and Robert P. Teulings. *Birds of the Carolinas.* Chapel Hill: University of North Carolina Press, 1980.

Powell, William S. *The North Carolina Gazeteer.* Chapel Hill: University of North Carolina Press, 1968.

Pratt, Joseph Hyde. "The Conservation and Utilization of Our Natural Resources." Elisha Mitchell Scientific Society, *Journal* 26 (April 1910): 1–25.

Preston, Daniel J. "The AOU's Fledgling Years." *Natural History* 92 (September 1983): 10–12.

Quaintance, Altus L. "Jottings from Florida." *Oologist* 5 (January 1888): 5–6.

————. "The Pileated Woodpecker in Florida." *Oologist* 7 (May 1890): 86–87.

Reiger, John F. *American Sportsmen and the Origins of Conservation.* New York: Winchester Press, 1975.

Reilly, Edgar M. *The Audubon Illustrated Handbook of American Birds.* New York: McGraw-Hill, 1968.

Rood, E. Irene, ed. *Papers Presented to the World's Congress on Ornithology.* Chicago: Charles H. Sergel Company, 1896.

Roosevelt, Theodore. *Theodore Roosevelt, an Autobiography.* New York: Macmillan, 1919.

Schenck, Carl A. *The Biltmore Story: Recollections of the Beginnings of Forestry in the United States.* St. Paul: American Forest History Foundation and Minnesota Historical Society, 1955.

Schmitt, Peter J. *Back to Nature: The Arcadian Myth in Urban America.* New York: Oxford University Press, 1969.

Seamster, Mike. "Big Bird Is Back!" *Wildlife in North Carolina* 52 (April 1988): 10–11.

Simpson, Marcus B. "The Letters of John S. Cairns to William Brewster, 1887–1895." *North Carolina Historical Review* 55 (Summer 1978): 306–38.

Smithwick, John W. P. "Ornithology of North Carolina. A List of Birds of North Carolina, with Notes of Each Species." North Carolina Agricultural Experiment Station, Raleigh, N.C. *Report, 1897–1898,* 197–227.

Sprunt, Alexander, Jr. *Florida Bird Life.* New York: Coward-McCann and National Audubon Society, 1954.

Sterling, Keir B. *Last of the Naturalists: The Career of C. Hart Merriam.* Rev. ed. New York: Arno Press, 1977.

Stick, David. *The Outer Banks of North Carolina, 1584–1958.* Chapel Hill: University of North Carolina Press, 1958.

Terres, John K. *The Audubon Society Encyclopedia of North American Birds.* New York: Alfred A. Knopf, 1980.

Trefethen, James B. *An American Crusade for Wildlife.* New York: Winchester Press and Boone and Crockett Club, 1975.

Webber, "Carl" [Charles H.] *The First Eden of the South . . . Alachua County, Florida. . . .* New York: Leve & Alden, 1883.

Welker, Robert H. *Birds and Men: American Birds in Science, Art, Literature, and Conservation, 1800–1900.* Cambridge: Belknap Press of Harvard University Press, 1955.

Williams, Robert W. *Game Commissions and Wardens.* Washington, D.C.: Government Printing Office, 1907. Biological Survey Bulletin No. 28.

Wilson, Edward O. *Biophilia.* Cambridge: Harvard University Press, 1984.

Wilson, Henry V. "The Laboratory of the U.S. Fish Commission at Beaufort, N.C." Elisha Mitchell Scientific Society, *Journal* 17 (1900), pt. 1: 1–4.

World's Columbian Exposition, 1893. *Report of the Committee on Awards. . . . Special Reports upon Special Subjects or Groups.* 2 vols. Washington, D.C.: Government Printing Office, 1901.

# Index

Abbey, George, 203
*Accipiter cooperii. See* Hawk, Cooper's
*Actitis macularia. See* Sandpiper,
    Spotted
Adams, Charles Francis, 51
Agassiz, Louis, 23, 43
Agassiz, Mrs. Louis, 51
*Agelaius phoeniceus. See* Blackbird, Red-
    winged
*Aix sponsa. See* Duck, Wood
*Ajaia ajaja. See* Spoonbill, Roseate
*Alca torda. See* Razorbill
Alderman, Edwin A., 40, 54, 66, 99
*Alle alle. See* Dovekie
Allen, Joel A.: in American Ornitholo-
    gists' Union, 22–29 passim; reviews
    Pearson's *Stories of Bird Life*, 89; in
    National Association of Audubon
    Societies, 143–44, 186, 227, 228;
    mentioned, 20, 70, 105, 167, 172
Ambler, Chase P., 97, 101, 118, 147
American Game Protective and Propa-
    gation Association, 232
American Game Protective Association.
    *See* American Game Protective and
    Propagation Association
American Humane Association, 29
American Ornithologists' Union: found-
    ed, 22–23; classification and
    nomenclature committee of, 23, 24;
    geographical distribution committee
    of, 23, 24; migration committee of, 23,
    24; bird protection committee, early
    work of, 23, 24–30
—model law: provisions, 25, 29, 111,
    113; adoptions, 84, 90, 115, 117, 129,
    153, 161, 201, 238

American Scenic and Historic Preserva-
    tion Society, 183
American Society for the Prevention of
    Cruelty to Animals, 45, 50
*Ammodramus maritimus. See* Sparrow,
    Seaside
*Anas rubripes. See* Duck, American Black
Angell, George T., 67
Anhinga, 10, 13, 22, 63
*Anhinga anhinga. See* Anhinga
Anthony, G. W., 123–24
Anti–Audubon Society bill. *See* Latham
    bill
*Ardea herodias. See* Heron, Great Blue
*Arenaria interpres. See* Turnstone, Ruddy
Ashe, William W., 59
*Asio flammeus. See* Owl, Short-eared
*Asio otus. See* Owl, Long-eared
Atkinson, George F., 57
*Atlantic Educational Journal*: begins, 82;
    ceases, 120–21
Audubon, John James, 26, 209
*Audubon Magazine* (first), 29–30
Audubon Millinery, 69–70
Audubon societies: Arizona, 238; Cal-
    ifornia, 69, 84, 104, 129, 222;
    Colorado, 129; Connecticut, 69, 70,
    125; Delaware, 84, 90; District of
    Columbia, 68, 90, 104, 105; Florida,
    84, 204; Georgia, 129, 137, 154–55,
    177–79, 214; Illinois, 68, 76; Indiana,
    69, 178; Iowa, 69, 104; Kansas, 238;
    Louisiana, 104, 130, 154, 186, 204;
    Maine, 68, 84, 234; Maryland, 84;
    Massachusetts, 50–51, 52, 68, 71, 82,
    85, 125; Michigan, 129, 236; Minne-
    sota, 68, 104; Missouri, 104;